THE TOURIST

Theory, Culture & Society

Theory, Culture & Society caters for the resurgence of interest in culture within contemporary social science and the humanities. Building on the heritage of classical social theory, the book series examines ways in which this tradition has been reshaped by a new generation of theorists. It will also publish theoretically informed analyses of everyday life, popular culture, and new intellectual movements.

EDITOR: Mike Featherstone, *Teesside Polytechnic*

Also in this series

Reproduction in Education, Society and Culture
Revised edition
Pierre Bourdieu and Jean-Claude Passeron

Global Culture
Nationalism, Globalization and Modernity
edited by Mike Featherstone

Theories of Modernity and Postmodernity
edited by Bryan S. Turner

THE TOURIST GAZE

Leisure and Travel in Contemporary Societies

JOHN URRY

SAGE Publications
London • Thousand Oaks • New Delhi

SAGE Publications Ltd
6 Bonhill Street
London EC2A 4PU

SAGE Publications Inc
2455 Teller Road
Thousand Oaks, California 91320

SAGE Publications India Pvt Ltd
32, M-Block Market
Greater Kailash – I
New Delhi 110 048

British Library Cataloguing in Publication data

Urry, John
   The tourist gaze: leisure and travel in contemporary
societies.
   1. Tourism – Sociological perspectives
   I. Title
   306.48

   ISBN 0–8039–8182–1
   ISBN 0–8039–8183–X pbk

Library of Congress catalog card number 90–061323

Typeset by Mayhew Typesetting, Bristol, England
Printed in Great Britain by
Redwood Books, Trowbridge, Wiltshire

'Tourists are "vulgar, vulgar, vulgar."' (Henry James, quoted in Pearce and Moscardo, 1986: 121)

'The United States makes the rest of the world seem authentic; California makes the rest of the United States seem authentic.' (MacCannell, 1976: 155)

'In the middle ages people were tourists because of their religion, whereas now they are tourists because tourism is their religion.' (Dr Robert Runcie, Archbishop of Canterbury, *Observer*, 11 December 1988)

'The Barbarian of yesterday is the Tourist of today.' (Mitford, 1959: 3)

'I am a traveller, you are a tourist, he is a tripper.' (Keith Waterhouse, 1989b: 18)

'Today everything exists to end in a photograph.' (Sontag, 1979: 24)

During the 1970s the Greek Orthodox Church recommended a new prayer: 'Lord Jesus Christ, Son of God, have mercy on the cities, the islands and the villages of this Orthodox Fatherland, as well as the holy monasteries which are scourged by the worldly touristic wave.' (quoted in Crick, 1988: 64)

'If the past is a foreign country, nostalgia has made it "the foreign country with the healthiest tourist trade of all."' (Lowenthal, 1985: 4)

CONTENTS

PREFACE

I am very grateful for the advice, encouragement and assistance of the following, especially those who have provided me with tourist gems from around the world: Paul Bagguley, Nick Buck, Peter Dickens, Paul Heelas, Mark Hilton, Scott Lash, Michelle Lowe, Celia Lury, Jane Mark-Lawson, David Morgan, Ian Rickson, Chris Rojek, Mary Rose, Peter Saunders, Dan Shapiro, Rob Shields, Hermann Schwengel, John Towner, Sylvia Walby, John Walton and Alan Warde. I am also grateful to professionals working in the tourism and hospitality industry who responded to my queries with much information and advice. Some interviews reported here were conducted under the auspices of the ESRC Initiative on the Changing Urban and Regional System. I am grateful to that Initiative in first prompting me to take holiday-making 'seriously'.

John Urry
Lancaster, December 1989

1

THE TOURIST GAZE

Why tourism is important

> The clinic was probably the first attempt to order a science on the exercise and decisions of the gaze . . . the medical gaze was also organized in a new way. First, it was no longer the gaze of any observer, but that of a doctor supported and justified by an institution . . . . Moreover, it was a gaze that was not bound by the narrow grid of structure . . . but that could and should grasp colours, variations, tiny anomalies . . . . (Foucault, 1976: 89)

The subject of this book would appear to have nothing whatsoever to do with the serious world of medicine and the medical gaze that concerns Foucault. This is a book about pleasure, about holidays, tourism and travel, about how and why for short periods people leave their normal place of work and residence. It is about consuming goods and services which are in some sense unnecessary. They are consumed because they supposedly generate pleasurable experiences which are different from those typically encountered in everyday life. And yet part at least of that experience is to gaze upon or view a set of different scenes, of landscapes or townscapes which are out of the ordinary. When we 'go away' we look at the environment with interest and curiosity. It speaks to us in ways we appreciate, or at least we anticipate that it will do so. In other words, we gaze at what we encounter. And this gaze is as socially organised and systematised as is the gaze of the medic. Of course it is of a different order in that it is not confined to professionals 'supported and justified by an institution'. And yet even in the production of 'unnecessary' pleasure there are in fact many professional experts who help to construct and develop our gaze as tourists.

This book then is about how in different societies and especially within different social groups in diverse historical periods the tourist gaze has changed and developed. I shall elaborate on the processes by which the gaze is constructed and reinforced, and will consider who or what authorises it, what its consequences are for the 'places' which are its object, and how it interrelates with a variety of other social practices.

There is no single tourist gaze as such. It varies by society, by social group and by historical period. Such gazes are constructed through difference. By this I mean not merely that there is no universal experience which is true for all tourists at all times. Rather the gaze in any historical period is constructed in relationship to its opposite, to non-tourist forms of social experience and consciousness. What makes a particular tourist gaze depends upon what it is contrasted with; what the forms of non-tourist experience happen to be. The gaze therefore pre-supposes a system of social activities and signs which locate the particular tourist practices, not in terms of some intrinsic characteristics, but through the contrasts implied with non-tourist social practices, particularly those based within the home and paid work.

Tourism, holiday-making and travel are more significant social pheno-mena than most commentators have considered. On the face of it there could not be a more trivial subject for a book. And indeed since social scientists have had plenty of difficulty explaining weightier topics, such as work or politics, it might be thought that they would have great difficulties in accounting for more trivial phenomena such as holiday-making. However, there are interesting parallels with the study of deviance. This involves the investigation of bizarre and idiosyncratic social practices which happen to be defined as deviant in some societies but not necessarily in others. The assumption is that the investigation of deviance can reveal interesting and significant aspects of 'normal' societies. Just why various activities are treated as deviant can illuminate how different societies operate.

This book is based on the notion that a similar analysis can be applied to tourism. Such practices involve the notion of 'departure', of a limited breaking with established routines and practices of everyday life and allowing one's senses to engage with a set of stimuli that contrast with the everyday and the mundane. By considering the typical objects of the tourist gaze one can use these to make sense of elements of the wider society with which they are contrasted. In other words, to consider how social groups construct their tourist gaze is a good way of getting at just what is happening in the 'normal society'. We can use the fact of difference to interrogate the normal through investigating the typical forms of tourism. Thus rather than being a trivial subject tourism is significant in its ability to reveal aspects of normal practices which might otherwise remain opaque. Opening up the workings of the social world often requires the use of counter-intuitive and surprising methodologies, such as in this case the investigation of the 'departures' involved in the tourist gaze.

Although I have insisted on the historical and sociological variation in this gaze there are some minimal characteristics of the social practices which are conveniently described as 'tourism'. I shall now set these out to provide a baseline for more historically and sociologically sensitive analyses later.

1   Tourism is a leisure activity which presupposes its opposite, namely regulated and organised work. It is one manifestation of how work and leisure are organised as separate and regulated spheres of social practice in 'modern' societies. Indeed acting as a tourist is one of the defining

characteristics of being 'modern' and is bound up with major transformations in paid work. This has come to be organised within particular places and to occur for regularised periods of time.

2   Tourist relationships arise from a movement of people to, and their stay in, various destinations. This necessarily involves some movement through space, that is the journey, and a period of stay in a new place or places.

3   The journey and stay are to, and in, sites which are outside the normal places of residence and work. Periods of residence elsewhere are of a short-term and temporary nature. There is a clear intention to return 'home' within a relatively short period of time.

4   The places gazed upon are for purposes which are not directly connected with paid work and normally they offer some distinctive contrasts with work (both paid and unpaid).

5   A substantial proportion of the population of modern societies engages in such tourist practices; new socialised forms of provision are developed in order to cope with the mass character of the gaze of tourists (as opposed to the individual character of 'travel').

6   Places are chosen to be gazed upon because there is an anticipation, especially through daydreaming and fantasy, of intense pleasures, either on a different scale or involving different senses from those customarily encountered. Such anticipation is constructed and sustained through a variety of non-tourist practices, such as film, TV, literature, magazines, records and videos, which construct and reinforce that gaze.

7   The tourist gaze is directed to features of landscape and townscape which separate them off from everyday experience. Such aspects are viewed because they are taken to be in some sense out of the ordinary. The viewing of such tourist sights often involves different forms of social patterning, with a much greater sensitivity to visual elements of landscape or townscape than is normally found in everyday life. People linger over such a gaze which is then normally visually objectified or captured through photographs, postcards, films, models and so on. These enable the gaze to be endlessly reproduced and recaptured.

8   The gaze is constructed through signs, and tourism involves the collection of signs. When tourists see two people kissing in Paris what they capture in the gaze is 'timeless romantic Paris'. When a small village in England is seen, what they gaze upon is the 'real olde England'. As Culler argues: 'the tourist is interested in everything as a sign of itself . . . . All over the world the unsung armies of semioticians, the tourists, are fanning out in search of the signs of Frenchness, typical Italian behaviour, exemplary Oriental scenes, typical American thruways, traditional English pubs' (1981: 127).

9   An array of tourist professionals develop who attempt to reproduce ever-new objects of the tourist gaze. These objects are located in a complex and changing hierarchy. This depends upon the interplay

between, on the one hand, competition between interests involved in the provision of such objects and, on the other hand, changing class, gender, generational distinctions of taste within the potential population of visitors.

In this book I will consider the development of, and historical transformations in, the tourist gaze. I shall mainly be concerned to chart such changes in the past century and a half; that is, in the period in which mass tourism has become widespread within much of Europe and north America. To be a tourist is one of the characteristics of the 'modern' experience. Not to 'go away' is like not possessing a car or a nice house. It is a marker of status in modern societies and is also thought to be necessary to health (see Feifer, 1985: 224).

This is not to suggest that there was no organised travel in premodern societies, but it was very much the preserve of elites (see Towner, 1988). In Imperial Rome, for example, a fairly extensive pattern of travel for pleasure and culture existed for the elite. A travel infrastructure developed, partly permitted by two centuries of peace. It was possible to travel from Hadrian's Wall to the Euphrates without crossing a hostile border (Feifer, 1985: ch. 1). Seneca maintained that this permitted city-dwellers to seek ever-new sensations and pleasures. He said: 'men [sic] travel widely to different sorts of places seeking different distractions because they are fickle, tired of soft living, and always seek after something which eludes them' (quoted in Feifer, 1985: 9).

In the thirteenth and fourteenth centuries pilgrimages had become a widespread phenomenon 'practicable and systematized, served by a growing industry of networks of charitable hospices and mass-produced indulgence handbooks' (Feifer, 1985: 29). Such pilgrimages often included a mixture of religious devotion and culture and pleasure. By the fifteenth century there were organised tours from Venice to the Holy Land.

The Grand Tour had become firmly established by the end of the seventeenth century for the sons of the aristocracy and the gentry, and by the late eighteenth century for the sons of the professional middle class. Over this period, between 1600 and 1800, treatises on travel shifted from a scholastic emphasis on touring as an opportunity for discourse, to travel as eyewitness observation. There was a visualisation of the travel experience, or the development of the 'gaze', aided and assisted by the growth of guidebooks which promoted new ways of seeing (see Adler, 1989). The character of the tour itself shifted, from the earlier 'classical Grand Tour' based on the emotionally neutral observation and recording of galleries, museums and high cultural artefacts, to the nineteenth-century 'romantic Grand Tour' which saw the emergence of 'scenic tourism' and a much more private and passionate experience of beauty and the sublime (see Towner, 1985). It is also interesting to note how travel was expected to play a key role in the cognitive and perceptual education of the English upper class (see Dent, 1975).

The eighteenth century had also seen the development of a consider-able tourist infrastructure in the form of spa towns throughout much of Europe (Thompson, 1981: 11–12). Myerscough notes that the 'whole apparatus of spa life with its balls, its promenades, libraries, masters of ceremonies was designed to provide a concentrated urban experience of frenetic socializing for a dispersed rural elite' (1974: 5). There have always been periods in which much of the mass of the population have engaged in play or recreation. In the countryside work and play were particularly intertwined in the case of fairs. Most towns and villages in England had at least one fair a year and many had more. People would often travel considerable distances and the fairs always involved a mixture of business and pleasure normally centred around the tavern. By the eighteenth century the public house had become a major centre for public life in the community, providing light, heat, cooking facilities, furniture, news, banking and travel facilities, entertainment, and sociability (see Harrison, 1971; Clark, 1983).

But before the nineteenth century few people outside the upper classes travelled anywhere to see objects for reasons unconnected with work or business. And it is this which is the central characteristic of mass tourism in modern societies, namely that much of the population in most years will travel somewhere else to gaze upon it and stay there for reasons basically unconnected with work. Travel is now thought to occupy 40 per cent of available 'free time' (Williams and Shaw, 1988b: 12). If people do not travel, they lose status: travel is the marker of status. It is a crucial element of modern life to feel that travel and holidays are necessary. 'I need a holiday' is the surest reflection of a modern discourse based on the idea that people's physical and mental health will be restored if only they can 'get away' from time to time.

The importance of this can be seen in the economic significance of tourism as an industry. I will now refer briefly to a variety of empirical indicators which show the importance of tourism in contemporary Britain. Such tourist-related services now employ about 1.5 million people and it is estimated that employment is increasing by 1,000 jobs per week (see Mills, 1989; Cabinet Office, 1983; Williams and Shaw, 1988c for various estimates). Worldwide tourism is growing at 5–6 per cent per annum and will probably be the largest source of employment by the year 2000. Tourist spending in the UK is currently worth at least £15 billion (Mills, 1989).

These striking increases reflect the fact that many new tourist sites have been opened in the past couple of decades. It was reported in a study conducted by the Cabinet Office that of those tourist sites open in 1983, half had been opened in the previous fifteen years. Indeed there were only 800 such sites in 1960 but 2,300 in 1983 (Cabinet Office, 1983). By 1987 233 million visits were made to over 3,000 sites within England, the most popular attractions being Blackpool Pleasure Beach (6.5 million visitors), Madame Tussaud's (2.5 million), Alton Towers Amusement

Park (2.33 million), the Tower of London (2.25 million), and National
Trust properties (6.5 million) (*The Guardian*, 12 December 1988).

Hotel accommodation has also greatly increased; the boom period for
opening new hotels, especially in London, was the early 1970s (see
Bagguley, 1987). In the 1980s many new hotels were opened in inland
towns and cities outside London (BTA/ETB, 1985). Such serviced
accommodation in England accounted for 46 per cent of all stays in
1974. This fell to 37 per cent in 1984, demonstrating the increasing
importance of self-serviced accommodation (Bagguley, 1987: 18).

In 1988 it was calculated £2 billion of investment was occurring in the
British tourist industry (Lee, 1988). A quarter of this was in hotels, a
fifth in themed attractions and museums, and an eighth in conference
centres.

These developments reflect dramatic increases in personal travel.
Between 1965 and 1985 there was a 60 per cent increase in total
passenger mileage within Britain (Dept of Transport, 1988: 7). This
increase was wholly accounted for by a doubling of travelling by car.
Between 1965 and 1985 the proportion of all journeys taken by car
increased from 47 per cent to 69 per cent, and this rose to 72 per cent
of all leisure journeys (Dept of Transport, 1988: 11). By 1985 70 per cent
of people lived in households which possessed a car.

Car ownership has permitted some increase in the number of domestic
holidays taken in Britain, which rose from 114 million in 1974 to 126
million in 1985, although this mainly consists of shorter holidays
(Cabinet Office, 1983: Key Note Report, 1987: 15). At the same time
there has been a marked rise in the number of holidays taken abroad.
In 1976 about 11.5 million visits were made abroad by UK residents. By
1986 28 per cent of Britons went abroad, making about 25 million
journeys, of which about a quarter were to Spain (Mitchinson, 1988: 48;
Business Monitor Quarterly Statistics, MQ6 Overseas Travel and
Tourism). In any year about 40 per cent of Britons go on holiday within
Britain, while about one-third have no holiday. This category ranges
from 9 per cent of the professional and managerial classes to 42 per cent
of semi- and unskilled workers.

There has been a smallish increase in the number of tourists coming
to the UK. There were about 11 million visits to the UK in 1976 and
about 15.5 million in 1987. It is estimated that this will rise to 19.9
million by 1993 and the opening of the Channel Tunnel (see Landry et
al., 1989: 45). Although overseas visitors to Britain spend more per head
than Britons spend abroad, partly because over a quarter are north
Americans, a serious deficit has appeared in the later 1980s in the
tourism account, in 1988 of £2 billion (Landry et al., 1989: 9).

Nevertheless, spending by such visitors accounts for 5 per cent of the
wider leisure market, much of it going on retailing expenditure (Martin
and Mason, 1987: 95–6). Domestic tourists spend a lower proportion on
shopping but even here the proportion is rising. Martin and Mason

conclude: 'shopping is becoming more significant to tourism, both as an area of spending and as an incentive for travelling' (1987: 96). More generally, tourist expenditure in the UK is the third-highest category of consumer expenditure after energy products and clothing and shoes. Tourism accounts for 6 per cent of all UK consumer expenditure (see Landry et al., 1989: 46).

In the next section I shall briefly consider some of the main theoretical contributions that have attempted to make sociological sense of this economically important set of social activities.

Theoretical approaches to the study of tourism

Making theoretical sense of 'fun, pleasure and entertainment' has proved a difficult task for social scientists. There is relatively little substance to the sociology of tourism. In this section I shall summarise some of the main contributions; they are not uninteresting but they leave a great deal of work still to be done. In the rest of the book I shall develop some notions relevant to the theoretical understanding of tourist activity, drawing on some of the contributions discussed here (also see chapter 3 for some of the approaches developed within economics concerned with issues of tourist congestion).

One of the earliest formulations is Boorstin's analysis of the 'pseudo-event' (1964; and see Cohen, 1988). He argues, partly anticipating Baudrillard, that contemporary Americans cannot experience 'reality' directly but thrive on 'pseudo-events'. Tourism is the prime example of these (see Eco, 1986; and Baudrillard, 1988). Isolated from the host environment and the local people, the mass tourist travels in guided groups and finds pleasure in inauthentic contrived attractions, gullibly enjoying the 'pseudo-events' and disregarding the 'real' world outside. As a result tourist entrepreneurs and the indigenous populations are induced to produce ever-more extravagant displays for the gullible observer who is thereby further removed from the local people. Over time, via advertising and the media, the images generated of different tourist gazes come to constitute a closed self-perpetuating system of illusions which provide the tourist with the basis for selecting and evaluating potential places to visit. Such visits are made, says Boorstin, within the 'environmental bubble' of the familiar American-style hotel which insulates the tourist from the strangeness of the host environment.

A number of later writers develop and refine this relatively simple thesis of a historical shift from the 'individual traveller' to the 'mass society tourist'. Particularly noteworthy is Turner and Ash's *The Golden Hordes* (1975), which fleshes out the thesis about how the tourist is placed at the centre of a strictly circumscribed world. Surrogate parents (travel agents, couriers, hotel managers) relieve the tourist of responsibility and protect him/her from harsh reality. Their solicitude restricts the tourist to the beach and certain approved objects of the tourist gaze. In a sense, Turner and Ash suggest, the tourists' sensuality and aesthetic sense are as restricted as they are in their home country. This is further heightened by the relatively superficial way in which indigenous cultures necessarily have to be presented to the tourist. They note about Bali that: 'Many aspects of Balinese culture and art are so bewilderingly complex and alien to western modes that they do not lend themselves readily to the process of over-simplification and mass-production that converts indigenous art forms into tourist kitsch' (Turner and Ash, 1975: 159).

The upshot of this and other processes is that in the search for ever-new places to visit, what is constructed is a set of hotels and tourist sights that is bland and lacking contradiction, 'a small monotonous world that everywhere shows us our own image . . . the pursuit of the exotic and diverse ends in uniformity' (Turner and Ash, 1975: 292).

Somewhat critical of this tradition is Cohen, who maintains that there is no single tourist as such but a variety of tourist types or modes of tourist experience (see 1972, 1979, 1988, for various formulations mainly drawn from the sociology of religion). What he terms the 'experiential', the 'experimental' and the 'existential' do not rely on the environmental bubble of conventional tourist services. To varying degrees such tourist experiences are based on the rejection of such ways of organising tourist activity. Moreover, one should also note that the existence of such bubbles does permit many people to visit places which otherwise they would not, and to have at least some contact with the 'strange' places thereby encountered. Indeed until such places develop a fully-fledged tourist infrastructure much of the 'strangeness' of such destinations will be impossible to hide and to package in a complete array of 'pseudo-events'.

The most significant challenge to Boorstin's position is developed by MacCannell, who is likewise concerned with the inauthenticity and super-ficiality of modern life (1976, and see 1989). He quotes Simmel on the nature of the sensory impressions experienced in the 'metropolis': 'the rapid crowding of changing images, the sharp discontinuity in the grasp of a single glance, and the unexpectedness of onrushing impressions' (MacCannell, 1976: 49). He maintains that these are symptomatic of the tourist experience. He disagrees with Boorstin's account, which he regards as reflecting a characteristically upper-class view that 'other people are tourists, while I am a traveller' (1976: 107). All tourists for MacCannell embody a quest *for* authenticity, and this quest is a modern version of the universal human concern with the sacred. The tourist is a kind of contemporary pilgrim, seeking authenticity in other 'times' and other 'places' away from that person's everyday life. Particular fascina-tion is shown by tourists in the 'real lives' of others which somehow possess a reality which is hard to discover in people's own experiences. Modern society is therefore rapidly institutionalising the rights of outsiders to look into its workings. 'Institutions are fitted with arenas, platforms and chambers set aside for the exclusive use of tourists' (MacCannell, 1976: 49). Almost any sort of work, even the backbreaking toil of the Welsh miner or the unenviable work of those employed in the Parisian sewer, can be the object of the tourist gaze.

MacCannell is particularly interested in the character of the social relations which emerge from this fascination people have especially in the work lives of others. He notes that such 'real lives' can only be found backstage and are not immediately evident to us. Hence, the gaze of the tourist will involve an obvious intrusion into people's lives, which would be generally unacceptable. So the people being observed and local tourist entrepreneurs gradually come to construct backstages in a contrived and artificial manner. 'Tourist spaces' are thus organised around what MacCannell calls 'staged authenticity' (1973). The development of the constructed tourist attraction results from how those who are subject to the tourist gaze respond, both to protect themselves from intrusions into their lives backstage and to take advantage of the opportunities it presents for profitable investment. By contrast then with Boorstin, MacCannell argues that 'psuedo-events' result from the social relations of tourism and not from an individualistic search for the inauthentic.

Pearce and Moscardo have further elaborated the notion of authenticity (1986; and see the critique in Turner and Manning, 1988). They maintain that it is necessary to distinguish between the authenticity of the setting and the authenticity of the persons gazed upon; and to distinguish between the diverse elements of the tourist experience which are of importance to the tourist in question. Crick, by contrast, points out that there is a sense in which all cultures are 'staged' and are in a certain sense inauthentic. Cultures are invented, remade and the elements reorganised (1988: 65–6). Hence, it is not clear why the apparently inauthentic staging for the tourist is so very different from what happens in all cultures anyway.

MacCannell also notes that, unlike the religious pilgrim who pays homage to a single sacred centre, the tourist pays homage to an enormous array of centres or attractions. These include sites of industry and work. This is because, according to MacCannell, work has become a mere attribute of society and not its central feature (1976: 58). He characterises such an interest in work displays as 'alienated leisure'. It is a perversion of the aim of leisure since it involves a return to the workplace.

He also notes how each centre of attraction involves complex processes of production in order that regular, meaningful and profitable tourist gazes can be generated and sustained. Such gazes cannot be left to chance. People have to learn how, when and where to 'gaze'. Clear markers have to be provided and in some cases the object of the gaze is merely the marker that indicates some event or experience which previously happened at that spot.

MacCannell maintains that there is normally a process of sacralisation

which renders a particular natural or cultural artefact a sacred object of
the tourist ritual (1976: 42–8). A number of stages are involved in this:
naming the sight, framing and elevation, enshrinement, mechanical
reproduction of the sacred object, and social reproduction as new sights
(or 'sites') name themselves after the famous. It is also important to note
that not only are there many attractions to which to pay homage, but
many attractions are only gazed upon once. In other words, the gaze of
the tourist can be amazingly fickle, searching out or anticipating
something new or something different.

The processes involved here are partly revealed in Turner's analysis of
pilgrims (1973; 1974). Important *rites de passage* are involved in the
movement from one stage to another. There are three such stages: first,
social and spatial separation from the normal place of residence and
conventional social ties; second, liminality, where the individual finds
him/herself in an 'anti-structure . . . out of time and place' – conventional social ties are suspended, an intensive bonding 'communitas' is
experienced, and there is direct experience of the sacred or supernatural;
and third, reintegration, where the individual is reintegrated with the
previous social group, usually at a higher social status.

Although this analysis is applied to pilgrimages, other writers have
drawn out its implications for tourism (see Cohen, 1988: 38–40; Lett,
1983; Shields, 1990). Like the pilgrim the tourist moves from a familiar
place to a far place and then returns to the familiar place. At the far
place both the pilgrim and the tourist engage in 'worship' of shrines
which are sacred, albeit in different ways, and as a result gain some
kind of uplifting experience. In the case of the tourist Turner and
Turner talk of 'liminoid' situations (1978). What is being pointed out
here is something left underexamined in MacCannell, namely that in
much tourism everyday obligations are suspended or inverted. There is
licence for permissive and playful 'non-serious' behaviour and the
encouragement of a relatively unconstrained 'communitas' or social
togetherness. Such arguments call into question the idea that there is
simply 'routine' or habitaul action, as argued for example by Giddens
(1984). What is often involved is semi-routine action or a kind of
routinised non-routine.

One of the most insightful analyses of this is Shields' exploration of
the 'honeymoon capital of the world', Niagara Falls (1990). Going on
honeymoon to Niagara did indeed involve a pilgrimage, stepping out into
an experience of liminality in which the codes of normal social experience
were reversed. In particular honeymooners found themselves historically
in an ideal liminal zone where the strict social conventions of bourgeois
families were relaxed under the exigencies of travel and of relative
anonymity and freedom from collective scrutiny. In a novel written in
1808 a character says of Niagara: 'Elsewhere there are cares of business
and fashion, there are age, sorrow, and heartbreak; but here only youth,
faith, rapture' (quoted Shields, 1990). Shields also discusses how Niagara,

just like Gretna Green in Scotland, has become a signifier now emptied of meaning, a thoroughly commercialised cliché.

Some writers in this tradition argue that such playful or 'ludic' behaviour is primarily of a restitutive or compensatory sort, revitalising the tourists for their return to the familiar place of home and work (see Lett, 1983 on ludic charter yacht tourism). Other writers, by contrast, adopt a less functionalist interpretation and argue that the rather general notions of liminality and inversion have to be given a more precise content. It is necessary to investigate the nature of the social and cultural patterns in the tourist's day-to-day existence in order to see just what is inverted and how the liminal experience will work itself out. Gottlieb argues, for example, that what is sought for in a vacation/holiday is inversion of the everyday. The middle-class tourist will seek to be a 'peasant for a day' while the lower middle-class tourist will seek to be 'king/queen for a day' (see Gottlieb, 1982). Although these are hardly very convincing examples they do point to a crucial feature of tourism, namely that there is a clear distinction between the familiar and the faraway and that such differences produce distinct kinds of liminal zones.

It therefore seems incorrect to suggest that a search for authenticity is the basis for the organisation of tourism. Rather, one key feature would seem to be that there is difference between one's normal place of residence/work and the object of the tourist gaze. Now it may be that a seeking for what we take to be authentic elements is an important component here but that is only because there is in some sense a contrast with everyday experiences. Furthermore, it has recently been argued that some visitors – what Feifer (1985) terms 'post-tourists' – almost delight in the inauthenticity of the normal tourist experience. 'Post-tourists' find pleasure in the multiplicity of tourist games. They know that there is *no* authentic tourist experience, that there are merely a series of games or texts that can be played. In later chapters I shall draw out some important connections between the notion of the post-tourist and the more general cultural development of postmodernism.

For the moment though it is necessary to consider just what it is that produces a distinctive tourist gaze. Minimally there must be certain aspects of the place to be visited which distinguish it from what is conventionally encountered in everyday life. Tourism results from a basic binary division between the ordinary/everyday and the extraordinary. Tourist experiences involve some aspect or element which induces pleasurable experiences which are, by comparison with the everyday, out of the ordinary (see Robinson, 1976: 157). This is not to say that other elements of the production of the tourist experience will not make the typical tourist feel that he or she is 'home from home', not too much 'out of place'. But potential objects of the tourist gaze must be different in some way or other. They must be out of the ordinary. People must experience particularly distinct pleasures which involve different senses or are on a different scale from those typically encountered in everyday life. There are many different ways in which such a division between the ordinary and the extraordinary can be established and sustained.

There is seeing a unique object, such as the Eiffel Tower, the Empire State Building, Buckingham Palace, the Grand Canyon, or even the very spot in Dallas where President Kennedy was shot (see Rojek, 1990 on the last). These are absolutely distinct objects to be gazed upon which everyone knows about. They are famous for being famous, although such places may have lost the basis of their fame (such as the Empire State Building, which still attracts 2 million people a year although it is no longer the tallest building in New York). Most people living in the west would hope to see some of these objects during their lifetime. They entail a kind of pilgrimage to a sacred centre, which is often a capital or major city.

There is the seeing of particular signs, such as the typical English village, the typical American skyscraper, the typical German beer-garden, the typical French château, and so on. This mode of gazing shows how tourists are in a way semioticians, reading the landscape for signifiers of certain pre-established notions or signs derived from various discourses of travel and tourism (see Culler, 1981: 128).

There is the seeing of unfamiliar aspects of what had previously been thought of as familiar. One example is visiting museums which show representations of the lives of ordinary people, revealing particularly their cultural artefacts. Often these are set out in a 'realistic' setting to demonstrate what their houses, workshops and factories were roughly like. Visitors thus see unfamiliar elements of other people's lives which had been presumed familiar.

There is the seeing of ordinary aspects of social life being undertaken by people in unusual contexts. Some tourism in China has been of this sort. Visitors have found it particularly interesting to gaze upon the carrying out of domestic tasks in a 'communist' country, and hence to see that the routines of life are not that unfamiliar.

There is the carrying out of familiar tasks or activities within an unusual visual environment. Swimming and other sports, shopping, eating and drinking all have particular significance if they take place against a distinctive visual backcloth. The visual gaze renders extra-ordinary activities that otherwise would be mundane.

Finally, there is the seeing of particular signs which indicate that a certain other object is indeed extraordinary, even though it does not seem to be so. A good example of such an object is moon rock which appears unremarkable. The attraction is not the object itself but the sign referring to it that marks it out as distinctive. Thus the marker becomes the distinctive sight (Culler, 1981: 139). A similar seeing occurs in art galleries when part of what is gazed at is the name of the artist, 'Rembrandt' say, as much as the painting itself, which may be difficult to distinguish from the many others in the same gallery.

I have argued that the character of the gaze is central to tourism. Campbell, however, makes an important point related more generally to the character of consumption as such (1987). He argues that covert day-dreaming and anticipation are processes central to modern consumerism. Individuals do not seek satisfaction from products, from their actual selection, purchase and use. Rather satisfaction stems from anticipation, from imaginative pleasure-seeking. People's basic motivation for consumption is not therefore simply materialistic. It is rather that they seek to experience 'in reality' the pleasurable dramas they have already experienced in their imagination. However, since 'reality' can never provide the perfected pleasures encountered in daydreams, each purchase leads to disillusionment and to longing for ever-new products. There is a dialectic of novelty and insatiability at the heart of contemporary consumerism.

Campbell seems to view 'imaginative hedonism' as a relatively auto-nomous characteristic of modern societies and separate from specific institutional arrangements, such as advertising, or from particular modes of social emulation (1987: 88–95). Both claims are dubious in general but particularly so with regard to tourism. It is hard to envisage the nature of contemporary tourism without seeing how such activities are literally constructed in our imagination through advertising and the media, and through the conscious competition between different social groups. If Campbell is right in arguing that contemporary consumerism involves imaginative pleasure-seeking, then tourism is surely the paradigm case. Tourism necessarily involves daydreaming and anticipation of new or different experiences from those normally encountered in everyday life. But such daydreams are not autonomous; they involve working over advertising and other media-generated sets of signs, many of which relate very clearly to complex processes of social emulation.

One further problem in Campbell's otherwise useful analysis is that he treats modern consumerism as though it is historically unchanging. He thus fails to address an issue much discussed in contemporary social science, namely the changing character of consumption and the possible parallel transformations in the nature of capitalist production (consumption is used here in the sense of 'purchase' and does not imply the absence of production within households). Many writers now argue that a sea change is taking place within contemporary societies. Elsewhere I refer to this as involving a shift from organised to disorganised capitalism (see Lash and Urry, 1987). Other writers have characterised it as a move from Fordism to post-Fordism, and in particular the claim that there is a shift in typical modes of consumption, from mass consumption to more individuated patterns of consumption (see Aglietta, 1987; Hirschhorn, 1984; Piore and Sabel, 1984; Leadbetter, 1988; Hall, 1988).

But this consumption side of the analysis is undeveloped, indicating the 'productivist' bias in much of the literature. I shall now set out two ideal types, of Fordist mass consumption and post-Fordist differentiated consumption.

Mass consumption: purchase of commodities produced under conditions of mass production; a high and growing rate of expenditure on consumer products; individual producers tending to dominate particular industrial markets; producer rather than consumer as dominant; commodities little differentiated from each other by fashion, season, and specific market segments; relatively limited choice – what there is tends to reflect producer interests, either privately or publicly owned.

Post-Fordist consumption: consumption rather than production dominant as consumer expenditure further increases as a proportion of national income; new forms of credit permitting consumer expenditure to rise, so producing high levels of indebtedness; almost all aspects of social life become commodified, even charity; much greater differentiation of purchasing patterns by different market segments; greater volatility of consumer preferences; the growth of a consumers movement and the 'politicising' of consumption; reaction of consumers against being as part of a 'mass' and the need for producers to be much more consumer-driven, especially in the case of service industries and those publicly owned; the development of many more products each of which has a shorter life; the emergence of new kinds of commodity which are more specialised and based on raw materials that imply non-mass forms of production ('natural' products for example).

There are obviously many consumption modes which cross-cut this division. However, there is considerable evidence that western societies have been broadly moving from the former to the latter type. If this is so then this shift will also be reflected in the changing character of contemporary tourism. In Britain the holiday camp was the quintessential example of Fordist holiday-making. In the move to post-Fordism such camps have become renamed 'centres' or 'holidayworlds' and now present themselves as places of 'freedom'. I shall show in later chapters that there are many other changes occurring in contemporary holiday-making of a broadly 'post-Fordist' sort. These changes have been characterised by Poon (1989) as involving the shift from 'old tourism', which involved packaging and standardisation, to 'new tourism' which is segmented, flexible and customised. The marketing director of British Airways writes for example of 'the *end of mass marketing* in the travel business . . . we are going to be much more sophisticated in the way we *segment* our market' (quoted in Poon, 1989: 94).

Some such changes are also transforming relations *between* tourism and other cultural practices. In chapter 5 I shall consider some of the current literature on 'postmodernism', an important feature of which is the importance placed on 'play, pleasure and pastiche', features which have always characterised the tourist gaze. Holiday centres are therefore a kind of prototype for what is now becoming much more widespread, what one might refer to as the aestheticisation of consumption.

The next chapter, offers a historical sociology of the seaside resort, the quintessential British holiday experience. The rise and fall of such resorts reflects important changes in British society, including the growth of post-Fordist consumption patterns (also see Pearce, 1982 for a social psychology of tourism, and Rojek, 1990, on the connections between tourism and leisure).

2

MASS TOURISM AND THE RISE AND FALL OF THE SEASIDE RESORT

Introduction

The development of the first example of mass tourism, which occurred amongst the industrial working class in Britain was an exceptionally novel form of social activity. The mass tourist gaze was initiated in the backstreets of the industrial towns and cities in the north of England. Why did this industrial working class come to think that going away for short periods to quite other places was an appropriate form of social activity? Why did the tourist gaze develop amongst the industrial working class in the north of England? What revolution in experience, thinking and perception led to such novel modes of social practice?

The growth of such tourism represents a democratisation of travel. We have seen that travel had always been socially selective. It was available for a relatively limited elite and was a marker of social status. But in the second half of the nineteenth century there was an extensive development of mass travel by train. Status distinctions then came to be drawn between different classes of traveller, but less between those who could and those could not travel. We will consider later how in the twentieth century the car and the aeroplane have even further democratised geographical movement (see Stauth and Turner, 1988: 521ff.). As travel became democratised so extensive distinctions of taste came to be established between different *places*: where one travelled to became of considerable social significance. The tourist gaze came to have a different importance in one place rather than another. A resort 'hierarchy' developed and certain places were viewed as embodiments of mass tourism, to be despised and ridiculed. Major differences of 'social tone' were established between otherwise similar places. And some such places, the working-class resorts, quickly developed as symbols of 'mass tourism', as places of inferiority which stood for everything that dominant social groups held to be tasteless, common and vulgar.

Explanations of the tourist gaze, of the discourses which established and sustained mass tourism for the industrial working class in the nineteenth century, have tended to be over-general. Such developments have normally been explained in terms of 'nineteenth-century industrialisation' (see Myerscough, 1974, for example). In identifying more precisely those aspects of such industrialisation which were especially important attention will be paid to the growth of seaside resorts, whose development was by no means inevitable. They stemmed from *particular* features of nineteenth-century industrialisation and the growth of new modes by which pleasure was organised and structured in a society based on large-scale industrial classes.

The growth of the British seaside resort

Throughout Europe a number of spa towns had developed in the eighteenth century. Their original purpose was medicinal: they provided mineral water which was used for bathing in and drinking. It is by no means clear exactly how and why people came to believe in its medicinal properties. The first spa in England appears to have been in Scarborough and dates from 1626 when a Mrs Farrow noticed a spring on the beach (see Hern, 1967: 2–3; and, more generally, Howell, 1974). Within a few decades the medical profession began to advocate the desirable effects of taking the waters, or taking the 'Cure'. Various other spas developed, in Bath, Buxton, Harrogate, Tunbridge Wells and so on. An amazing range of disorders were supposedly improved both by swallowing the waters and by bathing in them. Scarborough, though, was distinctive since it was not only a major spa but was also by the sea. A Dr Wittie began to advocate both drinking the sea water and bathing in it. During the eighteenth century there was a considerable increase in sea bathing as the developing merchant and professional classes began to believe in its medicinal properties as a general pick-me-up. At that stage it was advocated for adults and there was little association then between the seaside and children. Indeed since the point of bathing in the sea was to do one good, this was often done in winter and basically involved 'immersion' and not what is now understood as swimming (see Hern, 1967: 21). These dips in the sea were structured and ritualised and were prescribed only to treat serious medical conditions. Bathing was only to be undertaken 'after due preparation and advice' as the historian Gibbon put it (see Shields, 1990), and was also normally carried out naked. The beach was a place of 'medicine' rather than 'pleasure'.

Spa towns could remain relatively socially restrictive. Access was only possible for those who could own or rent accommodation in the particular town. Younger neatly summarises this:

> life in the seventeenth and eighteenth-century watering-places resembled in many ways life on a cruise or in a small winter sports hotel, where the company is small and self-contained, rather than the modern seaside resort, where the individual is submerged in the crowd. (1973: 14–15)

However, as sea bathing became relatively more favoured it was harder for dominant social groups to restrict access. Difficulties were caused in Scarborough because of its dual function as both a spa and as a resort by the seaside. In 1824 the spa property was fenced off and a toll gate opened to exclude the 'improper classes' (Hern, 1967: 16). Pimlott summarises the effects of the widespread development of specialised seaside resorts where this kind of social restriction was not possible:

> The capacity of the seaside resorts, on the other hand, was unbounded. While social life at the spas was necessarily focussed on the pump-room and the baths, and there was no satisfactory alternative to living in public, the sea coast was large enough to absorb all comers and social homogeneity mattered less. (1947: 55)

One precondition then for the rapid growth of seaside resorts in the later eighteenth and especially in the nineteenth centuries was space. Britain possessed an extensive coastline which had few other uses apart from as the location of fishing ports, and which could not be privately controlled since ownership of the shoreline and beach between high and low tide were invested in the Crown (see Thompson, 1981: 14).

The development of such resorts was spectacular. In the first half of the nineteenth century coastal resorts showed a faster rate of population increase than manufacturing towns: 2.56 per cent per annum compared with 2.38 per cent (Lickorish and Kershaw, 1975: 12). The population of Brighton increased from 7,000 to 65,000 in half a century, particularly because the Prince Regent had made it fashionable: 'a portion of the West End *maritimized*' (see Shields, 1990). The population of the 48 leading seaside towns increased by nearly 100,000 between 1861 and 1871; their population had more than doubled by the end of the century. By 1911 it was calculated that 55 per cent of people in England and Wales took at least one trip to the seaside and 20 per cent stayed for a longer period each year (Myerscough, 1974: 143).

A complex of conditions produced the rapid growth of this new form of mass leisure activity and hence of these relatively specialised and unique concentrations of services in particular urban centres, concentrations designed to provide novel, and what were at the time utterly amazing, objects of the tourist gaze.

There was a considerable increase in the economic welfare of substantial elements of the industrial population. The real national income per head quadrupled over the nineteenth century (see Deane and Cole, 1962: 282). This enabled sections of the working class to accumulate savings from one holiday to the next, given that at the time few holidays with pay were sought, let alone provided (see Walton, 1981: 252).

In addition to this was rapid urbanisation, as many small towns grew incredibly rapidly. In 1801 20 per cent of the population lived in towns; by 1901 80 per cent did. This produced extremely high levels of poverty and overcrowding. Moreover, these urban areas possessed almost no public spaces, such as parks or squares (see Lash and Urry, 1987: ch. 3). Unlike older towns and cities a fairly marked degree of residential segregation by class developed. This was crucial for the emergence of the typical resort, which relied on attracting particular social groupings from certain parts of these emerging industrial towns and cities. *The Economist* in 1857 summarised the typical pattern of urban development:

> Society is tending more and more to spread into classes – and not merely classes but localised classes, class colonies . . . . It is the disposition to associate with equals – in some measure with those who have similar practical *interests*, in still greater measure with those who have similar tastes and culture, most of all with those with whom we judge ourselves on a moral equality, whatever out real standard may be. (20 June 1857: 669; also see Johnson and Pooley, 1982)

One effect therefore of the economic, demographic and spatial transformation of the nineteenth-century town was to produce self-regulating working-class communities, communities which were relatively autonomous of either the old or new institutions of the wider society. Such communities were important in developing forms of working-class leisure which were relatively segregated, specialised and institutionalised (see Clarke and Critcher, 1985).

The growth of a more organised and routinised pattern of work led to attempts to develop a corresponding rationalisation of leisure: 'To a large extent this regularisation of the days of leisure came about because of a change in the daily hours of work and in the nature of work' (Cunningham, 1980: 147).

Particularly in the newly emerging industrial workplaces and cities, work came to be organised as a relatively time-bound and space-bound activity, separated off from play, religion and festivity. Over the course of the eighteenth and nineteenth centuries work was increasingly valued for its own sake and not merely as a remedy for idleness. Some attempts were made to move from an orientation to task towards an orientation to time (see Thompson, 1967). Industrialists attempted to impose a rigorous discipline on their newly constructed workforce (Pollard, 1965). Tough and quite unfamiliar rules of attendance and punctuality were introduced, with various fines and punishments. Campaigns were mounted against drinking, idleness, blood sports, bad language, and holidays (see Myerscough, 1974: 4–6; Cunningham, 1980: ch. 3 on 'rational recreation'). Many fairs were abandoned and Saints' Days and closing days at the bank of England were dramatically reduced. From the 1860s onwards the idea of civilising the 'rough' working class through organised recreation became much more widespread amongst employers, middle-class reformers and the state (see Rojek, 1990: ch. 2). The typical forms of preferred recreation were educational instruction, physical exercise, crafts, musical training and excursions. Country holidays for deprived city children, as well as the camps organised by the burgeoning youth movement (the Boys' Brigade, Scouts, Jewish Lads' Brigades and so on), were one element of the social engineering of the working class favoured by the rational recreation movement.

As work became in part rationalised so the hours of working were gradually reduced. Parliament introduced various pieces of protective legislation in the second half of the nineteenth century. Particularly

important was the attainment of the half-day holiday, especially on Satur-
days (see Cunningham, 1980: ch. 5). Phelps-Brown noted that: 'The
achievement of a work-week not exceeding 54 hours and providing a half-
holiday was unique in its time and was celebrated as "la semaine
anglaise".' (1968, 173; also see Cunningham, 1980: 142–5).

The achievement of longer breaks, of week-long holidays, was pioneered in the north of England and especially in the cotton textile areas of
Lancashire (see Walton, 1981). Factory owners began to acknowledge
'wakes weeks' as regularised periods of holiday which were in effect
traded for much more regular attendance at work during the rest of the
year: 'The total closure of a mill at a customary holiday was preferable
to constant disruption throughout the summer, and there were advantages
in channelling holiday observances into certain agreed periods' (Walton,
1981: 255).

Some employers thus began to view regular holidays as contributing to
efficiency. However, the gradual extension of holidays from the mid-
nineteenth century onwards mainly resulted from defensive pressure from
the workforce itself, particularly from the more affluent sections, who
saw such practices as ways of developing their own autonomous forms of
recreation. The factory inspector Leonard Horner ascribed the survival of
holidays to custom rather than to 'liberality on the part of the masters'
(Walton, 1978: 35). A particularly significant feature of such holiday-
making was that it should be enjoyed collectively. As Walton argues, at
wakes week 'as at Christmas, Easter and Whitsuntide, custom dictated
that holidays should be taken *en masse* and celebrated by the whole
community' (1978: 35). From the 1860s onwards wakes weeks came
mainly to involve trips to the seaside away from normal places of
residence (see Walton and Poole, 1982).

In the late eighteenth and early nineteenth centuries there was a certain
shift in values, which was partly connected with 'the Romantic movement'. Emphasis was placed on the intensity of emotion and sensation, on
poetic mystery rather than intellectual clarity, and on individual
hedonistic expression (see Feifer, 1985: ch. 5 on 'The Romantic' tourist,
as well as Newby, 1981). The high priests of romanticism in Britain were
the Shelleys, Lord Byron and the Wordsworths. The effects of romanticism were to suggest that one could feel emotional about the natural
world and that scenery was something one could gaze at with delight.
Individual pleasures were to be derived from an appreciation of impressive physical sights. Romanticism implied that the residents of the newly
emerging industrial towns and cities could greatly benefit from spending
short periods away from them, viewing nature. Romanticism not only led
to the development of 'scenic tourism' and an appreciation for magnificent stretches of the coastline. It also encouraged sea bathing. Considering
the generally inclement weather and the fact that most bathers were naked
since no suitable bathing attire had yet been designed by the early nineteenth century, some considerable development of a belief in the health-

giving properties of 'nature' must have occurred. Much nineteenth-century tourism was based on the natural phenomenon of the 'sea' and its supposedly health-giving properties (see Hern, 1967: ch. 2; Walton, 1983: ch. 2; Feifer, 1985: 216).

A further precondition for the growth of mass tourism was greatly improved transportation. In the late eighteenth century it took three days to travel from Birmingham to Blackpool. Even the trip from Manchester to Blackpool took a whole day. Only Brighton was reasonably well served by coach. By 1830 forty-eight coaches a day went between London and Brighton and the journey time had been cut to 4.5 hours (see Walvin, 1978: 34). But there were two major problems of coach travel. First, many of the roads were in very poor condition. It was only in the 1830s that the turnpike trusts created a reasonable national network and journey times fell dramatically. Second, coach travel was very expensive, costing something like 2½d. to 3d. a mile. Richard Ayton noted of Blackpool visitors in 1813 that: 'Most of them come hither in carts, but some will walk in a single day from Manchester, distant more than forty miles' (Walvin, 1978: 35).

At first in the 1830s the railway companies did not realise the economic potential of the mass, low-income passenger market. They concentrated instead on goods traffic and on transporting prosperous passengers. But Gladstone's Railway Act of 1844, an important piece of legislation, obliged the railway companies to make provision for the 'labouring classes' (see Walvin, 1978: 37). Even before this the opening of the railway lines between Preston and Fleetwood in 1840 had produced an extraordinary influx of visitors to the port – many of whom then travelled down the coast to Blackpool. By 1848 it was estimated that over 100,000 trippers left Manchester by train for the coast during Whit week; by 1850 it was over 200,000 (Walvin, 1978: 38). The effect on the social tone of Blackpool in the middle of the century was noted at the time:

> Unless immediate steps are taken, Blackpool as a resort for respectable visitors will be ruined . . . . Unless the cheap trains are discontinued or some effective regulation made for the management of the thousands who visit the place, Blackpool property will be depreciated past recovery. (quoted in Walvin, 1978: 38)

Indeed the 'social tone' of Blackpool appears to have fallen quickly since fifteen years earlier it was said to have been 'a favourite, salubrious and fashionable resort for "respectable families"' (see Perkin, 1976: 181).

But the role of the railways should not be overemphasised. Generally the railway companies found that the seasonal nature of the holiday trade meant it was not particularly profitable. It was only at the end of the century that they really set about promoting travel to different resorts by outlining the most attractive features of each resort (see Richards and MacKenzie, 1986: 174–9). And only very rarely, as in the case of Silloth in the north-west of England, did they try to construct a wholly new resort: in this case it conspicuously failed (see Walton, 1979).

It has also been argued that the pattern of railway development accounted for the difference in 'social tone' between the various rapidly emerging seaside resorts in the mid-nineteenth century. On the face of it a reasonable explanation of these differences would be that those resorts which were more accessible to the great cities and industrial towns were likely to be more popular and this would drive out visitors with higher social status. Thus Brighton and Southend were more popular and had a lower social tone than Bournemouth and Torquay, which were not in day-tripping range from London (Perkin, 1976: 182). But such an explanation does not fully work. Perkin notes that Scarborough and Skegness were practically the same distance from the West Riding, yet they developed very different social tones. Although the railway obviously made a difference to such places its arrival does not completely explain the marked variations that emerged. Nor, Perkin argues, do the actions of local elites. There were in fact strong campaigns in most of the places that became working-class resorts (such as Blackpool or Morecambe) to stop the local railway companies from running Sunday day trips because it was, correctly, thought that the trippers would drive out the wealthier visitors that all resorts were keen to attract.

Perkin argues instead that the effect of the local elites on the respective 'social tones' of different resorts resulted from the particular ways in which land and buildings were locally owned and controlled. The factor determining each resort's social tone was the competition for domination of the resort between three fractions of capital: local, large capital, especially owners of the main hotels, concert halls, shops etc.; local, small capital, especially boarding-house keepers, owners of amusement arcades, etc.; and large, externally owned, highly capitalised enterprises providing cheap mass entertainment (1976: 185). Particularly important was the prior ownership and control of land in each locality. Perkin shows this most convincingly in the contrast between Blackpool and Southport, the latter being located *nearer* to large centres of population and possessing fine wide beaches. Both resorts began with the more or less spontaneous provision of sea-bathing accommodation by local innkeepers, farmers and fishermen. But in Southport land was unenclosed and various squatters who provided sea-bathing facilities soon became tenants of the joint lords of the manor who in turn laid out the spacious and elegant avenue, Lords Street. The landlords also prevented new industrial and much commercial development, with the result that Southport became a resort of large hotels, residential villas, large gardens, and retirement homes for cotton magnates and the like (see Walton, 1981: 251).

Blackpool, by contrast, began as a community of small freeholders. By 1838 there were only twenty-four holdings of land in the town over 25 acres and most of these were well away from the seafront. Even the larger holdings on the front were sold off and divided up into plots for seafront boarding houses. Walton notes that no large resort was so dominated by small lodging houses as Blackpool. This was because:

There was no room for a planned, high-class estate to grow up on the landowner's own terms, for Blackpool's small freeholders were understandably more concerned with taking the maximum profit from a cramped parcel of land than with improving the amenities of the resort as a whole.

Land in Blackpool was thus developed at high densities from the first, and few restrictions were placed on developers by landowners, for the fragmented pattern of landownership meant that there was always competition to sell building estates. (Walton, 1978: 63)

As a result the whole central area became an ill-planned mass of smaller properties, boarding houses, amusement arcades, small shops and the like, with no space for the grand public buildings, broad avenues and gardens found in Southport. Although local small capital attempted to appeal to the rapidly expanding middle-class tourist market, Blackpool did not possess the scenic attractions necessary to appeal to this market, and simultaneously it was proving immensely popular, partly because of its cheapness, with the industrial working class. This included both trippers and those staying overnight. The numbers of visitors increased greatly during the 1870s and 1880s by which time, the *Morning Post* declared, in Blackpool 'more fun could be found, for less money, than anywhere else in the world' (24 August 1887). Efforts by the Corporation to exclude the traders selling cheap goods and services failed, and Perkin suggests that by the 1890s enough local ratepayers had acquired an interest in catering for the working-class holiday-maker for Blackpool's 'social tone' to be firmly set (1976: 187). The main exception to this pattern was to be found in the area known as the North Shore where the 'Blackpool Land, Building and Hotel Company' acquired control of three-quarters of a mile of seafront and carefully planned a socially select and coherent development (see Walton, 1978: 70–1). It is interesting to note that during the nineteenth century Southport in fact prospered more than Blackpool, with a larger population even in 1901 (Perkin, 1976: 186).

So differences in the 'social tone' of resorts (the 'resort hierarchy') seem to be explicable in terms of the intersection between land ownership patterns and scenic attractiveness. Those places which ended up as working-class resorts, or what might be described as 'manufacturing resorts' linked into a particular industrial city, were those which generally had had highly fragmented land ownership in the mid-nineteenth century and a relatively unattractive scenic landscape. Ashworth says of Skegness, or Nottingham-by-the-Sea, that it is situated on 'the most colourless, featureless, negative strip of coastline in England' (the *Guardian*, 21 June 1986). Such resorts developed as fairly cheap places to visit, with the resulting tourist infrastructure to cater for a mass working-class market, but a market normally derived from a specific industrial area. As the market developed, so wealthier holiday-makers went elsewhere looking for superior accommodation, scenery and social tone. Holiday-making is a form of conspicuous consumption in which status attributions are made on the basis of *where* one has stayed and that depends in part upon what the *other people* are like who also stay there. The attractiveness of a place and hence its location within a resort hierarchy also depends upon *how many* other people are staying in the same place, and especially how many other people there are like oneself.

There were some interesting differences in the nineteenth century between popular holiday-making in the south of the country and in the north (see Walton, 1981). In the south, day excursions were more popular and they tended to be organised by the railway companies, national interest groups like the National Sunday League, or commercial firms like Thomas Cook (see Farrant, 1987, on the development of south coast resorts, of 'London-by-the-Sea'). This last organisation was founded in 1841 when Thomas Cook chartered a train from Leicester to Lough-borough for a temperance meeting (see Feifer, 1985: 167). His first pleasure excursion was organised in 1844 and the 'package' included a guide to recommended shops and places of historic interest upon which to 'gaze'. Cook wrote eloquently of the desirability of mass tourism and the democratisation of travel:

> But it is too late in this day of progress to talk such exclusive nonsense . . . rail-ways and steamboats are the results of the common light of science, and are for the people . . . . The best of men, and the noblest of minds, rejoice to see the people follow in their foretrod routes of pleasure. (quoted in Feifer, 1985: 168–9)

Interestingly, amongst those undertaking Cook's 'packages' to the conti-nent women considerably outnumbered men. In restrictive Victorian Britain Thomas Cook provided a remarkable opportunity for (often single) women to travel unchaperoned around Europe. The immense organisational and sociological significance of Thomas Cook is well summarised by Younger: 'His originality lay in his methods, his almost infinite capacity for taking trouble, his acute sense of the needs of his clients . . . . He invented the now universal coupon system, and by 1864, more than a million passengers had passed through his hands' (1973: 21).

In the north of England the already existing voluntary associations played a more important organisational and financial role in the evolution of the holiday movement (see Myerscough, 1974: 4–5). Pubs, churches and clubs often hired an excursion or holiday train and provided saving facilities for their members. This also had the advantage that the prox-imity of friends, neighbours and local leaders provided both security and social control. Large numbers of quite poor people were thereby enabled to go on holiday, spending nights away from home. The pattern was soon established of holiday-makers returning again and again to the same accommodation in the same resort. Blackpool, with its high proportion of Lancashire-born landladies, enjoyed a considerable advantage in this respect. Holiday clubs became very common in many places in industrial Lancashire, although they remained a rarity elsewhere. Walton well summarises late nineteenth-century developments in industrial Lancashire:

> The factory communities, after early prompting by employers and agencies of self-improvement, thus created their own grassroots system of holiday

'Mass' tourism by the seaside

organisation in the later nineteenth century. Each family was enabled to finance its own holiday without assistance from above. The unique Lancashire holiday system was thus based on working-class solidarity in retaining and extending the customary holidays, and by cooperation and mutual assistance to make the fullest use of them . . . . Only in Lancashire . . . was a balance struck between the survival of traditional holidays and the discipline of industrial labour. Only here did whole towns go on holiday, and find resorts able to look after their needs. (1978: 39)

This pattern was particularly found in the cotton textile industry, partly because of the high employment of women. This meant higher family incomes and a greater interest in forms of leisure that were less male-based and more family/household-based (see Walton, 1981: 253). Elsewhere, Walton maintains, 'too great an attachment to customary holidays and ways of working retarded the development of the working class seaside holiday over much of industrial England' (1981: 263).

Indeed this was a period in which many other leisure events came to be organised – there was a plethora of traditions invented between 1870 and 1914, often promoted and rendered sacred by royal patronage. Examples included the Royal Tournament in 1888, the first Varsity match in 1872, the first Henry Wood Promenade Concert in 1895, the Highland Games (first made royal in 1852), and so on. As Rojek argues, in the late Victorian/Edwardian period there was a restructured system of moral regulation, which involved not the denial of pleasures but their cultivation. In this national spectacles played a key role, most spectacularly through the 'Trooping the Colour' on Horse Guards Parade (see 1990: ch. 2). Participating at least once in these leisure events came to be an important part of the emergent sense of Britishness in the late nineteenth century, a sense derived in part from people's leisure activities.

In the inter-war period the main developments affecting the tourist gaze in Britain were the growth of car ownership to over 2 million by 1939; the widespread use of coach transport; the considerable growth of air transport – with over 200 million miles flown in 1938; the development of new organisations such as the Cyclists' Touring Club, the Cooperative Holidays Association, Sir Henry Lunn's, the Touring Club of France, the International Union of Official Organizations for Tourist Propaganda, the Youth Hostels Association, the Camping Club of Great Britain and so on; the initial development of the holiday camp, beginning with Joseph Cunningham's Isle of Man camp in 1908 and culminating in this period in Billy Butlin's Skegness camp opened in 1936; and the development of pleasure cruises (see Brunner, 1945; Lickorish and Kershaw, 1975; Ward and Hardy, 1986). However, despite all these developments, Brunner maintained, the seaside resort remained the mecca for the vast majority of British holiday-makers throughout the period. Indeed she claimed that such resorts are 'essentially native to this country, more numerous and more highly specialised in their function as resorts than those of any other land' (1945: 8). Seaside holidays were still the predominant form of holiday in Britain up to the Second World War and had expanded faster than other type of holiday in the inter-war period (see Walvin, 1978: 116–18).

To cope with the millions of visitors the resorts had initiated an enormous programme of investment. Private investment in hotels and houses was worth between £200 and £300 million while the municipalities invested very heavily themselves, although these were often Conservative controlled (see Pickvance, 1990, on the importance of such 'municipal conservatism' in the Thanet resorts). In Blackpool, for example, £1.5 million was spent on the promenade and the gardens, £400,000 on swimming pools, £1.25 million on a park, and £1.25 million on the Winter Gardens (Walvin, 1978: 117). Four resorts, Blackpool, Bournemouth, Brighton and Southend, had become major urban centres by 1931, with populations of over 100,000. Such resorts had unusual demographic characteristics, with much higher proportions than the national average of personal service workers of men and especially of women; and an increasing proportion of retired people.

One final change in the pre-war pattern should be noted. There was a strong development of the holidays-with-pay movement which culminated in the Holidays Act of 1938 (see discussion in Brunner, 1945: 9; and Walvin, 1978: ch. 6). As early as 1920 fifty-eight agreements which guaranteed paid holidays had been signed by the unions; by the mid-1920s about 16–17 per cent of the wage-earning labour force received holidays with pay. Little further progress was made during the depression years especially as it became obvious that legislation would be necessary. Various Private Member's Bills were proposed but they all met stiff opposition. Finally a Select Committee was set up in 1937 and this culminated in the 1938 legislation, much of which only came into effect after the war had ended. Sir Walter Citrine, giving evidence to the Select Committee for the TUC, declared that going on holiday 'is an increasing factor in working-class life. I think most people now are appreciating the necessity for a complete change of surroundings' (quoted in Brunner, 1945: 9). It was estimated that the number of UK holiday-makers in the postwar period would double from 15 million to about 30 million. So by this time there had grown up an industry which had become particularly 'geared to dealing with people *en masse* and had become highly efficient and organized at attracting and coping with armies of working people from the cities' (Walvin, 1978: 107).

Thus by the Second World War there was widespread acceptance of the view that going on holiday was good for one, that it was the basis of personal replenishment. Holidays had become almost a marker of citizenship, a right to pleasure. And around that right had developed in Britain an extensive infrastructure providing specialist services, particularly in the resorts. Everyone had become entitled to the pleasures of the 'tourist gaze' by the seaside.

The next section details how that gaze came to be organised in one particular 'working-class resort', Morecambe in the top north-west corner of England south of the Lake District. It will be shown just how differentiated is the organisation of that gaze as different resorts came to specialise in the provision of services to distinct social groupings.

'Bradford-by-the-Sea', beaches and bungalows

As we have seen, it was in the north of England, and especially in the Lancashire textile towns, that the development of working-class holidays was pioneered in the 1850s and 1860s:

> It was here that the seaside holiday, as opposed to the day excursion, became a mass experience during the last quarter of the nineteenth century. Elsewhere, even in London, the process was slower and patchier. But working-class demand became the most important generator of resort growth in northern England in late Victorian times. (Walton, 1983: 30–1)

Up to the mid-nineteenth century almost all of the largest resorts were located in the south of England, close to the middle-class patrons and sources of finance (see King, 1984: 70–4). Only these resorts could attract visitors from a national market; resorts away from the south coast had to rely on a local or regional market. But by the beginning of the twentieth century this had dramatically changed. A number of major resorts had developed in the north of England. By 1911 Blackpool had become the fifth-largest resort in the country while Lytham, Morecambe, Southport and St Anne's all showed major population increases. This was therefore a period which 'saw the swift and emphatic rise of the specialized working-class resort' (Walton, 1983: 67). Compared with the previous period the fastest growing resorts were much more widely dispersed throughout the country.

The pattern of growth in Morecambe has been described as follows: 'Morecambe . . . tried to become a select resort and commuter terminus for West Riding business men, but became instead the Yorkshireman's Blackpool' (Perkin, 1976: 104; and see Quick, 1962).

A condition essential to the growth of the working-class holiday resort was the strong ties of community found in the industrial centres in the north of England (see Walton, 1978: 32). But Morecambe could not hope to compete with Blackpool for the bulk of the holiday trade from Lancashire because Blackpool had established a sizeable tourist infrastructure somewhat earlier. It had better rail links (using the same company throughout the journey) and it was considerably nearer the rapidly expanding towns and cities in south and east Lancashire and could therefore develop a huge day-tripper clientele. Once a resort had established a pull over its 'industrial hinterland' it was unlikely that its position would be challenged, since visits to that resort became part of the 'tradition' of holiday-making in those industrial centres. Resorts that developed later, such as Bournemouth or Skegness, generally were able to do so because they had no obvious or similar rivals close by (see Walvin, 1978: 161). In the case of Morecambe it had become clear in the second half of the century that it would be unable to compete with Blackpool for the bulk of the Lancashire holiday market. Thus the Wigan coalowner and alderman Ralph Darlington declared to a Commons Committee in 1884 that: 'Morecambe does not stand in estimation with us as a watering place. I should say it is not one at all' (quoted in Grass, 1972: 6). Likewise Thomas Baxter, chairman of the Morecambe Board of Health in 1889, observed that: 'there was no doubt that Blackpool had always had the pull all over Lancashire' (*Observer*, 11 October 1889).

The inability to compete for the Lancashire holiday market combined with the rail link to the Yorkshire woollen towns meant that much of the Morecambe trade came from the West Riding. This was because the connections with Yorkshire extended not only to the holiday trade but also to patterns of migration. Considerable numbers of people from Yorkshire, both workers and employers, came to live in Morecambe, some of whom commuted to Bradford or Halifax daily (Perkin, 1976: 190). The first mayor of the new Corporation, Alderman E. Barnsbee, was a Bradford man who retired to Morecambe. In addition Morecambe

Postcard from Morecambe

was not the only holiday destination for those living in the West Riding. It had to face considerable competition from the resorts on the east coast, in both Yorkshire and Lincolnshire. Yet it did become increasingly popular. A *Daily Telegraph* correspondent wrote in 1891:

> as Margate is to the average Cockney, so is Morecambe to the stalwart and health-loving Yorkshireman. For it is allowed on all sides that Morecambe is true Yorkshire to the backbone . . . Yorkshiremen, Yorkshire lads, and Yorkshire lasses have selected to colonise and to popularise this breezy, rainy, wind-swept, and health-giving watering-place. (quoted in Grass, 1972: 10)

While in the inter-war period a Lord Mayor of Bradford proclaimed that: 'most of the citizens of Bradford, to say nothing of the children, have enjoyed spending some of their leisure time in this wonderful health resort' (*Visitor*, July 1935, Diamond Jubilee Souvenir).

Morecambe, however, could not attract sufficient numbers of the middle-class visitors that were wanted. Partly this was because the town leaders could not prevent the growth of the day-tripper trade, described by the *Lancaster Guardian* as a 'disorderly and riotous mob' (22 August 1868). And partly this was because the existence of very many relatively small houses (often 'back houses') made it impossible to stop the establishment of new boarding houses and small hotels which provided accommodation for less well-off visitors, especially those from West

Yorkshire. There was a considerable debate between the champions of 'respectability', who were organised through the Board of Health until 1894 and the Urban District Council after then, and the providers of 'mass holiday consumption' such as the large entertainment companies. In an editorial in 1901 the *Visitor* supported the latter group on the grounds that in a town with 'no public band, no public parks, no pier supported from the rates', they had 'done their work catering for the visitors admirably this season' (2 October 1901). As early as the late 1890s the advocates of commercial development had won the day and attempts by the Urban District Council to maintain 'respectability' had failed. The *Daily Telegraph* summed up Morecambe in 1891: 'It may be that, to the fastidious, rough honest-hearted Morecambe is a little primitive, and slightly tinged with vulgarity. But it is never dull' (quoted in Perkin, 1976: 191).

In the later parts of the century there were a number of related developments in Morecambe: a rapid rate of population increase (over 10 per cent per annum); a considerable growth of capital expenditure, especially on major facilities including a revolving tower; and an extensive growth of lodging-house and hotel accommodation (see Denison-Edson, 1967).

But its prosperity was dependent upon the level of prosperity, particularly in the west Yorkshire area. When Bradford, and especially the woollen industry, was doing well then Morecambe seemed to prosper. As the *Observer* noted in 1883, when 'the Bradford trade has been at a low ebb it has not been at all plain sailing for "Bradford-by-the-Sea"' (25 May). Also Morecambe remained the prisoner of the railway companies and the quality and quantity of the train services they provided.

In the inter-war period Morecambe was successful, partly because there was an extensive growth of paid holidays for those in work, and partly because most holidays were still taken at the seaside and family-households were transported there by rail and to a lesser extent by coach. Spokesmen from Morecambe advocated that all workers should receive a week's holiday with pay (*Visitor*, 22 January 1930). By 1925 there were two holiday camps in Heysham, which was part of the same borough. Morecambe experienced considerable annual growth in population, 3.8 per cent during the 1930s, and its total rateable value rose by 54 per cent between 1930 and 1946 (Denison-Edson, 1967: 28). The 1930s and 1940s were particularly prosperous, with the town council investing heavily in new objects for the tourist gaze, a clear example of how a Conservative council in a resort may well engage in 'municipal conservatism'.

I shall now very briefly describe two other resorts by way of comparison: Brighton, on the south coast, and Birchington, in Kent. Each is responsible for having been first to develop new objects of the tourist gaze at the seaside, Brighton with the first beach devoted to 'pleasure', and Birchington with the first bungalows.

We have already noted the early and extensive development of Brighton in the eighteenth century. The beach was viewed as a site for medical treatment and was regulated by the 'dippers', the women responsible for immersion (on the following, see Shields, 1990: Part 2, ch. 2). In the mid-nineteenth century this medicalised beach was replaced by a pleasure beach, which Shields characterises as a liminal zone, a built-in escape from the patterns and rhythms of everyday life. Such a zone had a further characteristic, of carnival, as the beach became noisy and crowded, full of unpredictable social mixing, and involving the inversion of social hierarchies and moral codes. In the classic medieval carnival, the grotesque body was counterposed to the disciplined body of propriety and authority; in the nineteenth century holiday carnival the grotesque body was shamefully uncovered and open to the gaze of others. Literally grotesque bodies became increasingly removed from actual view and were gazed upon through commercialised representations, especially the vulgar picture postcard. Shields summarises the carnival of the beach rendered appropriate for pleasure:

> It is this foolish, impudent, undisciplined body which is the most poignant symbol of the carnivalesque – the unclosed body of convexities and orifices, intruding onto and into others' body-space, [which] threatens to escape, transgress, and transcend the circumscriptions of the body. (1990)

The fact that Brighton was the first resort in which the beach became constructed as a site for pleasure, for social mixing, for status reversals, for carnival, is one reason why in the first few decades of the twentieth century Brighton came to have a reputation for sexual excess and particularly for the 'dirty weekend'. This has become part of the place image of Brighton, although the beach no longer functions as a site of the carnivalesque.

Whereas Brighton's class associations were with royalty and the aristocracy, the resorts in Kent in the mid-nineteenth century were associated with the relatively new middle class (see King, 1984: 72–8). But as early as 1870 both Margate and Ramsgate were becoming less attractive to this holiday market, especially to the professional middle class, which was increasingly staying in Cliftonville and Westgate. In the latter all the roads were private and only detached houses were allowed. The first bungalows in Britain thus came to be built in 1869–70 in Westgate and more extensively in Birchington in 1870–3, just next door (King, 1984: 74). Until this development there was no specialist house building by the seaside. Indeed in the earlier fishing villages houses were often built with their 'backs' to the sea, as at Ravenglass in the Lake District. The sea was there for fishing not for gazing on. Nineteenth-century resorts were public places with some distinctive public buildings, such as assembly rooms, promenades, public gardens, dance halls and so on. Residential provision was similar to that found in inland towns and was not distinctive.

By contrast, the development of the bungalow as a specialised form of housing by the seaside resulted from a number of developments: the heightened attraction of visiting the seaside not for strictly medical reasons but for the bracing air and fine views; the increasing demand from sections of the middle class for accommodation well away from other people, for being able to gaze at the sea in relative solitude; and the rising popularity of swimming as opposed to dipping and hence the perceived need for semi-private access for the whole family and especially for children. Birchington ideally met these conditions; there were no public facilities, there was an attractive coastline for building, the first bungalows were 'rural looking' and offered attractive contrasts with the urban, and tunnels could be built linking each bungalow with the beach. In the twentieth century there has been an extensive 'bungaloid growth' at the seaside so that in some sense in the twentieth century the bungalow is the seaside. And as it has become the housing of the lower middle class so its earlier fashionability and bohemianism has disappeared, and indeed it has become an object of considerable status hostility (see King, 1984: ch. 5).

It is worth considering for a moment holiday developments in a country much influenced by British culture but where the outcome has been quite different – New Zealand. There are basically no seaside resorts, the closest being Day's Bay, near Wellington, but even here there are no facilities except for one municipally owned teashop. In addition the bungalow could hardly become associated with the seaside in New Zealand since it is the form of house building found everywhere. There seem to be several main reasons for the lack of resort development in New Zealand: since all the major towns are on the coast it was unlikely that 'going to the seaside' would be seen as in any way special: population growth only occurred after the development of the motor car, so leisure became more privatised and less geographically dependent upon the railway, which was important in Britain, as we have seen; and finally the very strong emphasis on family-organised leisure has been associated with a tendency to self-provisioning rather than purchasing the required services.

The postwar period saw both the rapid growth of the British seaside resort in the 1950s and rapid decline in many places in the 1970s and 1980s. I shall deal with these processes fairly briefly here since much of the rest of the book is taken up with a rather broader analysis of how the tourist gaze is being transformed in western societies with the result that the British seaside resort has become a much less favoured object of that gaze.

The end of the pier?

In this section I shall chart what has happened to seaside resorts in the postwar period, and try to make sense of the following paradox. In Britain tourism has become a massively important industry, yet the places which were the most developed in terms of their infrastructure to take advantage of this, namely seaside resorts, have not shared in this growth. In the past ten years the proportion of total tourist expenditure spent in the resorts has fallen from about one-half to one-third and the number of bed nights has declined by 25 per cent (Wickers and Charlton, 1988: F6). For example, between 1973 and 1987 in Morecambe the number of small hotels and guesthouses fell from 640 to 267 and the number of bed-spaces from 12,340 to 7,115 (Bagguley et al., 1989: ch. 3). Many of the hotels have been converted into accommodation for those released from psychiatric hospitals, for those on income support, and for the elderly. Resorts have thus become merely one of a large number of potential objects of the tourist gaze. The spending of a week or fortnight's holiday by the seaside in Britain is now viewed as a less attractive and significant touristic experience than in the decades around the Second World War.

In the immediate postwar period there was no hint of the troubles to come. As Parry says, if the 1920s and 1930s were the heyday of the resorts then the 1950s and early 1960s were a kind of Indian summer: 'rationing ended, "austerity" ceased and business boomed; the holiday abroad was still the preserve of the few and package tours were non-existent' (Parry, 1983: 189). Moreover, the majority of northerners stayed loyal to their own resorts. This traditional or organised pattern continued, with whole towns moving off to the seaside in a given week. A central role in sustaining such patterns was played by the railway. British Railways organised many specials or excursion trains, taking visitors from particular destinations to the resorts which had been traditionally visited. For example, at Easter 1960 at least forty-eight specials arrived at Morecambe, whose stationmaster declared it the busiest Easter in the past eighteen years. Major new investments were planned although most of the visitors still stayed either in traditional hotel or bed-and-breakfast accommodation (which was unlicensed), or in a holiday camp. The latter expanded greatly in the 1950s particularly with the arrival of Pontins (see Ward and Hardy, 1986: ch. 4).

In this period the holiday experience was remarkably regulated. Even where people stayed in apartments this generally involved the provision of set meals for a week. The holiday was based on the time zone of the week (see Colson, 1926). It was almost impossible to book mid-week. Visitors knew when they were to eat, what they would eat, and exactly how long they were to stay. If people were staying in a holiday camp then much else was organised and indeed 'from one camp to the next the mix was identical – the same pattern of entertainment, the same diet, the same type of accommodation, the same weekly routine' (Ward and Hardy, 1986: 161). Although television was appearing in such places the emphasis was still upon the provision of live entertainment. In the 1950s big-name artists were regularly attracted to Morecambe, while Blackpool boasted fourteen live shows (Parry, 1983: 191).

However, much of this began to change dramatically in the 1960s, and the rest of the book charts a series of transformations in the organisation of the tourist gazes away from many of these resorts. I shall now describe changes in what is ordinary and hence what is taken to be extraordinary in what is gazed upon at the seaside.

Seaside resorts in Britain normally possessed at least one pier (Blackpool had three) and often one tower. Both such constructions involved an attempt to conquer nature, to construct a 'man-made' object which at all times and for ever would be there dominating either the sea or the sky. Their domination is what gives them a reason for being there, that is their function. Barthes says of the similar Eiffel Tower that it enables the visitor to participate in a dream (1979). The Tower is no normal spectacle because it gives observers a wholly original view of Paris. Indeed it transforms Paris into nature, 'it constitutes the swarming of men into a landscape . . . the city joins up with the great natural themes that are offered to the curiosity of men [sic]: the ocean, the storm, the mountains, the snow, the rivers' (1979: 8). The most famous such building in Britain is the tower at Blackpool, opened in 1894 and an imitation of the Eiffel Tower. It is a unique building in Britain, and effectively stands for the town. Such towers, and to a lesser extent, piers, enable people to see things in their structure, to link human organisation with extraordinary natural phenomena, and to celebrate the participation within, and the victory of, human agency over nature. They are part of that irreducibly extraordinary character of the ideal tourist site. Thompson says of Blackpool Tower:

> It also adds a third dimension to the east/west and north/south axes of move-ment. Rather like the beach/sea interface, it offers some specific pleasures by transcending the normal and day-to-day. It enables the holidaymaker to enjoy Blackpool from a different perspective. (1983: 126)

In the past two or three decades, the extraordinary character of piers and towers has dramatically declined. Piers have been falling into the sea and do not demonstrate the domination *of* nature, rather the reverse. In Morecambe for example one pier has been washed away and the other is half burnt down and may be demolished. For years both Brighton piers were derelict. Piers and towers now stand for nostalgia, for the 'theme' of the old seaside holiday which is well expressed in the 1988 Isle of Man advertising slogan 'You'll look forward to going back'. At the same time, much more spectacular and modern examples of the mastery of the sea can now be found, in bridges, tunnels, hovercraft, ships, and marinas (with one even planned for Morecambe). Likewise towers connecting the land and the sky are now dwarfed by skyscrapers, hotels, space capsules, and of course by aircraft, all of which are much more obviously 'modern' and extraordinary.

A second major attraction at the seaside resort was the funfair or pleasure park. In Britain Blackpool Pleasure Beach has been since its beginnings in 1906 the leading site for such a regime of pleasure (see

Parry, 1983: chs 17, 18; Bennett, 1983). From the 1920s onwards it has always tried to look resolutely modern. 'Its architecture of pleasure has taken on a streamlined, functional appearance' (Bennett, 1983: 145). The employment of the architect Joseph Emberton created a wholly new 'Architecture of Pleasure' in which everything was light, sun, fresh air and fun (Parry, 1983: 152–4). And it has been periodically updated. The designer of the Festival of Britain, Jack Radcliffe, gave it a new look during the boom period in the 1950s. New rides kept being added, mostly based either on innovations pioneered in world fairs (for example, a ferris wheel based on one exhibited at the Chicago World Fair of 1893), or on futuristic rides found in American amusement parks (for example, the *Starship Enterprise* introduced in 1980). Central to the strategy of the management of the Pleasure Beach has been progress, being first (at least in the UK), biggest and best. It even has its own tower using latest technology and which makes *the* Blackpool Tower seem rather quaint (Bennett, 1983: 147). The Park is still owned by a local company; it has not gone the way of much of Blackpool's entertainment facilities, which became part of London-based leisure companies, such as THF and EMI, in the 1960s and 1970s (Bennett, 1983: 146). It attracts 6.5 million visitors a year. Most other places at the seaside cannot compete with it. For example, people staying at Morecambe often travel to Blackpool to visit the Pleasure Park.

The main competition to Blackpool now comes from the new-style amusement and theme parks, the most successful in the north of England being that at Alton Towers. These new parks are not normally located at the seaside, although they generally have a very attractive 'rural' location close to the motorway (rather than the rail) network. Apart from Blackpool Pleasure Beach the pleasure parks located at the existing seaside resorts will struggle to compete. Such places should exhibit 'modernity', high technology, youth, controlled danger, anticipation and pleasure. But if they are located in 'old-fashioned' resorts (almost anywhere but Blackpool or Brighton) there are many counter-messages, of previous technologies, age, danger through neglect, and regret at not being elsewhere. In Morecambe the major pleasure park has been turned into a theme park, bizarrely based on the theme of the wild West.

Blackpool, by contrast, has more generally tried to construct itself as irreducibly modern, as a cosmopolitan, international leisure centre, the 'Las Vegas of the North', having less now to do with its previous Lancashire/northern/working-class associations. As Bennett notes: 'At Blackpool, everything is new no matter how old it is' (1986: 146). It is the biggest seaside resort in Europe with more visitors than the whole of Greece, and more beds than Portugal (Wickers and Charlton, 1988: F6; Waterhouse 1989a: 10). There are currently 2,700 hotels, tourism accounts for 12,000 jobs, 16 per cent of all short-break holidays in Britain are made to Blackpool, and an incredible 25 per cent of day visitors have made at least fifty previous day trips to the resort (Lancashire County

Council, 1987: 24). Keith Waterhouse summarises its over-the-top charms: 'it would have been, in all its gaudy tattiness, the greatest show on earth. It still is, outvulgarised . . . only by Las Vegas' (1989a: 10). By contrast, all other seaside resorts appear old-fashioned and cannot offer anything like the same range of facilities. The few that have prospered, such as Bridlington, Torquay or Southport with its proposed £300 million marina, have the advantage of few modernist buildings to spoil the image of what a typical resort (apart from Blackpool) ought to look like (see Wickers, 1987: 8).

Another feature of most resorts were holiday camps (see Ward and Hardy, 1986). They had begun before the First World War when they literally consisted of a camp of tents. Even at that time their development was said to be a reaction against the relatively poor quality of accommodation and services in the typical seaside boarding house. The most significant development came with the 'luxury' camps started by Billy Butlin, beginning with that in Skegness which opened in 1936. Compared with what was available at the typical hotel or guesthouse, Butlin provided really luxurious facilities, with extensive on-site amusement, good-quality food, high-class entertainments and modern sanitation – what Ray Gosling has termed a 'veritable Beveridge of leisure' (quoted in Ward and Hardy, 1986: 60). Interestingly, when the first camp was opened the visitors appeared bored and Butlin concluded that holiday-makers required some degree of organisation. The famous 'Redcoats' were invented – they '*would* lead, advise, explain, comfort, help out, and generally make themselves the closest thing to holiday angels on earth' (quoted in Ward and Hardy, 1986: 63).

The heyday of such camps was in the immediate postwar period up to 1959 when the BBC television series *Hi-de-Hi!* is set. This prosperity resulted from a number of factors including the coming into effect of the 1938 Holidays with Pay Act, the high levels of employment, and the reduced age of marriage and high rate of family formation. In 1948 one in twenty of all holiday-makers stayed at Butlin's. The holiday camp was a symbol of the postwar society, reflecting the modernist architectural style of the period. Some camps looked little better than scaled-down council estates, such as Pontin's at Middleton Sands near Morecambe. Others, that at Prestatyn in Wales for example, captured something of the glamour and fantasy of the ocean liner in its clean, functional styling (see Ward and Hardy, 1986: ch. 5).

In the 1950s a considerable effort was made to construct the camps as places for 'family holidays' and to limit the number of single visitors. There was also an attempt to prevent the majority of visitors to the camps being mainly from the 'working class'. This was unsuccessful as the camps, like their host resorts, became unable to attract large numbers of middle-class visitors, although it should be noted how the camps tried to construct their clientele as classless through treating them all as 'campers'. There was also a shift in the camps towards 'self-catering' especially by

Pontin's. They tried to construct this as involving increasing 'freedom' and indeed the term 'camp' has itself been dropped since it implies regimentation. They are now known as 'centres', 'villages' or 'holiday-worlds'. Nevertheless their attraction has undoubtedly diminished, with the number of such camps in England falling from 114 in 1939 to 83 in 1986. In 1983 two of the largest, the Butlin's camps at Filey and Clacton, were closed. Ward and Hardy concluded from their study that by the 1970s and 1980s:

> holiday camps are something of a period piece . . . new concepts of holidaymaking have been developed . . . . Package holidays to exotic places, coupled with more individualistic off-season breaks, increase the difficulties of the camps . . . . Much about the holiday camp is now commonplace. (1986: 152)

They are no longer the stuff of which dreams are made. The response of their owners has been both to concentrate on larger centres (as at Butlin's), and to segment the market with different centres tailored to different tastes, including adult-only centres, special-interest holidays, and short breaks (as at Warner's) (see Glancey, 1988).

Such camps will certainly be weakly placed to compete with the newest 'concept' in holiday provision in Europe, the Center Parc development in Sherwood Forest, Nottinghamshire. This is a £34 million holiday village in which an artificial 'seaside' has been constructed within a giant double-skinned plastic dome which sustains a constant temperature of 84°F. In this complex, swimming is entertainment, fun and pleasure with tropical heat, warm water lagoons, palm trees and waterside cafes. Other features include sailing, canoeing and a immense variety of vegetation. Such centres do not have to be located near the sea since the technology in effect permits the seaside to be constructed anywhere. The second Center Parc is being built in East Anglia.

Resorts were believed to be extraordinary because concentrated there were the sea, the sand, sometimes the sun, as well as the absence of the manufacturing industry that was present in almost all other substantial towns and cities. But in recent years a number of transformations have changed all this. As I pointed out, the seaside can now be constructed and gazed upon anywhere. But the relative attraction of the sea itself has also declined. In the nineteenth century the development of the resorts was based on the presumed health-giving properties of sea bathing. Sun-bathing, by contrast, was relatively uncommon partly because of the high value placed upon pale skin which signified delicacy, idleness and seclu-sion. However, this began to change within the upper classes from the 1920s onwards, particularly with the development of newly fashionable resorts such as Cannes and Biarritz. Amongst such groups a tan was associated with the presumed spontaneity and natural sensuality of black people. Sunbathing was presumed to bring people closer to nature (see Turner and Ash, 1975: 79–83).

In the postwar period it has been the sun, not the sea, that is presumed to produce health and sexual attractiveness. *The* ideal body has come to be viewed as one that is tanned. This viewpoint has been diffused downwards through the social classes with the result that many package holidays present this as almost the reason for going on holiday. The north European resorts have thus come to be seen as less attractive, less fashionable, because they cannot guarantee to produce a tanned body (see Fiske, 1989: ch. 3, on the semiotics of the Australian beach for contrast). Although this may change with the current panic about malignant melanoma and it may become fashionable again to be pale, so far in Europe this concentration on the sun has enormously benefited the development of resorts around the Mediterranean. This began in France and Spain, then spread to Greece, Italy, Yugoslavia, and then to north Africa and most recently to Turkey.

Beaches in Britain cannot guarantee the sun. Nor can they guarantee clean water, if one wishes to swim in the sea. Of the 392 beaches in Britain listed by the government, 40 per cent do not meet EEC standards, including almost all of those in the north-west of England (see Scott, 1988). By comparison France had 1,498 and Italy 3,308 beaches. It should be noted that beaches are complex spaces, anomalously located between land and sea, nature and culture. Different stretches of beach are to be read quite differently – with strikingly different possible forms of activity possible.

Seaside resorts have also become less distinctive because of the widespread de-industrialisation of many towns and cities so that there is less need to escape from them to the contrasting seaside. As the everyday has changed, as towns and cities have become de-industrialised and many have themselves become objects for the tourist gaze, with wave machines and other features of the beach, so seaside resorts are no longer extraordinary.

People used to go to the seaside in order to find concentrations of those services specifically organised for the provision of pleasure. Now, however, many resorts boast poorer services than comparably sized towns. A recent report on Morecambe stated that:

> In 1973 the resort boasted two piers, five cinemas, theatres, a dance hall, a wealth of live entertainment and many other attractions. Today the piers and cinemas have ceased operating, the theatres have closed and the range of live entertainment is extremely limited. (quoted in *Lancashire Evening Post*, 23 December 1987)

A number of processes have reduced the distinctiveness of the resorts in this way. The growth of television has at a stroke evened out the provision of entertainment so that now one does not need to go to resorts in order to see the big names. As Parry expresses it: 'television paraded the top talent every night of the week' (1983: 192). Further, most resorts are in population terms fairly small and cannot support a high concentration of entertainment services. Often therefore they rely on some level of public provision. However, since they are generally run by Conservative councils there is considerable reluctance to pay for such activities 'on the rates'. And even if they do develop such facilities they are often still less impressive than those to be found in the potential visitor's home town. Many councils away from the coast have built sports and leisure centres, while national entertainment companies have expanded almost anywhere except at the seaside. More generally, as we shall see later, many towns and cities have developed as centres of consumption, both for their own residents and for potential tourists. Harvey notes that increasingly every town and city has: 'to appear as an innovative, exciting, creative and safe place to live, play, and consume. Spectacle and display became the symbols of [a] dynamic community' (1987: 13).

I shall examine such changes in the following chapters. Just why have 'spectacle and display' become characteristics of almost everywhere? What processes have produced the generalising of the tourist gaze? And what does this mean for the organisation of those industries which have developed to provide services for the tourist gaze?

One important point to consider is the internationalisation of contemporary tourism. Every potential object of the tourist gaze now has to compete internationally, and this has led to substantial changes in just what is extraordinary and what is internationally ordinary. Parry well expresses how the cheap 'package tour' had devastating effects upon the northern seaside resort:

> The holidaymaker of the 1930s had no choice and was prepared to take a chance. If he [sic] lived in a mill town at least all his neighbours would have suffered from the same 'poor week'. Not so his counterpart in the 1970s. He wanted sun – and if half the street was to come back from Marbella or Torremolinos with burned backs, peeling noses and queasy stomachs he wasn't going to be left out. (1983: 192–3)

3
THE CHANGING ECONOMICS OF THE TOURIST INDUSTRY

Introduction

The relationship between the tourist gaze and those industries which have been developed to meet that gaze is extremely problematic.

Initially, it should be noted that almost all the services provided to tourists have to be delivered at the time and place at which they are produced (see Urry, 1987). As a consequence the quality of the social interaction between the provider of the service, such as the waiter, flight attendant or hotel receptionist, and the consumers, is part of the 'product' being purchased by tourists. If aspects of that social interaction are unsatisfactory (the offhand waiter, the unsmiling flight attendant, or the rude receptionist), then what is purchased is in effect a different service product. The problem results from the fact that the production of such consumer services cannot be entirely carried out backstage, away from the gaze of tourists. They cannot help seeing some aspects of the industry which is attempting to serve them. But furthermore, tourists tend to have high expectations of what they should receive since 'going away' is an event endowed with particular significance. People are looking for the *extra*ordinary and hence will be exceptionally critical of services provided that appear to undermine such a quality.

Other features of tourist industries are likely to produce difficulties for the producers of such services. Such services cannot be provided anywhere: they have to be produced *and consumed* in very particular places. Part of what is consumed is in effect the place in which the service producer is located. If the particular place does not convey appropriate cultural meanings, the quality of the specific service may well be tarnished. There is therefore a crucial 'spatial fixity' about tourist services (see Bagguley, 1987). In recent years there has been enormously heightened competition to attract tourists. In relationship to Britain there has been a 'Europeanisation' of the tourist market and increasingly a 'globalisation'. So while the producers are to a significant extent spatially fixed, in that they have to provide particular services in particular places, consumers are increasingly mobile, able to consume tourist services on a global basis. The industry is inevitably competitive since almost every place in the world could well act as an object of the tourist gaze. Such services are inherently labour-intensive and hence employers will seek to minimise labour costs. A variety of strategies is employed to bring this about but some at least will result in tarnishing or wholly undermining the extraordinary character of the consumers' tourist gaze.

The emphasis on the quality of the social interaction between producers and consumers of tourist services means that developments in the industry are not explicable simply in terms of 'economic' determinants. As will be shown later in the book it is also necessary to examine a range of cultural changes which transform people's expectations about what they wish to gaze upon, what significance should be attached to that gaze, and what effects this will have upon the providers of the relevant tourist services. This is an industry which has always necessitated considerable levels of public involvement and investment and in recent years this has increased as all sorts of places attempt to construct or reinforce their position as favoured objects of the tourist gaze. The economics of tourism cannot be understood separately from the analysis of cultural and policy developments to be found later in the book, just as work in tourist industries cannot be understood separately from the cultural expectations that surround the complex delivery of such services. Work relationships in tourist industries are significantly culturally defined.

In this present chapter attention will be directed to some of the more obvious recent developments in what can loosely be termed the changing political economy of the tourist industry. The next section gives a brief account of the concept of positional goods, the main economic concept used to account for the economics of tourism, before moving on to the changing UK tourist industry, noting particularly its tendencies to globalisation; and to some of the main changes in the political economy of overseas tourism.

The social limits of tourism

The economist Mishan presents one of the clearest accounts of the thesis that there are fundamental limits to the scale of contemporary tourism (1969; and see Urry, 1990, on the following). These limits derive from the immense costs of congestion and overcrowding. In the 1960s Mishan perceptively wrote of: 'the conflict of interest . . . between, on the one hand, the tourists, tourist agencies, traffic industries and ancillary services, to say nothing of governments anxious to augment their reserves of foreign currencies, and all those who care about preserving natural beauty on the other' (1969: 140). He quoted the example of Lake Tahoe, whose plant and animal life had been destroyed by sewage generated by the hotels built along its banks. A 1980s example would be the way in which the coral around tourist islands like Barbados is dying because of the pumping of raw sewage into the sea from the beachside hotels and because locals remove both plants and fish from the coral to sell to tourists.

Mishan also notes that here is a conflict of interests between present and future generations which stems from the way in which travel and tourism are priced. The cost of the marginal tourist takes no account of the additional congestion costs imposed by the extra tourist. These congestion costs include the generally undesirable effects of overcrowded beaches, a lack of peace and quiet, and the destruction of the scenery. Moreover, the environmentally sensitive tourist knows that there is nothing to be gained from delaying a visit to the place in question: if anything, it is the opposite. There is a strong incentive to go as soon as possible – to enjoy the unspoilt view before the crowds get there! Mishan's perspective as someone horrified by the consequences of mass tourism can be seen from the following: 'the tourist trade, in a competitive scramble to uncover all places of once quiet repose, of wonder, beauty and historic interest to the money-flushed multitude, is in effect literally and irrevocably destroying them' (1969: 141). His middle-class elitism is never far from the surface. For example, he claims that it is the 'young and gullible' who are taken in by the fantasies dreamt up by the tourist industry.

His main criticism is that the spread of mass tourism does not produce a democratisation of travel. It is an illusion which destroys the very places which are being visited. This is because geographical space is a strictly limited resource. Mishan says: 'what a few may enjoy in freedom the crowd necessarily destroys for itself' (1969: 142). Unless international agreement is reached (he suggests the immensely radical banning of all international air travel!), the next generation will inherit a world almost bereft of places of 'undisturbed natural beauty' (1969: 142). So allowing the market to develop without regulation has the effect of destroying the very places which are the objects of the tourist gaze. Increasing numbers of such places are suffering from the same pattern of self-destruction. One resort that has recently been thought to be so damaged is St Tropez, the place initially made famous by Brigitte Bardot. She now claims that it is being swept by a 'black tide of human filth'; that tourists 'are mediocre, dirty, ill-mannered and rude'; and that she intends 'leaving it to the invaders' (see Rocca, 1989).

This pessimistic kind of argument is criticised by Beckerman, who makes two useful points (1974: 50–2). First, concern for the effects of mass tourism is basically a 'middle-class' anxiety (like much other environmental concern). This is because the really rich: 'are quite safe from the masses in the very expensive resorts, or on their private yachts or private islands or secluded estates' (Beckerman, 1974: 50–1). Second, most groups affected by mass tourism do in fact benefit from it, including even some of the pioneer visitors who find available services that were previously unobtainable when the number of visitors was rather small. Hence Beckerman talks of the 'narrow selfishness of the Mishan kind of complaint' (1974: 51).

This disagreement over the effects of mass tourism is given more theoretical weight in Hirsch's thesis on the social limits to growth (1978; also see the collection Ellis and Kumar, 1983). His starting point is similar to Mishan's: he notes that individual liberation through the exercise of consumer choice does not make those choices liberating for all individuals together (1978: 26). In particular he is concerned with the positional economy. This term refers to all aspects of goods, services, work, positions and other social relationships which are either scarce or subject to congestion or crowding. Competition is therefore zero-sum: as any one person consumes more of the good in question, so someone else is forced to consume less. Supply cannot be increased, unlike the case of material goods where the processes of economic growth can easily produce more. People's consumption of positional goods is inherently relational. The satisfaction derived by each individual is not infinitely expandable but depends upon the position of one's own consumption to that of others. This can be termed coerced competition. Ellis and Heath define this as competition in which the status quo is not an option (1983: 16–19). It is normally assumed in economics that market exchanges are voluntary so that people freely choose whether or not to enter into the exchange relationship. However, in the case of coerced consumption people do not really have such a choice. One has to participate even though at the end of the consumption process one is not necessarily better off. This can be summarised in the phrase: 'one has to run faster in order to stay still'. Hirsch cites the example of suburbanisation. People move to the suburbs to escape from the congestion of the city and to be nearer the quietness of the countryside. But as economic growth continues, the suburbs get more congested, they expand, and so the original suburbanites are as far away from the countryside as they were originally. Hence they will seek new suburban housing closer to the countryside, and so on. The individually rational actions of others make one worse off and one cannot avoid participation in the leap-frogging process. No one is better off over time as a result of such coerced consumption.

Hirsch clearly believes that much consumption has similar characteristics to the case of suburbanisation, namely that the satisfaction people derive from it depends on the consumption choices of others. This can be seen most clearly in the case of certain goods which are scarce in an absolute sense. Examples cited here are 'old masters' or the 'natural landscape', where increased consumption by one leads to reduced consumption by another (although see Ellis and Heath, 1983: 6–7). Hirsch also considers the cases where there is 'direct social scarcity': luxury or perhaps snob goods which are enjoyed because they are rare or expensive and possession of them indicates social status or good taste. Examples here would include jewellery, a residence in a particular part of London, or designer clothes. A third type Hirsch considers is that of 'incidental social scarcity': goods whose consumption yields satisfaction which is influenced by the extensiveness of use. Negative examples here would include the purchase of a car and no increase of satisfaction because of

increased congestion, as everyone does the same; and the obtaining of
educational qualifications and no improved access to leadership positions
because everyone else has been acquiring similar credentials (Ellis and
Heath, 1983: 10–11).

It is fairly easy to suggest examples of tourism that fit these various
forms of scarcity. On the first, the Mediterranean coastline is in the
condition of absolute scarcity where one person's consumption is at the
expense of someone else. On the second, there are clearly many holiday
destinations which are consumed not because they are intrinsically
superior but because they convey taste or superior status. For Europeans,
the West Indies, West Africa and the Far East would be current examples,
although these will change as mass tourist patterns themselves alter. And
third, there are many tourist sites where people's satisfaction depends
upon the degree of congestion. Perhaps the best example would currently
be Greece. Hirsch quotes a middle-class professional who remarked that
the development of cheap charter flights to such a previously 'exotic'
country meant that: 'Now that I can afford to come here I know that it
will be ruined' (1978: 167).

Although I have set out these different types of positional good identified by Hirsch the distinctions between them are not fully sustainable
and they merge into each other. Furthermore, there are a number of
major difficulties in Hirsch's argument. It is ambiguous about what is
meant by consumption in the case of much tourism. Is it the ability to
gaze at a particular object if necessary in the company of many others?
Or is it to be able to gaze without others being present? Or is it to be able
to rent accommodation for a short period with a view of the object close
at hand? Or is it the ability to own property with a view of the object
nearby? The problem arises because of the importance of the gaze to
touristic activity. A gaze is after all visual, it can literally take a split
second, and the other services provided are in a sense peripheral to the
fundamental process of consumption, which is the capturing of the gaze.
This means that the scarcities involved in tourism are more complex than
Hirsch allows for. One strategy pursued by the tourist industry has been
to initiate new developments which have permitted greatly increased
numbers to gaze upon the same object. Examples include building huge
hotel complexes away from the coastline; the development of off-peak
holidays so that the same view can be gazed upon throughout the year;
devising holidays for different segments of the market so that a wider
variety of potential visitors can see the same object; and the development
of time-share accommodation so that the facilities can be used all of the
year.

Moreover, the notion of scarcity is problematic for other reasons. I shall
begin here by noting the distinction between the physical carrying capacity
of a tourist site, and its perceptual capacity (see Walter, 1982). In the
former sense it is clear when a mountain path literally cannot take any
more walkers since it has been eroded and has effectively disappeared.

Nevertheless, even in this case there are still thousands of other mountain paths that could be walked along and so the scarcity only applies to *this* path leading to this particular view, not to all paths along all mountains.

The notion of perceptual capacity changes the situation. Walter is concerned here with the subjective quality of the tourist experience (1982: 296). Although the path may still be physically passable, it no longer signifies the pristine wilderness upon which the visitor had expected to gaze. Thus its perceptual carrying capacity would have been reached, but not its physical capacity. Walter goes on to note that perceptual capacity is immensely variable and depends upon particular conceptions of nature and on the circumstances in which people expect to gaze upon it. He cites the example of an Alpine mountain. As a material good the mountain can be viewed for its grandeur, beauty and conformity to the idealised Alpine horn. There is almost no limit to this good. No matter how many people are looking at the mountain it still retains these qualities. However, the same mountain can be viewed as a positional good, as a kind of shrine to nature that individuals wish to enjoy in solitude. There is then a 'romantic' form of the tourist gaze, in which the emphasis is upon solitude, privacy and a personal, semi-spiritual relationship with the object of the gaze. Barthes characterises this viewpoint as found in the *Guide Bleu*; he talks of 'this bourgeois promoting of the mountains, this old Alpine myth . . . only mountains, gorges, defiles and torrents . . . seem to encourage morality of effort and solitude' (1972: 74).

Walter discusses the example of Stourhead Park in Wiltshire, which illustrates:

> the romantic notion that the self is found not in society but in solitudinous contemplation of nature. Stourhead's garden is the perfect romantic landscape, with narrow paths winding among the trees and rhododendrons, grottoes, temples, a gothic cottage, all this around a much indented lake . . . . The garden is designed to be walked around in wonderment at Nature and the presence of other people immediately begins to impair this. (1982: 298)

When discussing Mishan I noted his emphasis that 'undisturbed natural beauty' constituted the typical object of the tourist gaze. However, this is in fact only one kind of gaze, what I will call the 'romantic'. There is an alternative: the 'collective' tourist gaze, with different characteristics. Here is a description of another Wiltshire house and garden, Longleat:

> a large stately home, set in a Capability Brown park; trees were deliberately thinned . . . so that you can see the park from the house, and house from the park. Indeed the house is the focal point of the park . . . the brochure lists twenty-eight activities and facilities . . . . All this activity and the resulting crowds fit sympathetically into the tradition of the stately home: essentially the life of the aristocratic was public rather than private. (1982: 198)

Such places were designed as public places: they would look strange if they were empty. It is other people that make such places. The collective gaze thus necessitates the presence of large numbers of other people, as were found for example in the seaside resorts discussed in chapter 2. Other people give atmosphere or a sense of carnival to a place. They indicate that this is *the* place to be and that one should not be elsewhere. And as we saw, one of the problems for the British seaside resort is that there are not enough people to convey these sorts of message. As Walter says: 'Brighton or Lyme Regis on a sunny summer's day with the beach to oneself would be an eerie experience' (1982: 298). It is the presence of other *tourists*, people just like oneself, that is actually necessary for the success of such places, which depend upon the collective tourist gaze. This is also the case in major cities, whose uniqueness is their cosmopolitan character. It is the presence of people from all over the world (tourists in other words) that gives capital cities their distinct excitement and glamour (see Walter, 1982: 299).

Large numbers of other tourists do not simply generate congestion, as the positional good argument would suggest. The presence of other tourists provides a market for the sorts of service that most tourists are in fact desperate to purchase, such as accommodation, meals, drink, travel and entertainment. New Zealand is an interesting case here. Once one leaves the four major cities there are almost no such facilities because of the very few visitors in relation to the size of the country. The contrast with the Lake District in north-west England is most striking, especially given the scenic similarity.

Thus Hirsch's arguments about scarcity and positional competition mainly apply to those types of tourism characterised by the romantic gaze. Where the collective gaze is to be found there is less of problem of crowding and congestion. And indeed Hirsch's argument rests on the notion that there are only a limited number of objects which can be viewed by the tourist. Yet in recent years there has been, as we noted in chapter 1, an enormous increase in the objects of the tourist gaze, far beyond Mishan's 'undisturbed natural beauty'. Part of the reason for this increase results from the fact that contemporary tourists are collectors of gazes and appear to be less interested in repeat visits to the same auratic site. The initial gaze is what counts.

Those who do really value solitude and a romantic tourist gaze do not see this as merely *one* way of regarding nature. Instead they attempt to make everyone sacralise nature in the same sort of way (see Walter, 1982: 300–3). Romanticism, which as we noted in chapter 2 was involved in the early emergence of mass tourism, has become widespread and generalised, spreading out from the upper middle classes, although the notion of romantic nature is a fundamentally invented and variable pleasure. And the more its adherents attempt to proselytise its virtues to others, the more the conditions of the romantic gaze are undermined: 'the romantic tourist is digging his [sic] own grave if he seeks to evangelize others to his own religion' (Walter, 1982: 301). The romantic gaze is an important mechanism which is helping to spread tourism on a global scale, drawing almost every country into its ambit as the romantic seeks ever-new objects of that gaze, and minimising diversity through the extension of what Turner and Ash term the 'pleasure periphery' (1975).

The contemporary tourist gaze is increasingly signposted. There are markers which identify the things and places worthy of our gaze. Such signposting identifies a relatively small number of tourist nodes. The result is that most tourists are concentrated within a very limited area. As Walter says: 'the sacred node provides a positional good that is destroyed by democratisation' (1982: 302). He by contrast favours the view that there are 'gems to be found everywhere and in everything . . . there is no limit to what you will find' (Walter, 1982: 302). We should, he says, get away from the tendency to construct the tourist gaze at a few selected sacred sites, and be much more catholic in the objects at which we may gaze. Undoubtedly this has began to occur in recent years, particularly with the development of industrial and heritage tourism. However, there is little doubt that Walter's analysis of the class character of the romantic gaze is highly persuasive and I will end this section on the economic theory of tourism by noting his thoroughly sociological analysis of the pervasiveness of the romantic as opposed to the collective gaze and the consequential problem of the positional good of many tourist sites:

> professional opinion-formers (brochure writers, teachers, Countryside Commission staff, etc.) are largely middle class and it is within the middle class that the romantic desire for positional goods is largely based. Romantic solitude thus has influential sponsors and gets good advertising. By contrast, the largely working class enjoyment of conviviality, sociability and being part of a crowd is often looked down upon by those concerned to conserve the environment. This is unfortunate, because it . . . exalts an activity that is available only to the privileged. (Walter, 1982: 303)

Globalisation and the economics of tourism

We have already seen that the English seaside resort went into decline in the mid-1960s, at the moment when mass tourism, at least in Europe, became internationalised. There has continued to be massive growth of international tourist flows. By 1984 there were almost 300 million tourist arrivals worldwide and international tourism was the second-largest item in world trade. International tourist receipts increased 47.6 times over the period 1950–84. About three-quarters of this involves industrial countries, with the USA, Japan, Germany and Canada having a large deficit, and Austria, France, Italy, Spain and Switzerland large credits (IMF, 1986: Table C-5). In the case of the UK, overseas earnings and expenditure more or less balanced in the early 1980s, having been well in credit in the 1970s. Britain ranks after the US, Spain, Italy and France in terms of overseas earnings from tourism. But in the mid- to late 1980s a strong deficit developed, resulting from increased visits being made by UK citizens abroad, the tendency for UK holiday-makers to increase their expenditure when abroad, and the fact that overseas visitors to the UK are now spending relatively less, in part because fewer of them now come from north America (Department of Employment, 1988).

This internationalisation of tourism means that we cannot explain tourist patterns in any particular society without analysing developments taking place in other countries. The internationalisation of tourism especially in Europe means that every tourist site can be compared with those located abroad. So when people visit somewhere in their own country they are in effect choosing not to visit a site abroad. The internationalisation of tourism means that all potential objects of the tourist gaze can be located on a scale, and can be compared with each other.

The result of such internationalisation is that different countries, or different places within a country, come to specialise in providing particular kinds of objects to be gazed upon. An international division of tourist sites has emerged in the last decade or two. Britain has come to specialise in its tourism on history and heritage and this affects both what overseas visitors expect to gaze upon, and what attracts UK residents to spend time holiday-making within Britain. Moreover, this internationalisation of holiday-making is more advanced and developed in the UK than in most other countries. This is partly because of the early and innovative development of the package or inclusive holiday in Britain, and partly because of the availability of an exceptional number of historical sites suitable for attracting large numbers of overseas tourists. Just as the UK economy in general is an open economy so this is specifically true of tourism. I shall briefly consider the nature of the package holiday industry before considering the main features of the UK domestic holiday industry.

Tour operators based in Britain seem to sell their inclusive or package holidays at a considerably cheaper price than in comparable European countries. In a sample survey of 57 hotels in Spain, Portugal and Greece, it was noted that in the case of 40 it was a British tour operator that offered the lowest price. In 39 out of 57 hotels a German company charged the most (Milner, 1987: 21). British-based companies have been particularly effective at reducing unit costs and at generating a huge market in the UK. There are now about 11 million package holidays sold each year (compared with around 5 million in 1980). The main reason why the inclusive holiday has had such an impact in Britain is because of the early emergence of integrated companies, the tour operators, who made spectacularly successful use of the new technologies of jet transport and computerised booking systems (see Reynolds, 1989: 330–3, on Thompson Holidays, which is incidentally part of the Canadian media and marketing multinational).

The expansion of the package tour industry in Britain has been accompanied by a considerable degree of concentration. In 1988 the Thompson Group (which includes Portland and Skytours) accounted for 28 per cent of the market and International Leisure Group (which includes Intasun and Club 18–30) 17 per cent. The third major company with about 8 per cent of the market, Horizon, has recently been taken over by Thompson (see *The Economist*, 27 August 1988: 59–60). The strength of the main tour operators partly results from the fact that either they own their own airline (Thompson owns Brittannia for example), or that they are themselves owned by an airline (British Airways owns Martin Rooks). When Thompson takes over Horizon, the new airline will be larger than Swissair and twice as big as SAS (*The Economist*, 1988: 59; see Goodall, 1988: 28–9 on vertical integration in much of the European tourist industry). Indeed, to a significant extent, the tour operators tend to make more money through their subsidiary airline than through the inclusive holiday operations, where it is claimed that the profit to the operator may be as little as £1–2 per £275 holiday (see Williams, 1988; *The Economist*, 27 August 1988).

Yet there are still many small companies providing inclusive holidays. In 1988 there were 679 tour operators licensed with the Civil Aviation Authority. However, the share taken by the large companies has steadily increased. It seems that this is partly because they have began to cater for more exotic destinations and for more specialised tastes – for what I will discuss later as the 'post-tourist'. Thompson, for example, has twenty-four brochures orientated to different market segments and the purchase of Horizon will probably involve further market segmentation (Williams, 1988; *The Economist*, 27 August 1988).

In a survey of their readership in 1987 *Holiday Which?* found that none of the largest three tour operators were placed into even the top twenty in terms of popularity. The people surveyed preferred smaller, more specialised operators. But in a different survey Lewis and Outram found that clients could perceive little difference between tour operators (1986: 209–10). They also found a high level of satisfaction with the operators among their respondents, who had particularly positive attitudes towards the convenience and value aspects of their package holiday (Lewis and Outram, 1986: 213). This perhaps runs counter to the image of such holidays which has been effectively summarised by Pile. He quotes an industrial psychologist who writes of such holidays that:

> they are based upon all the most stressful features of 20th century life. It is amazing that people never question why they are going on them . . . . They leave a comfortable, civilised home and basically go to live on a beach for a fortnight in acute discomfort . . . . They arrive in a strange hotel where they can't even eat when they want to. (Pile, 1987)

A number of important changes will affect this sector of the tourist industry. First, the inclusive holiday will enable much more distant destinations to become accessible to a mass market, such as the Caribbean for £300 or the Far East for £400–500.

Consumers will in future be able to put together much more flexible packages, a kind of holiday 'mix n' match' or what the industry terms 'Free and Independent Travel' or FITs (see Hart, 1988: 19). This will mean that travel agents must become more skilled than surveys suggest they are at present (see Welsh, 1989, for a damning indictment of the leading travel agencies).

At present the markets for inclusive holidays are regulated or organised by the central aviation authority within each country (see *The Economist*, 27 August 1988). However, after 1992 and the formation of a single market, the tour operators in Europe will operate in each of the major countries to a much greater extent. This will have the effect of increasing competition and reducing the level of concentration within a single country. It will be interesting to see whether this is associated with increased vertical integration, with the operators continuing to purchase travel agents, hotels and airlines (see Buck, 1988, on the complex relationship between tour operators and travel agents).

And finally, this is an industry where new technologies are particularly appropriate because of the immense informational and communication problems involved. The most recent innovation has been the adoption of interactive videotext. This was first introduced in 1979 and has now spread to about 90 per cent of all UK travel agencies, the best known being Thompson's TOPS system (see Bruce, 1987: 115). In the future one development will be systems which permit customers to 'self-serve' themselves with tickets and other standardised products. Indeed if these were available in the home then it is possible to envisage a 'paperless travel agency'. Expert systems developments would enable the prospective traveller to provide some parameters of intended travel and then allow the computer to generate a number of possible consumer products (Bruce, 1987: 117–18).

In 1989 in Britain a million fewer inclusive holidays were sold by the main operators than in the previous year. And it is predicted that the number will be below 9 million in 1990 (Barrett, 1989b). Yet the number of overseas holidays taken by UK residents continues to rise (8 per cent in 1988–9). It seems that with increased leisure time people are increasingly moving away from the somewhat standardised package holiday and seeking out a wider variety of forms of leisure activity, including independent travel (see McRae, 1989). This will force tour operators to develop the more flexible kinds of travel arrangements discussed earlier. There has been a marked increase recently in seats-only flights, partly because of the demand for more flexibility and partly because of the growth in overseas property ownership (see Ryan, 1989, for a very useful survey of future developments). These factors are also likely to force the tour operators to seek greater quality control over all aspects of the holiday, something they have not been very successful in achieving so far: 'The result has been inconsistent quality. There is no Marks and Spencer in tourism. As a result the operators have been losing the up-market, high value-added segment of the trade' (McRae, 1989).

Barrett also suggests that the switch to independent travel 'is partly a reaction to the "naffness" of package holidays', that they are no longer viewed as fashionable or smart (1989b). So far I have looked at some features of the industry concerned with transporting British and other north European holiday-makers mainly to certain south European countries, within which there is intense spatial concentration (see Goodall, 1988: 25–6). In the next section I shall consider the organisation of the tourist industry in societies that host large numbers of such visitors. But before this I shall examine some features of the tourist industry concerned with the provision of services *within* Britain.

I have noted that there is currently a large tourism deficit in Britain. The response from the minister with (at the time) special responsibility for tourism, John Lee, was as follows:

> Hopefully the British public will increasingly appreciate that holiday taking in the United Kingdom is not only a stimulating and enjoyable experience but will help our balance of payments as well. Any potential visitors from overseas should realise that there can be few countries in the world offering such a range of heritage, countryside, resorts, sporting and cultural opportunites and attractions (in England 30% of our existing visitor attractions have been opened since 1980, 60% since 1970). (Lee, 1988)

Not only does the minister make it clear that 'heritage' is the first feature likely to appeal to overseas visitors, but also that there has been an exceptional investment in new tourist attractions.

As far as overseas visitors are concerned there is a huge potential market. Only 7 per cent of US citizens possess a passport; this figure would merely have to reach 10 per cent for there to be very large increases in the number of potential US visitors (see Cabinet Office, 1983). Of foreign visitors coming to Britain only about 20 per cent visit the seaside, and even Blackpool attracts relatively few for all its efforts to market itself as an international leisure centre. Only 7 per cent of overseas visitors visit 'funfairs and entertainment parks' (BTA/ETB Research Services, 1988a: 58).

The preferences of foreign visitors are highly localised, most being attracted to London and to various small inland towns and cities. In fact about 80 per cent began their visit in London and this is reflected in, for example, the fact that 40 per cent of those visiting London West End theatres are foreign visitors (BTA/ETB Research Services, 1988a; SWET, 1982). The build-up of overseas visitors in London in 1984–5 produced no significant deflection to provincial centres that were not already attracting significant numbers of such visitors. Indeed it may be that if there is no shift in visitor patterns and if hotel space in London remains in short supply, then some overseas visitors will divert to other destinations in Europe rather than to the rest of Britain (see Jeffrey and Hubbard, 1988).

Over 75 per cent of overseas visitors made their own travel arrangements rather than booking an inclusive tour. There has been no increase in the absolute numbers coming to the UK on inclusive tours (BTA/ETB Research Services, 1988a).

There has been no increase in the number of new visitors to the UK and all of the increase has been in 'repeat' visitors. Such 'repeats' are more common amongst business travellers, West Europeans, visitors aged over 35 and people travelling outside London (BTA/ETB Research Services, 1988a).

At present the six most popular leisure pursuits for overseas visitors are visiting shops or markets (82 per cent), restaurants or cafés (77 per cent), churches, cathedrals etc. (69 per cent), historic sites/buildings (69 per cent), museums and art galleries (64 per cent), and historic cities or towns (62 per cent) (BTA/ETB Research Services, 1988a, and see Key Note Report, 1987). Overseas visitors were also asked which faciles provided good value for money. All bar one facility were thought to provide good value by a higher proportion than those thought to be offering not good value. The one exception were London hotels, where three times as many visitors thought that they provided poor value compared with those who thought they provided good value (BTA/ETB Research Services, 1988a). This low level of satisfaction reflects the very strong demand for accommodation in London. Average room occupancy rates are the highest in the country, 78 per cent, compared with 47 per cent in seaside towns, 51 per cent in the countryside and 57 per cent in England overall in 1984 (Bagguley, 1987: 16). A number of other features of the economic and geographical organisation of British tourism will now be considered.

An initial point is that accommodation in Britain is still mainly provided in small units. In the early 1980s it was estimated that there were almost 10,000 hotels, 20,000 guesthouses, 18,000 bed-and-breakfast outlets, 4,800 farms providing accommodation, 300 motels and 90 holiday camps (Bagguley, 1987: 8). Only 1.5 per cent of hotels had more than 200 rooms, while almost 85 per cent had fewer than 50. In a slightly later survey it was calculated that of the 0.5 million hotel bedrooms in Britain, 30 per cent were corporately owned and 70 per cent owned by independents, most with fewer than 50 bedrooms (Slattery and Roper, 1986). Small capital is thus of enduring significance in the provision of tourist accommodation in Britain (see Goffee and Scase, 1983: my account here is taken from Bagguley, 1987). Amongst these small capitals four different sectors can be usefully distinguished.

There are the 'self-employed' with no outside labour and a reliance upon family labour and trade-based skills. They are economically marginal, formal management skills are weak, and there is no divorce of ownership from control. Many bed-and-breakfast units are of this type. There is the category of 'small employers' who are distinguished from the self-employed by the intermittent employment of outside labour. Many guesthouses and small hotels are of this sort. There are 'owner controllers' who do not use family labour and employ outside labour which may receive a considerable degree of training. Levels of capital investment are higher and there are more formal means of managerial control. These are less economically marginal, although there is no divorce of ownership and control. Many so-called country house hotels where the proprietor is directly involved are of this sort. Finally there are 'owner directors', where there is considerable capital investment, formal training, and the separation of ownership and control. This is most common amongst those city centre hotels which are not part of any chain.

All these different types of small capital in the hotel and catering industry show enormous vulnerability in the market. Between 1980 and 1986 121,700 hotel and catering establishments were established in the sense that they came on to the register for paying value added tax (VAT); and yet a staggering 115,900 came off the register (Smith, 1988: 22). A quarter of such establishments close within two years, half within four. About one-quarter do survive while the remaining three-quarters are in a continuous state of flux. The rate of turnover is considerably higher in this industry than in most others, which means that there is great job insecurity. The Hotel and Catering Industry Training Board estimates that a quarter of the workforce will lose or leave their job within a year (Smith, 1988: 22). The category of 'owner controllers' appears best able to survive. Drew Smith, former editor of *Good Food Guide*, maintains that: 'it is the personally run restaurant [and hotel] that has bucked the trend, often by the sheer dedication of the owner. At the other end of the market this has usually been because the family has kept the freehold of the site' (1988: 22). This therefore is an industry of enormous volatility. And although there are some very large operators, as we will see, there are very few restrictions on entry (and exit!). Drew Smith estimates that fifty new restaurants open each month in London. Indeed there are almost certainly large variations in the propensity to start new restaurants and hotels in different parts of the country. Cornwall, for example, seems to have relatively weak traditions of local entrepreneurship in all sectors of the economy including tourism, although most tourist-related enterprises are in fact small. In a study of Looe it was found that there was a very high level of geographical mobility amongst entrepreneurs. For example, 90 per cent of the owners of hotels and guesthouses came from outside the south-west region, the majority coming from the south-east (Hennessy et al., 1986: 16). Cornwall in general seems important in attracting entrepreneurs rather than generating its own.

One major influence on the kinds of tourist-related activities found in different areas (London compared with Looe) is the growth of business tourism and its differential impact. There was a 30 per cent increase in the number of business 'nights' spent in Britain between 1980 and 1984. This makes up for the more or less static number of hotel 'nights' demanded by domestic holiday-makers over the same period (Bagguley, 1987: 13–18). Business tourism is made up of a number of components: genuine meetings held in other parts of the country; conferences – in 1984 there were 14,000 international conferences of which the majority were held in the UK; and the provision of travel as a non-taxable perk – something provided by about one-third of Britain's top companies (see Williams and Shaw, 1988b: 19).

The effect of business tourism in particular has generated periodic hotel building booms. For example, in the late 1960s and early 1970s there was a spate of hotel building especially in London following the 1969 Hotel Development Incentive Scheme. In March 1970 there were 61 hotels planned for London, all but 7 with more than 75 bedrooms. This was three times as many as were planned for traditional 'holiday areas' (Bagguley, 1987: 17). However, in the early 1980s the pattern was quite different. Only 3 per cent of new hotels completed between 1981 and 1984 were in London and the largest proportion, 38 per cent, were located in 'small towns' (BTA/ETB, 1985). By 1988 (January–June) investment in new hotels is fairly evenly spread amongst the different tourist regions, with London getting about 10 per cent. Interestingly though, most expenditure on hotel refurbishment is to be found in London, as is the largest expenditure on the building of 'themed attractions'. Overall about one-third of all tourist investment is currently taking place in London (BTA/ETB, 1988a: Table A).

It was noted earlier that much accommodation in the UK is provided by a very large number of small hotels and guesthouses. It seems that the number of these declined between 1951 and 1971 (Stallinbrass, 1980). In recent years the data are less clear although it is certain that there has been an increase in the share of accommodation provided by the very large hotel groups. The major chains in 1984 were Trusthouse Forte, Ladbroke Group, Crest and Thistle (Key Note Report, 1986, and see Shaw et al., 1988).

The most significant development in the past few years has been the development of hotel consortia. In 1984 there were 170 Best Western hotels in the UK, 103 in the Inter Hotel consortium and 22 Prestige hotels (*Financial Times*, 2 January 1984; Bagguley, 1987: 19–22). Such consortia grew up in the 1960s to compensate for the decentralised structure of capital and the problems this created for capital accumulation and systematic cost cutting. Corporate growth is difficult given the low levels of concentration, small unit size and the varying combination of meals, drinks and accommodation for which demand is both seasonal and volatile (see Litteljohn, 1982; Slattery et al., 1985; Bagguley, 1987). Consortia enable hotels to gain economies of scale and hence to be able to compete much more effectively with the economies obtainable by the large chains listed earlier. Consortia fall into a number of different types:

marketing consortia: to provide access to a corporate marketing department on the basis of either regional grouping (such as Thames Valley Hotels) or a specific market segment (such as Prestige);
marketing and purchasing consortia: apart from marketing economies they also negotiate reduced prices for bulk orders (Best Western, Inter Hotel);
referral consortia: to provide a national or international system of referrals particularly connected with airlines (British Airways Associate Hotels);

personnel and training consortia: to provide common training and personnel functions (Concord Hotels);
reservations systems: to provide a system of national or international reservations often linked to various other tourist offices (Expotel Hotels).

Some of the groups just considered are highly internationalised. In 1986, for example Trusthouse Forte owned 793 hotels worldwide, as well as many other catering-related establishments (see Williams and Shaw, 1988b: 26). The second largest British group, Ladbrokes, also own 140 Hilton International hotels. The largest international groups in 1986 were Holiday Inns with 1907 hotels and Quality Inns with 801. Since then Holiday Inns sold, first in 1988 control of all their non-north American hotels, and then in 1989 their north American hotels, to the British company Bass (see Jamieson, 1989). Holiday Inns control 10 per cent of all hotel beds in the USA. Bass have not bought outright ownership since most of the hotels are franchised. They now have control of 1,700 hotels worldwide.

Grand Metropolitan is also a major international force but recently it has sold the whole of the huge Intercontinental Hotels group for £1.3 billion to the Japanese company Seibu Saisson (the *Guardian*, 14 November 1988). Another major company operating in Britain is Novotel which is French-owned, while the largest hotel company in West Germany is Queens Moat Houses which was also the sixth largest British group (in 1984).

It is useful to distinguish between a number of different kinds of hotel group. First, there is the relatively specialist hotel chain such as Queens Moat Houses. Second, there is the more general hotel and catering group such as Trusthouse Forte which, apart from its 700 or so hotels, also owns Little Chef, Happy Eater and operates 200 Kentucky Fried Chicken outlets (the *Guardian*, 14 November 1988). Overall it has reduced its degree of diversification since 1970 (see Gratton and Taylor, 1987: 48–50). Third, there are hotel chains such as Sheraton, which is part of the American conglomerate ITT, or in Britain Rank hotels which are part of the much wider Rank group, which includes Butlins and Top Rank bingo (Gratton and Taylor, 1987: 41–4). Fourth, there are the hotels owned by tour operators or travel agents. This is more common in western Europe than north America – Thompson in the UK or Vingressor in Sweden would be good examples. And finally, there are the hotel chains owned by airlines: Pan-Am, for example, used to own Intercontinental Hotels (see Williams and Shaw, 1988b: 26).

Internationalisation of leisure provision also occurs in other parts of the tourist-related services. This can be seen most obviously in the case of McDonalds, as well as in the rather larger one-off investments. Currently, for example, the Walt Disney Company is building a $2 billion theme park near Paris to be called Euro Disneyland. This will be a 5,000-acre development with 500 hotel rooms, shopping centres, offices, up-market housing, camp grounds, golf courses and a rail link – a full 'destination resort' rather than a 'day trip' as at the Disneyland in California (for more detail see Shamoon, 1989).

The tourist-related industries analysed here are thus intensely competitive. Moreover, although the very large operators can move their capital around in response to changing market pressures, most of the industry cannot, certainly in the short run. This is an industry with great spatial fixity, an exceptional degree of decentralisation, and immense volatility of taste. Since many visitors to hotels and restaurants are only there because of the attractions available in the area so there may well be much support given to enhancing local facilities, to increasing the number or attraction of potential objects of the tourist gaze. Hence, tourist-related capital may well be in favour of large-scale public investment by local authorities to provide new or enhanced objects upon which visitors can gaze.

In the past decade or so companies involved in the industry have pursued a number of cost-reduction strategies.

1 The expansion of self-serviced accommodation which in Britain in 1984 accounted for 152 million nights, compared with 91 million nights in serviced accommodation (Bagguley, 1987: 18).

2 The extensive use of information technology (IT). This results from the fact that slack resources in the industry such as a hotel bed cannot be stored; the immense volatility of demand; and the fact that tourist units are necessarily geographically dispersed. IT enables various kinds of network to be established between potential consumers and the many locally specific and decentralised units.

3 Changing the labour input especially via the growth of part-time female employment. The proportion of such workers in the UK hotel and catering industry rose from 32.5 per cent in 1971 to 44.7 per cent in 1981 (Census of Employment).

4 Economising on costs through joining a group or consortium.

5 Closing down in slack periods or alternatively trying to generate extra business during the often very long off-season.

6 Generating extra income by improving the quality of the product provided, such as better meals, more trained labour or *en suite* facilities.

The overseas impact of tourism

Tourist development outside the UK has had a broad economic, social and cultural impact. Drawing in part on the concept of the positional good discussed earlier, I shall consider some Mediterranean countries, and shall follow this with comments on north America and South-East Asia.

As we saw in chapter 1, there are complex relationships between tourists and the indigenous populations of the places at which those tourists gaze; the resulting artificiality of many tourist attractions results from the particular character of the social relations that come to be established between 'hosts' and 'guests' in such places (see Smith, 1978, for much of the following). There are a number of determinants of the particular social relations that are established between 'hosts' and 'guests'.

1   The *number* of tourists visiting a place in relationship to the size of the host population and to the scale of the objects being gazed upon. For example, the geographical size of new Zealand would permit many more tourists to visit without either environmental damage or an undesirable social effect. By contrast the physical smallness of Singapore means that extra tourists cannot easily be accommodated except by even more hotel building which would only be possible by demolishing the remaining few Chinese shophouses which in the past have been one of the main objects of the tourist gaze. Similarly the magnificently preserved medieval city of Dubrovnik has an absolute physical limit determined both by the city walls and by the fact that over 4,000 people live within those walls. The resident population cannot but be numerically overwhelmed during the height of the summer season.

2   The predominant *object* of the tourist gaze, whether it is a landscape (the Lake District), a townscape (Chester), an ethnic group (Maoris in Rotorua, New Zealand), a life-style (the 'wild West'), historical artefacts (Canterbury Cathedral or Wigan Pier), bases of recreation (golf courses at St Andrews), or 'sand, sun and sea' (Majorca). Those tourist activities which involve observation of physical objects are clearly less intrusive than those which involve observing individuals and groups. Moreover, within the latter category, the observation of the private lives of host groups will produce the greatest social stress. Examples here include the Eskimo, or the Masai who have responded to the gaze by charging a '£ for car' for visits to their mud huts. By contrast, where what is observed is more of a public ritual then social stress will be less pronounced and indeed wider participation may be positively favoured, as in various Balinese rituals (see Smith, 1978: 7).

3   The *character* of the gaze involved and the resulting spatial and temporal 'packing' of visitors. For example, the gaze may be something that can take place more or less instantaneously (seeing/photographing New Zealand's highest mountain, Mount Cook), or it may require prolonged exposure (seeing/experiencing the 'romance' of Paris). In the case of the former, Japanese tourists can be flown in for a visit lasting just a few hours, while the experience of the romance of Paris will necessitate a longer and 'deeper' immersion.

4   The *organisation* of the industry that develops to service the mass gaze: whether it is private or publicly owned and financed; whether it is locally owned or involves significant overseas interests; whether the capital involved is predominantly small or large scale; and whether there are conflicts between the local population and the emergent tourist industry. Such conflicts can occur around many issues: conservation as opposed to commercial development, the wages to be paid to locally

recruited employees, the effects of development on local customs and family life, what one might call the 'trinketisation' of local crafts, and how to compensate for the essential seasonality of labour (see Smith, 1978: 5–7).

5 The effects of tourism upon the *pre-existing agricultural and industrial activities*. These may range from the destruction of those activities (much agriculture in Corfu); to their gradual undermining as labour and capital are drawn into tourism (parts of Spain); to their preservation as efforts are made to save pre-existing activities as further objects to be gazed upon (cattle farming and hence grazing in the Norfolk Broads).

6 The economic and social *differences* between the visitors and the majority of the hosts. In northern Europe and north America tourism creates fewer strains since the mass of 'hosts' will themselves be 'guests' on other occasions. It may be that tourism can in a rather inchoate way develop 'international understanding'. The shift in public attitudes in Britain towards a pro-Europeanism in the 1980s is difficult to explain without recognising that some role is played by the European tourism industry and the way in which huge flows of visitors have made Europe familiar and unthreatening. Elsewhere, however, there are usually enormous inequalities between the visitors and the indigenous population, the vast majority of whom could never envisage having either the income or the leisure time to be tourists themselves. These differences are reinforced in many developing countries by the nature of the tourist development, which appears to be exceptionally opulent and highly capitalised, as for example in many hotels in India, China, Singapore, Hong Kong and north Africa, partly because there are so few service facilities otherwise available to either visitors or the host population.

7 The degree to which the mass of visitors demand *particular standards of accommodation and service*, that they should be enclosed in an environmental bubble to provide protection from many of the features of the host society. This demand is most marked amongst inclusive tour visitors, who not only expect western standards of accommodation and food but also bilingual staff and well-orchestrated arrangements. Such tourists rarely leave the security of the western tourist bubble and to some degree are treated as dependent 'children' by the tourist professionals (see Smith, 1978: 10–11). In some cases the indigenous culture actually is dangerous, as in Sicily, parts of New York, and recently in Florence. This demand is less pronounced amongst individual exploring 'travellers', poorer tourists such as students, and those visitors for whom 'roughing it' is part of their expected experience as tourists.

8 The degree to which the *state* in a given country actively seeks to promote tourist developments or alternatively endeavours to prevent them. Good examples of the former are Spain, Tunisia and Hawaii which are all actively developing a fully-fledged tourist culture where large numbers of tourists have become part of the 'regional scenery' (Smith,

1978: 12). By contrast many of the oil states have for moral/social reasons explicitly decided to restrict tourism by refusing visas (Saudi Arabia is a good example). Likewise during the Cultural Revolution in China the state actively sought to prevent the growth of tourism. When this changed in the early to mid-1970s western visitors were so unusual that they were often applauded as though they were royalty.

9 The extent to which *tourists can be identified and blamed* for supposedly undesirable economic and social developments. This is obviously more common when such visitors are economically and/or culturally and/or ethnically distinct from the host population. It is also more common when the host population is experiencing rapid economic and social change. However, such change is not necessarily the outcome of 'tourism'. In the case of Tonga, for example, it is not the annual influx of visitors but rather gross overpopulation which accounts for the high inflation rate. And yet of course it is much easier to blame the 'nameless, faceless foreigner' for indigenous problems of economic and social inequality (see Smith, 1978: 13). Moreover, some local objections to tourism are in fact objections to 'modernity' or to modern society itself: to mobility and change, to new kinds of personal relationships, to a reduced role of family and tradition, and to different cultural configurations (see discussion in Welsh, 1988, of the 'Ecumenical Coalition of Third World Tourism').

The social impact of tourism will thus depend on the intersection of a wide range of factors. For example, great concern has been expressed about the likely consequences of tourism in various Mediterranean countries. The growth of tourism in the Mediterranean is one of the most significant economic and social developments in the postwar period. It is a particularly striking symbol of postwar reconstruction in Europe, or at least in western Europe.

There is a high income elasticity of demand for tourist services and as incomes have grown in West Germany, France, Scandinavia, the Low Countries and the British Isles, so there has been a more than corresponding increase in demand for overseas travel. Western Europe in fact accounted for 68 per cent of all international tourists in 1984 (Williams and Shaw, 1988a: 1). In response to such demand the countries of southern Europe have developed enormous tourist industries. And those industries have been particularly cost effective, which in turn has lowered the real cost of overseas travel and hence led to further expansion of demand. Spain was the first and has remained the largest of the Mediterranean destinations. The number of foreign visitors increased from 6 million in 1960 to over 40 million by the early 1980s (Williams et al., 1986: 5). Other major destination countries are France, Italy, Greece, Portugal, Yugoslavia and, most recently, Turkey. In 1984 tourism receipts accounted for over 4 per cent of the national income of Spain and Portugal, over 3 per cent of that of Greece, and 2.6 per cent of that of Italy (Williams et al., 1986: 13; it should also be noted that the highest proportion in Europe is in fact Austria, with 7.8 per cent). Overall, the Commission of the European Community argues, tourism generates a net distribution of wealth from northern to southern Europe, and especially to Spain and Italy. It should however be noted that developments in such countries tend to be highly geographically concentrated. In the case of Spain for example 26 per cent of all high-season employment in the Balearic Islands is to be found in hotels although attempts are now being made to encourage travel into inland Spain (Valenzuela, 1988). Likewise in Yugoslavia 86 per cent of all tourists stay in coastal resorts (Williams and Shaw, 1988b: 36).

The problematic effects of such tourist developments in at least some of the countries concerned are fairly well known. They result from the huge number of tourists and their seasonal demand for services, the deleterious social effects particularly resulting from the gendered work available, the geographical concentration of visitors, the lack of concerted policy response, the cultural differences between hosts and guests, and the demand by many visitors to be enclosed in expensive 'environmental bubbles'. One place that has been overrun by tourists is Florence, where the resident population of 500,000 accommodates 1.7 million visitors each year. This has led to the plan to remove the city's academic, commercial and industrial functions from the centre and to turn it over entirely to tourism. It would mean the 'Disneyfication of Florence' (Vulliamy, 1988: 25).

Robert Graves has written of the similar tourist transformation of Majorca:

> the old Palma has long ceased to exist; its centre eaten away by restaurants, bars, souvenir shops, travel agencies and the like . . . . Huge new conurbations have sprung up along the neighbouring coast. . . . The main use of olive trees seems to be their conversion into . . . salad bowls and boxes for sale to the tourists. But, as a Majorcan wag remarked, once they are all cut down we will have to erect plastic ones for the tourists to admire from their bus windows. (1965: 51)

A recent UN report has moreover suggested that there is a very serious threat to the whole Mediterranean coastline. At present, with 100 million visitors (in 1985), it is the world's most popular tourist destination. The UN report suggests that this number could increase to 760 million in 2025, thereby placing a huge strain upon food, water and human resources. The growth of existing coastal cities needs to be dramatically slowed down (the *Guardian*, 2 November 1988). But the opposite is occurring with Turkey, the latest country to develop as a major tourist destination. The immediate attraction for local investors in Turkey is that most revenue comes in the form of foreign exchange which protects them against a domestic inflation rate of around 80 per cent. Private sector tourist investment in 1988 was more than double that for 1987 although interestingly the source of much of that investment was the state-owned Turizm Bankasi (Bodgener, 1988). Turkish tourism has so far involved the proliferation of some exceptionally ugly unplanned developments, such as those in Bodrum and Marmara, which may have to be demolished fairly soon. One specialist operator, Simply Turkey, withdrew from selling holidays in Gumbet because it was 'No longer small and pretty, it is a sprawling building site, noisy and dusty, with a beach not large enough to cater for its rapid development' (quoted in Whitaker, 1988: 15). In other words, it is no longer suitable for the up-market holidays that company had been selling. So far the demand has grown very rapidly, with 400,000 inclusive holidays to Turkey sold in 1988. The impact of such rapid growth is felt particularly keenly because this area of south-west Turkey has always attracted considerable numbers of individual travellers due to the exceptional quality of its antiquities. Turkey is hence poised between the conflicting interests of mass tourism and a more socially select tourism.

The second most important area of tourist activity worldwide is north America. Developments here are, interestingly, different from Europe. Central to north American tourism has been the car, the highway, the view through the windscreen and the commercial strip. Jakle talks of how, in the postwar period, cities, towns and rural areas were all remade in what he calls 'universal highway order' (1985: ch. 9 for the following). In 1950 80 per cent of all long-distance trips were made by automobile and by 1963 43 per cent of American families took long vacation trips each year, averaging 600 miles.

There was a rapid improvement of the quality of the road system, to cope with faster travel and higher traffic volume. Unfortunately there was little to see from the new roads except the monotony of the road itself. John Steinbeck wrote that 'it will be possible to drive from New York to California without seeing a single thing' (quoted in Jakle, 1985: 190). Roads came to be built for the convenience of driving, not for the patterns of human life that might be engendered. The ubiquitousness of the radio and to some extent of air conditioning in American cars insulates the passengers from all almost all aspects of the environment except the view through the windscreen (see Wilson, 1988).

And this view reveals almost nothing because even townscapes consist of commercial strips, the casual eradication of distinctive places and the generation of a standardised landscape. Jakle terms this the production of 'commonplaceness'. The commercial strips are common places lacking the ambiguities and complexities that generally make places interesting. They were 'unifunctional landscapes' which became even more uniform in appearance as large corporations developed which operated chains of look-alike and standardised establishments (such as McDonalds, Howard Johnson, Col. Saunders, Holiday Inn and so on). The automobile journey has become one of the icons of postwar America, reflected in novels like Kerouac's *On the Road* or the film *Easy Rider*. In *Lolita* Humbert Humbert concludes 'We have been everywhere. We have seen nothing' (quoted in Jakle, 1985: 198).

Probably the most famous tourist site in north America is Niagara Falls. Reaction to it has always involved superlatives (see Shields, 1990, for the following). Observers reported themselves lost for words. It was an exotic wonder; it had an immense natural aura. However, a series of transformations that have taken place have rendered Niagara as a series of different objects of the tourist gaze. First, in the late nineteenth century the Falls became the most favoured of places for honeymoons and for courtship more generally. Shields links this to the way in which the Falls constituted an admirable liminal zone where strict social conventions of the bourgeoisie were relaxed under the exigencies of travel and relative anonymity. The historic association of waterfalls with passion, whether of love or death, further enhanced the salience of such a zone. Travellers expected the Falls to be exceptional, a place where the limits of ordinary experience were transcended. The trip was analogous to a pilgrimage. Nathaniel Hawthorne wrote of going 'haunted with a vision of foam and fury, and dizzy cliffs, and an ocean tumbling down out of the sky' (quoted in Shields, 1990). More recently however the honeymoon has been emptied of its symbolic liminal status. It has become a meaningless nuptial cliché, referring to nothing but itself. All the emphasis at the Falls is placed on the props, on honeymoon suites and heart-shaped 'luv tubs'. The Falls now stand for kitsch, sex and commercial spectacle. It is as though the Falls are no longer there as such: they can only be seen through their images.

Thus the same object in a physical sense has been transformed by a variety of commercial and public interests. The nature of the gaze has undergone immense changes. In the eighteenth century the Falls were an object of intense natural aura; in the nineteenth century they functioned as a liminal zone gazed upon and deeply experienced by courting couples; and in the later twentieth century they have become another 'place' to be collected by the immensely mobile visitor for whom the gaze at the Falls stands for spectacle, sex and commercial development.

A related kind of development has been the growth of so-called 'sex-tourism' in South-East Asia. In South Korea this has been specifically encouraged by the state. Its main form consists of the kisaeng tour specifically geared to Japanese businessmen (see Mitter, 1986: 64–7). Many Japanese companies reward their outstanding male staff with all-expenses tours of kisaeng brothels and parties. South Korean ministers have congratulated the 'girls' for their contribution to their country's economic development. Other countries with a similarly thriving sex industry are the Philippines and Thailand. In the case of the former the state encourages the use of 'hospitality girls' in tourism, and various brothels are recommended by the Ministry of Tourism (Mitter, 1986: 65). Package tours organised in conjunction with a Manila agent include preselected 'hospitality girls'. Of the money earned only about 7–8 per cent will be retained by the women themselves. In Thailand it is calculated that there are 500,000 women working in the sex industry, with perhaps

200,000 in Bangkok alone (see Lea, 1988: 66–9). Particular processes which have helped to generate such a pattern are: the exceptionally strong set of patriarchal practices which cast women as either 'madonna/virgin' or 'whore'; the belief amongst people from affluent countries that women of colour are more available and submissive; the high rate of incest and domestic violence by fathers/husbands in some such societies; and rural depopulation which draws people into the cities looking for any possible work (see Enloe, 1989: ch. 2 for more detail, especially on attempts by women to organise to protect the prostitutes).

Similar factors apply elsewhere but such patterns are less obvious. Singapore provides an interesting contrast. In the advertising material provided for tourists there are no references to sex-tourism. The only clubs listed are various discos and Asian-style shows. Singapore is never-theless an extremely successful object of the tourist gaze but this has been achieved by playing down its exotic character. Much of the emphasis in the publicity material is on Singapore's attractions as a modern shopping centre, and there is indeed an extraordinary complex of shopping centres along the now wholly misnamed Orchard Road. Singapore has also trans-formed many of the old areas of Chinese shophouses into modern hotel complexes, including what is claimed to the the tallest hotel in the world. This has been built next to the world-famous Raffles Hotel, which has an impressive range of historical and literary connections as well as superb colonial atmosphere. However, it was announced in 1989 that the Raffles is going to be shut for a year or so while it is 'modernised'. Singapore is 'in the east' but not really any more 'of the east'. It is almost the ultimate modern city and does not construct itself as 'exotic/erotic' for visitors.

An interesting development in Singapore is the leisure island of Sentosa, which is best entered by cable car. A wholly artificial environment is being created although much of it has a (vaguely) colonial appearance including especially the new ferry terminal. It is only when one gets close to it that one realises that it is built almost entirely of plastic. The capacity of the island is very large and visitors are transported from site to site by a purpose-built monorail. This curious combination of the ultra-modern and the historical pastiche will no doubt be seen as a model tourist development for other parts of Asia and Africa.

Conclusion

It is clear that the effects of tourism are highly complex and contradic-tory, depending on the range of considerations outlined earlier. Not surprisingly there has been much discussion about the desirability of tourism as a strategy for economic development in so-called developing societies. This raises many difficult issues, which I am not going to enter into here. Instead I shall make some points of clarification.

It is important to appreciate that the growth of tourism in developing countries, such as 'game tourism' in Kenya, 'ethnic tourism' in Mexico, 'sports tourism' in the Gambia and so on, does not simply derive from processes internal to those societies. Such a development possibility results from a number of external conditions: technological changes such as cheap air travel and computerised booking systems; developments in capital including the growth of worldwide hotel groups (Ramada), travel agencies (Thomas Cook), and personal finance organisations (American Express); the widespread pervasion of the 'romantic' gaze so that more and more people wish to isolate themselves from the existing patterns of mass tourism; the increased fascination of the developed world with the cultural practices of less developed societies; the development of the tourist as essentially a 'collector' of places often gazed upon and experienced on the surface; and the emergence of a powerful metropolitan lobby concerned to promote the view that tourism has a major development potential (see Crick, 1988: 47–8).

The economic benefits from tourism are often less than anticipated. Much tourist investment in the developing world has in fact been undertaken by large-scale companies based in north America or western Europe, and the bulk of such tourist expenditure is retained by the transnational companies involved; only 22–25 per cent of the retail price remains in the host country (Lea, 1988: 13; and see de Kadt, 1979). In Mauritius, for example, 90 per cent of foreign exchange earned from tourism is repatriated to companies based elsewhere. This repatriation is particularly likely to happen with the presently high level of vertical integration in the industry – in 1978, for instance, just sixteen hotel groups owned one-third of all hotels in the developing countries (see Crick, 1988: 45). An interesting exception to this pattern of repatriation (in addition to Singapore and the central role of Singapore Airlines) is Yugoslavia and the near monopoly on inclusive tours at least from Britain exercised by the state-owned Yugotours.

A further problem, again avoided in Singapore, occurs where tourism accounts for a really high proportion of the national income of the country. Some of the islands in the West Indies experience this difficulty. It means that if anything serves to undermine tourist demand, an enormous loss of national income will result. This is also what happened, for example, in Fiji in 1987 following military coups (see Lea, 1988: 32–6, particularly on the scale of advertising needed to restore consumer confidence, especially in Australia). It must also be asked: development *for whom*? Many of the facilities that result from tourism (airports, golf courses, luxury hotels and so on) will be of little benefit to the mass of the indigenous population. Likewise much indigenous wealth that is generated will be highly unequally distributed and so most of the population of developing countries will gain little benefit. This does of course depend on patterns of local ownership. Finally, much employment generated in tourist-related services is relatively low-skilled and may well reproduce the servile character of the previous colonial regime, what one critic has termed 'flunkey training' (quoted in Crick, 1988: 46).

However, it has to be asked whether many developing countries have much alternative to tourism as a development strategy. Although there are serious economic costs, as well as social costs which I have not even considered here, it is very difficult in the absence of alternatives to see that developing societies have much choice but to develop their attractiveness as objects of the tourist gaze, particularly for visitors from north America, western Europe and increasingly from Japan (see Dogan, 1989, on an assessment of costs and benefits).

In the next chapter I shall consider an issue just mentioned: the nature of the jobs that are to be found in tourist-related services, an issue of importance in both developing and developed countries as tourism accounts for an increasing proportion of paid employment throughout the world.

4

WORKING UNDER THE TOURIST GAZE

Introduction

I have so far analysed a number of different aspects of the tourist gaze. In the last chapter it was noted that the gaze can take two forms, the romantic and the collective, and that this distinction relates to the kinds of organisation possible of the tourist-related industries that develop to meet these different gazes. I also noted that in some cases, Niagara Falls for example, the gaze we experience is structured by pre-existing cultural images in which the physical object is barely 'seen' at all. It was also noted that some enormously significant organisational innovations have occurred within the tourist industry, including Thomas Cook's coupon system, the luxury holiday camp, the tour operator, computerised booking systems, fast-food outlets and so on.

In this chapter I shall consider in detail the complex relationship between two elements involved in the provision of services to tourists. On the one hand, there are the cultural practices of tourism, which constitute a set of preferred social activities highly structured by distinctions of taste. Such practices lead people to want to be in certain places, gazing at particular objects, in the company of specific other types of people. And on the other hand, a wide variety of services are provided, mainly under conditions of profit maximisation, for such tourists. And as we saw, huge international industries have developed so that the provision of services can be provided at a cost which permits large segmented markets to develop.

Various contradictions may develop between such cultural practices and the particular industries that have emerged (see Bagguley, 1987: 5–6). Such industries, particularly of transport, hotels, catering and entertainment, are all concerned with the provision of consumer *services* (sometimes known as the 'hospitality' industry). Such provision is often highly problematic, even to the extent that it is often unclear just what the product is that is being purchased. Furthermore, the tourist gaze is structured by culturally specific notions of what is extraordinary and therefore worth viewing. This means that the services provided, which may of course be incidental to the gaze itself, must take a form which does not contradict or undermine the quality of the gaze, and ideally should enhance it. This in turn poses, as we shall see, immense problems of management of such industries, to ensure that the service provided by the often relatively poorly paid service workers is appropriate to the almost sacred quality of the visitors' gaze on some longed-for and remarkable tourist site.

Two geographical or spatial features should be noted about tourist-related services. First, such services have to be provided in, or at least near to, the objects of the tourist gaze; they cannot be provided just anywhere. Tourist services develop in very particular places and cannot be shifted elsewhere; they have a particular 'spatial fix'. Second, much service production involves close spatial proximity between the producers and the consumers of the service in question. This results from the nature of many service products provided for tourists, such as a meal, a drink, a ride at the funfair, and so on. Such consumer services involve a necessarily close connection between producers and consumers.

Providing a 'service'

In the case of manufactured products it is normally clear just what the product consists of. In many service industries this is not nearly so straightforward (see discussion in Bagguley et al., 1990: ch. 3; and Bagguley, 1987). Mars and Nicod describe the problem of specifying the boundary of a given service:

> 'service' as we use it, refers to an action or material thing that is more than one might normally expect. In a transport cafe it can mean no more than pass-ing the sauce bottle with a smile. In the Savoy it might mean making prodigious efforts to supply a rare delicacy or indulging a customer's particular preference or foible.
>
> The more people actually pay for service, the more exacting will be their demand for better *and more individual* service. (1984: 28)

This quotation also demonstrates that the expenditure of labour is central to service work, whether this labour merely consists of passing the sauce or of some much more extensive and discriminating activity. Tourist-related services in particular are labour-intensive and this means that labour costs represent a significant proportion of total costs. Some examples of the proportion that the wages bill constituted as a proportion of sales minus pre-tax profits were, in the early 1980s: Aberdeen Steak Houses Group Ltd 21 per cent (1982); Berni Inns Ltd 27.7 per cent (1982); Grandmet Catering Services 40.8 per cent (1983); Pizza Express Ltd 28.1 per cent (1983); Trusthouse Forte 28.6 per cent (1983) (Pine, 1987: 62).

Moreover, since in manufacturing technical change can more radically reduce unit costs, services will over time come to be relatively more expensive. Employers in the various service sectors will seek to monitor and, where possible, to minimise such costs. However, most service enterprises will not be able to lower costs in the manner achieved by

McDonald's – now to merely 15 per cent of the value of sales (Percy and Lamb, 1987).

As noted, labour is to varying degrees implicated in the delivery of many tourist-related services. This occurs as the intended outcome of a necessarily *social* process in which some interaction occurs between one or more producers and one or more consumers. The quality of the social interaction is itself part of the service purchased (see Leidner, 1987). To buy the service is to buy a particular social or sociological experience. Sasser and Arbeit, for example, suggest that: 'Even if the hamburger is succulent, if the employee is surly, the customer will probably not return' (1976: 63). Many services are what are known as high-contact systems in which there is considerable involvement of the customer in the service. As a result it is more difficult to rationalise the system, partly because the customer may provoke a change in the system of operation (see Pine, 1987: 64–5).

The production of services normally involves some social interaction between producers and consumers at the point of production. First, unless the service can be more or less entirely materialised, then there has to be, as noted earlier, some geographical or spatial proximity between one or more of the service producers and consumers. Second, a distinction may be made between two classes of employee: those who have minimal contact with the service consumers and those who have high contact. In the case of the former, what may then be pursued by employers will be technical change and the extensive rationalisation of labour; with the latter employees would be recruited and trained on the basis of inter-personal attributes and public relations skills (see discussion in Pine, 1987: 65). There are difficulties in such divisive strategy: there is potential resentment between the two groups, such as between chefs and waiters; the maintenance of the distinction between the groups may be hard to sustain in complex organisations like hotels where customers cannot be confined to very restricted areas; and the variability in demand for many services means that a considerable premium is placed on the flexible use of labour, something difficult to organise if a strong demarcation is made between different groups.

Furthermore, the social composition of the producers, at least those who are serving in the front line, may be part of what is in fact 'sold' to the customer. In other words, the 'service' partly consists of a process of production which is infused with particular social characteristics, of gender, age, race, educational background and so on. When the individual buys a given service, what is purchased is a particular social composition of the service producers (see Hochschild, 1983, on how this applies in the case of flight attendants). In some cases what is also bought is a particular social composition of the other service *consumers*. Examples of this point are to be found in tourism/transport where people spend considerable periods of time consuming the service in relatively close proximity to others and hence part of what is being bought is the social composition of the other consumers. We will return to this in later chapters.

For the present I will examine in more detail the significance of 'labour' for the delivery of services. As labour is itself part of the service product, this poses particular difficulties for management. These difficulties are particularly significant: the longer the delivery takes, the more intimate the service, and the greater the importance of 'quality' for the consumer. This has the consequence that in some such cases employees' speech, appearance and personality may all be treated as legitimate areas of intervention and control by management, as in the case of service in the Savoy noted earlier.

Mars and Nicod note more generally the significance of the distinction between what is a routine and what is an emergency (1984: 34–5). There is a chronic tension between service receivers who regard all sorts of issues as an emergency (such as an overcooked steak), and service producers who have to learn to deal with such incidents as perfectly routine. This tension is most marked in highly prestigious hotels where customers pay for and expect very high levels of personal service and where such problems cannot be treated as purely matters of routine. By contrast, in much less prestigious and cheaper hotels staff have to develop techniques which suggest that everything is under control when there may in fact be all sorts of emergencies that routinely develop because of the intensity of work that is expected.

There are obviously very considerable variations in the expectations held by different customers. Mars and Nicod suggest that in cheaper hotels people expect a fast service but are not particularly bothered about its quality more generally (1984: 37). In top-quality hotels customers expect a wide range of idiosyncratic requests to be met, and indeed that waiters are almost able to anticipate such requests in advance. Mars and Nicod suggest that particular difficulties are caused in middle-ranking establishments where the level and forms of service to be provided are relatively unclear and contestable.

Gabriel provides an interesting and related discussion of the services provided by a gentleman's club (1988: ch. 4). As far as its members are concerned, the club offers them far more than a decent, traditional English meal. The club also offers a:

> whole range of *intangible products*, a place where important contacts can be made, where guests can be offered hospitality, where information can be exchanged, where certain rituals can be preserved and daily re-enacted. The very anachronistic nature of the club is part of this appeal; it is the appeal of the old. (1988: 141)

Gabriel goes on to say that the only way of assessing its success is through its ability to survive 'by providing those "intangible" services which cannot be rationalized and incorporated in the catering machinery' (1988: 141). The members of staff therefore serve more than meals; they are providing an intangible ambience which would be lost if the catering were to be rationalised.

Such services require what can loosely be called 'emotional work'. Amongst other requirements this involves the need to smile in a pleasant, friendly and involved way to consumers (Hochschild, 1983). Marshall notes that in the restaurant he studied: 'Staff were constantly encouraged to "cater for" the customers: to smile, exchange pleasantries, and, if there was time, longer conversations' (1986: 41). Crucial therefore to many consumer services is 'emotional work' of a public and recognisable sort. In the case of flight attendants specific training has brought this about, which results in a commercialisation of human feeling. In other occupations it is not nearly so publicly identifiable. Indeed the emphasis may be more on establishing a more 'genuine' emotional relationship between producers and consumers (as in a hospice) rather than one which is obviously contrived or artificial (see James, 1989). Nevertheless all such emotional work might well be said to be difficult and demanding, under-recognised and relatively under-rewarded. The fact that a great deal of it is provided by women is clearly no coincidence.

Hochschild argues that this emotional work has been made more difficult for flight attendants with the intensification of labour on American airlines since deregulation from the mid-1970s onwards: 'The workers respond to the speed-up with a slowdown: they smile less broadly, with a quick release and no sparkle in the eyes, thus dimming the company's message to the people. It is a war of smiles' (1983: 127).

Such a decline in quality is exceptionally hard for management to monitor and control, even if they are well aware that the attendants are no longer providing the complete service that passengers expect.

Yet in some further research conducted amongst KLM aircrews a rather different and more complex picture emerges (see Wouters, 1989). What seems to have happened more recently is that the demands made by the company with regard to sex, age, weight, jewellery, make-up, shoes, smile, behaviour and so on have become rather looser, particularly with the increased diversity of contemporary air travellers. Wouters explains this as follows:

> an aeroplane now has become a melting-pot, not only of nationalities but also of social classes. Behaviour in contacts between flight attendants and passengers correspondingly had to become less uniform or standardized and more varied and flexible . . . in each contact there is a need to attune one's behaviour to the style of emotion management of the individual passenger. (1989: 113)

What is also important is that in many services the actual delivery is provided by relatively low-level workers who are badly paid (at least relatively) and who may have little involvement or engagement with the overall enterprise. In London this problem of low pay is now being officially recognised since it is reported that an unattractive image is conveyed to prospective employees in the hotel and catering industry (the *Guardian*, 17 December 1988). A major shortage of such workers is predicted in London by the early 1990s. It is estimated that about one-third more employees will be needed by 1993 compared with the late 1980s, and the image of poor pay is causing problems.

These relatively low-level workers are normally female, the main exception being in the older forms of transport and in societies where occupations like 'waiting' have had historically a much higher status than in Britain. Overlying the interaction, the 'service', are often particular assumptions and notions of gender-specific forms of behaviour. And yet for many consumers what is actually consumed as a service *is* the particular moment of delivery by the relatively low-level service deliverers: the smile on the flight attendant's face, the pleasantness of the manner of the waitress, the sympathy in the eyes of the nurse, and so on. The problem for management is how to ensure that these moments do in fact work out appropriately, while minimising the cost of an undesirably intrusive (and hence resented) system of management/supervision, as well as minimising friction with other more highly paid, often male, workers backstage (see Whyte, 1948).

Jan Carlzon, President of the Scandinavian airline SAS, terms these 'moments of truth' for any organisation (1987). He suggests that in SAS there are something like 50 million moments of truth each year, each of which lasts perhaps 15 seconds when a customer comes into contact with an employee. It is, he says, these moments of truth that determine whether or not SAS will succeed or fail. He argues that the importance of such moments means that organisations have to be completely re-organised, towards service to the customer as the primary objective. As a consequence, the actual service deliverers, the company's 'foot soldiers' who know most about the 'front line' operations, have to be given much more responsibility to respond effectively, quickly and courteously to the particular needs of the customer. This in turn means that the efforts of the front-line employees need to be much more highly valued. Since they are the providers of the 'moments of truth' their motivation is crucial. And, Carlzon argues, in such a service-oriented organisation individual decisions should be made at the point of responsibility not higher up the hierarchy. The service deliverers have themselves to be the 'managers' and to be much more consumer-orientated (for related changes in British Airways, see Reynolds, 1989).

Another example can be seen in the management literature on hotels. Greene askes what is it that makes visitors return again and again to the same hotel (1982). He suggests that this has little to do with a hotel's physical features but rather results from two-way recognition between staff and the hotel's guests. Greene argues that there is nothing more satisfying than walking into a hotel and seeing a familiar face, and then in turn being greeted by name and not by one's room number. Greene proposes a number of techniques by which hotel staff are reminded of guests' names so that they can be used at each 'moment of truth'. This strategy is carried to considerable lengths by the Porterhouse Restaurant Group, which devised a scheme to motivate its staff to identify as many customers as possible by name. Those who could identify 100 or more became members of the '100 Club', those who could identify 250, members of the '250 Club' and so on. One manageress achieved a UK record of being able to recognise an amazing 2,000 visitors (Lunn, 1989).

Some other examples of 'moments of truth' are provided by Welsh (1989). He sought help and advice for a possible Mediterranean holiday from twelve different travel agents and found the service in many far from satisfactory, and in some conspicuously bad. Welsh summarised how this poses problems for the image of service provided by what were well-known high-street agents: 'an employee who wears the corporate uniform of a large travel agency surely reflects to some degree the attitude of the company as a whole towards its customers' (1989).

Four concluding points should be noted about services. The production of many services is *context* dependent, they depend for their successful production upon aspects of the social and physical setting within which they occur. Examples include the style of furnishings in a travel agent's reflecting an appropriate corporate image, the apparently safe interior of an aeroplane, the antique furniture in the country hotel, the particular historically interesting set of buildings in a resort and so on. In other words, the delivery of many services is interconnected with aspects of the environment and especially with the nature of design and architecture. In certain cases the service cannot be received in an inappropriate physical and social context – part of the 'service', part of what is consumed, is in effect the context. This is particularly the case with tourist-related services.

Further, the quality of many services has become intensely *contested* in contemporary societies. This is for a number of reasons: that services meet an increasingly wide range of people's needs; that their consumption normally involves spending considerable amounts of time since it has to occur serially and not simultaneously (see Gershuny, 1987); that the consumers movement has encouraged people to be much more critical and inquisitive about the quality of services being received; and that consumers are increasingly choosy, eclectic and fickle. Service providers thus have all sorts of difficulties to face when confronted with the essentially contested character of 'service'.

The service product is predominantly *intangible*. So although there are certain tangible elements, such as the food or journey or drink, the crucial elements are intangible. This is shown in a study of small country hotels:

> service is not concerned with the product itself, but with the way in which the product is created and handled, with the manner, knowledge and attitude of the people who deliver it and with the environment in which it is deliverd . . . in general terms quality is manifestly incapable of measurement. (Callan, 1989: 245)

Finally, there are considerable differences between the perceived quality of service in different societies. In a recent survey by Mintel, one-third of shoppers in Britain considered shop staff incompetent and unhelpful.

Standards of service in Britain seem lower than in, say, the USA (but not New York!) or Japan (see *The Sunday Times*, 8 October 1989).

These fairly general points about services will now be applied to the problems involved in providing one particular category of services central to tourism: food and drink.

Catering for the customer

The development of the catering industry has been long and complex. Catering has now become publicly available. Restaurants, bars and cafes are part of the public space of contemporary societies. This is in marked contrast to London even in the nineteenth century, when all the best places to eat were private or semi-private (see on the following Mennell, 1985: ch. 6). Two particular forms should be noted: the private London clubs which grew more numerous from 1820 onwards, and private hotels where meals were served in the private suites of rooms and there was no 'public dining room'. This began to change in the 1880s and 1890s with the construction of many grand hotels, stemming from the increased mobility brought about by the development of the railway. The new hotels were no longer private. Their public dining romms were open at least to the wealthy 'public' – and rapidly became fashionable. As Mennell notes, their exclusiveness stemmed not from semi-private association with a particular social circle, but from expense. Such hotels were no longer the preserve of men. They were public, or perhaps semi-public, spaces for wealthy men and women, to see and to be seen in.

The new hotels entailed innovative forms of organisation, particularly because the new clientele demanded much faster preparation of meals. The key figure in this rationalisation of the kitchen was Escoffier, who brought about a transformation of catering work. Traditionally the kitchen had been divided into a number of distinct sections, each responsible to a chef and for a particular category of dishes, and in which each chef worked independently of the others. Escoffier, by contrast, organised his kitchen into five sections, based not on the type of dish to be prepared but on the kind of operation to be undertaken (such as the *rôtisseur* who did roasts, grilled and fried dishes, the *saucier* who made sauces, and so on). These different sections were highly interdependent so that any particular dish resulted from the work carried out by chefs working in a number of different sections. The effect of this reform was to break down traditional craft demarcations and to generate a new division of labour based upon novel forms of specialisation and interdependence of activites (Mennell, 1985: 155–9).

I will now consider some recent evidence and debate surrounding the contemporary division of labour in the kitchen (see Bagguley, 1987, 1990, for more detail on much of the material here).

It is useful to begin by outlining some of the main features of hotel and catering workplaces according to Mars and Nicod (1984). One is *ad hoc management*. Because the level of demand for such services is highly volatile and unpredictable, management has to develop *ad hoc* ways of responding to varying demands and unanticipated crises. To cope with this unpredictability, managements largely avoid collective contracts and favour *individual contract-making*. Each employee will negotiate separate arrangements with management. What is of most significance to such employees is the *total reward system*, which includes not only basic pay, but also formalised perks such as accommodation, semi-formalised perks such as tips, and non-formal opportunities for perks and pilferage (see especially Mars and Nicod, 1984: ch. 6, 'The Waiter's Informal Career: Learning to be Bent'). And there is the distinction between *core and peripheral workers*; the former benefit most from the informal system of rewards that operates.

These four features, in part at least, derive from the key characteristics of restaurants identified in Whyte's classic study: the *combination* of production and service (1948: 17). A restaurant thus differs from a factory which is solely a unit of production; and it differs from a shop which is purely a unit of service:

> The restaurant operator produces a perishable product for immediate sale within his establishment. Success in such a business requires a delicate adjustment of supply to demand and skilful cooordination of production and service . . . . This situation puts a premium upon the skilful handling of personnel . . . . The restaurant must provide a satisfactory way of life for the people who do the work or else it cannot provide the satisfactions sought by its customers. (Whyte, 1948: 17–18)

There are important implications of the fact that restaurants represent a combination of both production and service. Because employees are dealing with a perishable product, the tempo of work is highly variable; it is difficult to generate a rhythm by which to work and it also means that there are immense problems of co-ordination (Whyte, 1948: 18–19). The restaurant worker has essentially two bosses, the supervisor/employer and the customer. The total reward depends upon satisfactory relationships with both. Moreover, low-status employees, waiters and waitresses, are able to demand prompt action from their status superiors, the chefs and cooks. But this is something that often generates resentment and a slowdown to demonstrate status superiority. Mars and Nicod suggest that these conflicts are likely to be less significant in very high-class hotels and restaurants where there is a common commitment to quality and less pressure on time (1984: 43–7). Whyte discusses various means of overcoming any such problems, that is, to preserve communication between the kitchen and the waiters while limiting face-to-face interaction and hence the possibilities of friction.

Marshall, however, examines a further aspect of the catering industry which Whyte ignores, namely the fact that when staff and customers meet there is a complex intertwining of labour and leisure. Marshall argues that had Whyte 'investigated the staff–customer relationship with similar resolve he would have realised that the proximate culture of restaurant employees is only in part that of the "workplace"' (1986: 34). And it is the mixing of labour and leisure that is the central characteristic of the restaurant he investigates.

Marshall is particularly interested in the contradiction between the poor conditions of work in the restaurant and the lack of resentment about them expressed by the workforce. The pay was bad, the hours worked were exceptionally long, and all the staff had to demonstrate complete job flexibility. And yet there was remarkably little discontent either about the nature of the work or about the obvious wealth of the owner. There was more or less no unionisation, like most of the rest of the industry (see Mars and Nicod, 1984: 109). There was also, rather unusually, little turnover of staff.

It was initially presumed by Marshall that the employer's somewhat idiosyncratic paternalism, combined with the material and symbolic significance of the total reward system, were sufficient to explain the apparent loyalty of the workforce. However, through participant observation Marshall came to conclude that these 'employees were convinced that they weren't really "working" for their pay packets at all' (1986: 40). The staff rarely used the language of work. They did not say thay were going to work, or were going home from work. The business after all involved the provision of leisure. Many of the customers were friends or relatives of the employees and, at least during slack times, staff were encouraged to talk to and even participate in the leisure activities going on around them. Little attention was paid to punctuality and staff were given freedom to organise their own routines of work. Moreover, much of the employee's leisure time was in fact also spent at the restaurant drinking in the bars. Thus many symbolic boundaries between work and leisure did not really operate. The daily round of activities (that is, of what was formally 'work' and what was formally 'leisure') were to be seen as much more a way of life. Marshall suggests that many other workplaces may have rather similar features, especially where what is provided are leisure or tourist-related services.

However, at the same time, a range of rather significant transformations is occurring in the nature of catering work, particularly concerned with the introduction of new technologies, which I shall now briefly consider. I will begin here with Chivers' extensive survey of the labour process of over 600 chefs and cooks (1973; and see Bagguley, 1987: Section 3).

Some features of the work culture and situation of the cook make it unlikely that there will be active trade unionism and class consciousness amongst cooks and chefs. Chefs and cooks, particularly in private hotels and restaurants, typically have an orientation to service. There is the dedication to task because of the belief that the work they do is skilled, interesting and offers extensive scope for expressing their craft-like abilities. There are status differences between 'chefs' and 'cooks' in that the former view themselves as an elite serving an upper-class clientele in high 'quality' establishments. Such status differences with deep historical roots undermine the perception of a homogeneous 'occupation'. There are many opportunities in the industry to acquire managerial or employer positions. In the early 1970s, for example, there were three times as many 'managerial/employer' positions in hotels and catering than the proportion in the UK economy as a whole (see Chivers, 1973). This has led to the perception among cooks of a distinct career structure through which they can progress upwards and come to run their own establishment.

But Chivers goes on to argue that extensive technical change occurred amongst such chefs and cooks in the 1970s. This was partly because of the introduction of various electrical devices, which replaced many routine hand operations, but mainly because of the widespread development of 'convenience foods':

> where the very nature of the craft was being invaded by technological change in the form of convenience foods (dried, tinned and frozen), opinions revealed doubts and distress. There was recognition of the advantages of such foods in speeding up operations, increasing control over work and reducing wastage, but between a half and three-quarters of chefs and cooks feared a loss of skill and dishes would suffer. Where convenience foods have taken over, they transplant the need for skill from the kitchen to earlier stages of food preparation in factories. The result is that frozen meats, fish, vegetables and desserts enter the kitchen in a condition which requires no more than the semi-skilled operation of reconstitution before service. (Chivers, 1973: 650–1)

However, Gabriel's research in a hospital kitchen in the 1980s suggests that the situation may be more complex than this. He shows that what was more common was the juxtaposition of convenience foods *and* highly skilled craft cooking, depending upon the numbers of staff available and the particular catering requirements on a particular day (1988: 33, 54). The craft skills had certainly not been eliminated and if anything had been partly reintroduced. Nevertheless, in further research in a cook-freeze kitchen Gabriel shows that it is possible to transform a kitchen into a production line. One employee said; 'This is not a kitchen, it is a production line, but we don't get production money' (Gabriel, 1988: 57). But in relationship to cooking it is often difficult to establish just what skilled work really amounts to. This is because it often involves tacit skills which are not learnt through formal apprenticeships. It involves judgement and intelligence, sensitivity and subjectivity.

The other major labour process in hotel and catering that has been extensively restructured through technical change in the postwar period is dishwashing. The proportion of all employees in hotel and catering who were kitchen hands fell from 21.0 per cent in 1951 to only 4.2 per cent in 1971 (Bagguley, 1987: 25). The kitchen hand's work has been highly automated and often involves no more than the loading of dishes in and out of the machine as well as simple 'fetching and carrying' around the kitchen. Smith estimates that some 140,000 'kitchen-hand' jobs disappeared as the result of the introduction of dishwashing machines over the twenty-year period, something which particularly reduced the levels of women's employment (1986).

Bagguley interestingly suggests that there have been two distinct 'phases' of technical change in hotel kitchens in Britain, and that these have had rather different gender implications (1987: Sections 3 and 4). The first, in the 1950s and 1960s, was the mechanisation of routine manual tasks and resulted in the reduction of women's employment as kitchen hands, chefs and cooks. The second phase – mostly during the 1970s – was the introduction of pre-prepared foods, the initial consequence of which Chivers analysed. During this phase there was a considerable increase in the numbers and proportion of women employed as chefs and cooks.

It may also be suggested that the 1980s represent a third phase, where there has been extensive investment in the fast-food industry and what Levitt terms the 'industrialisation of service' (1981). In the UK as a whole over 1,350 pizza, 1,000 hamburger and 650 chicken outlets have opened in the past fifteen or so years (Gabriel, 1988: 94). The growth of such fast-food competition has also transformed traditional fish and chip outlets in Britain, the numbers of which have perhaps surprisingly increased in total in recent years (Gabriel, 1988: 143). An executive interviewed by Gabriel admitted more generally that fast food is 'not a chef system, but a food management system' (1988: 92). One particularly striking feature of such fast-food outlets has been the promotion of easy accessibility and flexible consumption more or less at any time. They have broken down the tyranny of fixed mealtimes and the rigid timetabling of the day. Eating food often now involves 'grazing'.

One dominant employment effect of these changes has been to increase the proportion of the catering workforce who are aged under 21. In 1986 75 per cent of the 15,000 workers employed by McDonald's nationally were under 21 and most worked part-time. Annual staff turnover in the industry is around 300 per cent. Working in fast food is now the commonest choice of first-time job in Britain. A fast-food manager explained the recruiting policy: 'We *just* have to recruit young people because of the pace of work. Older people couldn't stand the pace . . . this job, with its clean, dynamic image, appeals to younger people' (quoted in Gabriel, 1988: 97).

In such places the young staff have to learn how to present themselves in particular programmed ways to customers. There are stereotyped forms of address, which are sometimes even printed on the back of the menu. Staff must also learn the company smile. A fast-food worker nevertheless explained: 'It's all artificial. Pretending to offer personal service with a smile when in reality no one means it. We know this, management knows this, even the customers know this, but we keep pretending' (Gabriel, 1988: 93).

Yet, Gabriel argues, although almost everything in the fast-food business is rule-bound, these rules are often broken in order to meet the immense demand at particular times of the day and to break the drudgery of the work involved. Management regularly turns a blind eye to the ways in which employees maintain a measure of autonomy and put their mark on work that they otherwise would find immensely monotonous (Gabriel, 1988: 107).

I have so far assumed that the same processes apply in each country. However, Mennell conclusively shows that the French and English experiences have been strikingly different. There has been a long-standing dominance in England of the job of 'management', particularly of large hotels, and a corresponding disdain until recently for the occupations of chef and cook (1985: 195). France, by contrast, has seen the development of the chef as a professional. The *chef-patron* enjoyed immensely high status in French society. Mennell suggests that the situation in England has facilitated the more extensive implementation of deskilling strategies compared with France.

A 'flexible' labour force

Here I shall show that the so-called new restructuring strategy of the 1980s, the flexible use of labour, is something that has characterised many tourist-related services for some decades, and that the understanding of such services necessitates a careful examination of the changing gender relations in such industries, since particular kinds of labour flexibility presuppose a certain gendering of the labour force (see generally here Walby, 1987, and, for all this section, Bagguley, 1990).

In the UK the most systematic analysis of the flexible use of labour has been carried out by Atkinson, who identified four forms of flexibility (see 1984). First, there is *numerical flexibility*, where firms vary the level of labour input in reponse to changes in the level of output. This may involve the use of part-time, temporary, short-term contract and casual workers. Second, there is *functional flexibility*, which refers to the ability of employers to move employees between different functional tasks according to changes in the work load. Third, there is the strategy of *distancing*, which involves the displacing of internal employment relations by commercial market relations through subcontracting and similar arrangements. Fourth, there is *pay flexibility*, whereby employers attempt to reward individual employees who have for example become 'multi-skilled' and functionally flexible employees. These management strategies have the effect of restructuring employment in firms into 'core' and 'peripheral' workers. The core group consists of functionally flexible highly remunerated permanent employees working part time, on temporary contracts, or in subcontracting.

The thesis has been almost entirely discussed in relationship to manufacturing industry, particularly during the 1980s (see NEDO, 1986;

Pollert, 1988). However, much service industry has for a much longer period been characterised by many of these forms of flexibility. In tourist-related services for example we have already noted the use of pay flexibility, something which seems related to the low levels of unionisation, even in large hotels, and the relative absence of industrial disputes (see Johnson and Mignot, 1982). Furthermore, Bagguley notes that both functional and numerical flexibility have been clear management goals in hotel and catering from the 1960s onwards. This is demonstrated in Department of Employment research conducted at that time. It was noted for example that:

> The essential need for full and flexible use of staff has led to a considerable move away from traditional staffing patterns. In many hotels both the occupational structure of the staff and the content of their jobs have changed. The more flexible use of staff was evident in all departments. (Department of Employment, 1971: 31)

A typical day for a functionally flexible 'chamber maid' in the 1960s was described as follows:

> . . . make and serve early morning teas; assist in preparation and service of breakfast; make beds and clean bedrooms and bathrooms, and after an afternoon break, assist with the preparation and service of the evening meal; or part-time staff might be engaged for the evening duties. (Department of Employment, 1971: 31)

Similar functional flexibility was noted in the kitchen:

> Few hotels retained the full traditional kitchen brigade. Boulangiers, rôtisseurs and sauciers especially were less frequently employed, often being replaced by less specialised sous-chefs. Similarly the employment of separate breakfast cooks was tending to decline, their work being undertaken by assistant cooks, who combined it with other, wider, kitchen duties. The increased use of convenience foods and the consequent reduction in the preparation of vegetables, etc., has enabled the introduction of kitchen assistants with a wider range of duties, previously covered by separate grades. (Department of Employment, 1971: 31)

The report also notes the widespread use of part-time employees to meet fluctuations in demand during the day, of temporary seasonal workers to offset the well-known seasonality of demand, and of subcontracting certain functions, especially laundering (see Ball, 1988, on seasonality).

Bagguley further notes that more recent evidence of the importance of functional flexibility is revealed in the Hotel and Catering Industry Training Board's research on hotel and catering skills (1990; ETAC, 1983). Six categories of tasks were identified: food preparation and cookery; serving food and drink; handling and storing food and drink before preparation; cleaning activities; administrative and clerical work; supervisory and managerial activities. It was concluded from an extensive survey that:

> Two thirds of the sample worked in three or more of these areas on occasion. About 90 per cent worked in at least two of them. People in managerial or administrative positions had the most diversity in their work, followed by

people in kitchen jobs. People working in reception or the front office had the least. Over one third of crafts people said they worked in four or more of these areas . . . . People in smaller establishments, where one would expect greater flexibility of working, tended to work in more areas than people in larger establishments. (ETAC, 1983: 9)

There is also a distinct gender division in the form and extent of these various flexible working practices (Bagguley, 1990). It seems that it was much more common for men to have jobs which involved functional flexibility. The ETAC report again notes: 'There was a marked tendency for men to be doing a wider variety of tasks than women, which no doubt reflects the high proportion of women in operative positions, which have the least diversity in their work' (1983: 9).

The 'operative positions' – cooks, waiting and bar staff, kitchen hands, domestic staff and cleaners – are overwhelmingly filled by women. Moreover, it is in these positions that such women employees work part-time, that is, demonstrating what Atkinson terms 'numerical flexibility'. In 1984 over 80 per cent of part-time employees in hotels in Britain were women (Dept of Employment, 1987). Such numerically flexible workers are also usually the least functionally flexible. Most part-time employees (mostly women) do not have the opportunity to develop a wide range of skills and experience to become functionally flexible as full-time employees, who are more likely to be male (see Bagguley, 1990, for further discussion). Thus the gender of the employee determines which form of flexible working is likely to be experienced; and these forms contradict each other.

The development of such flexible forms of employment is affected by various factors. The fact that most tourist-related services have to be provided when the customer demands them and this increases the use of temporary, part-time and functionally flexible workers. In many tourist-related services there is an exceptional variety of functions which have to be met – food production, food service, entertainment, accommodation, bars, etc. – and this provides many opportunities for developing task flexibility. The industrial relations climate in these firms needs to be taken into account. Lack of extensive unionisation and of employees' organisations around occupational groups within the industry means there is little formally organised opposition to new working practices. We have already seen that the managerial style is casual and particularistic depending on informal regard systems (Whyte, 1948; Mars and Nicod, 1984). Such a style is less likely to inhibit flexibility compared with one that is part of a large and tightly rule-bound organisation (see Bagguley, 1990).

So far, then, there is plenty of evidence to support the view that flexible working practices have for some time been a key feature of tourist-related industries in Britain. However, it does not follow that the workforce can be seen as easily divided up into a core and a peripheral labour force, as the flexibility literature hypothesises (see Atkinson, 1984). Guerrier and Lockwood (1989) suggest that two particular groups in the hotel workforce do not conveniently fit into the core–periphery model. First, there are what they call the 'operative core' – staff, receptionists, kitchen staff, waiting staff and so on – who in large hotels are often relatively functionally inflexible rather than multi-skilled as the model would suggest. Second, there is a peripheral group who carry out more or less identical tasks to the employees just identified. But this peripheral group enjoys much less job security and fewer career prospects. Especially in London, hotels appear to make great use of mobile, transient staff often recruited from abroad. With such staff demonstrating very high turnover it is often difficult to sustain adequate skill levels and develop appropriate training programmes. Sometimes it appears that companies use 'numerical flexibility' instead of developing the multiple skills of their core staff.

Indeed more generally there appears to be a paucity of career paths in tourist-related services except for those in managerial and chef positions. Metcalf summarises the situation for many workers in what is usually described as the hospitality industry: 'Very few career jobs were identified . . . . Most jobs were characterised by young recruits, no promotion and high turnover. And leavers went into a variety of unskilled jobs . . .' (1988: 89).

There are relatively few exceptions to this in the industry, an interesting one in the north of England being Betty's tearooms, which are to be found in four Yorkshire towns (see Burton, 1989). Training is taken very seriously. Each trainee is allocated to a trainer for a month before working on their own. Also the company has deliberately not expanded beyond the control exercised by the family. There is a customer panel of food samplers to report back on any shortcomings and there are good career prospects.

This relatively unusual example proves the general rule that tourist-related services are amongst the most difficult of 'products' to produce. This is particularly so because of the changing cultural expectations about tourism, and hence about those services.

5
CULTURAL CHANGES AND THE RESTRUCTURING OF TOURISM

Introduction

I have so far conceptualised the tourist gaze as being relatively distinct from other social activities and occurring at particular places for specific periods of time. This viewpoint was reinforced by the analysis in chapters 3 and 4 of some salient characteristics of the tourist industry. Although it is difficult to demarcate just what is and what is not part of that industry, I presumed a reasonably tight formulation. In chapter 4, for example, I discussed the specific character of service delivery in the so-called hospitality industry.

But changes in the nature of western societies in the past two or three decades have seriously undermined such a precise notion. I shall argue the following. There has been a reversal of the long-term process of structural differentiation by which relatively distinct social institutions had come to specialise in particular tasks or functions. Part of this reversal is that 'culture' has come to occupy a more central position in the organisation of present-day societies, whose contemporary culture can be at least in part characterised as 'postmodern'. Postmodernism involves a dissolving of the boundaries, not only between high and low cultures, but also between different cultural forms, such as tourism, art, education, photography, television, music, sport, shopping and architecture. In addition, the era of mass communications has transformed the tourist gaze and many of the features of postmodernism have already been partly prefigured in existing tourist practices. What I have termed the tourist gaze is increasingly bound up with and is partly indistinguishable from all sorts of other social and cultural practices. This has the effect, as 'tourism' *per se* declines in specificity, of universalising the tourist gaze – people are much of the time 'tourists' whether they like it or not. The tourist gaze is intrinsically part of contemporary experience, of postmodernism, but the tourist practices to which it gives rise are experiencing rapid and significant change. Such change cannot be separated from these more wide-ranging structural and cultural developments in contemporary society.

In earlier chapters I referred to certain notions which I will develop in this half of the book. In chapter 1 it was shown that daydreaming was important in most forms of consumption, and it is obviously central to much holiday-making. But daydreaming is not a purely individual activity; it is socially organised, particularly through television, advertising, literature, cinema, photography and so on. The idea of the 'post-tourist' was introduced, again referring to the fact that tourist patterns are not themselves unchanging. In particular it suggests that tourism might be viewed by some at least as a 'game' and that there are no authentic tourist experiences. In chapter 2 the development of mass tourism in Britain was analysed, in particular the development of the English seaside resort and the emergent resort hierarchy. Explanations for the demise of such resorts, partly because of the changing powers of different social classes, will be considered later in this chapter.

In chapter 3 the romantic and the collective tourist gazes were distinguished and some of the social and environmental effects of each were considered. In this chapter it will be suggested that the former has become considerably more significant and is part of the mechanism by which contemporary tourism has been 'globalised'. It will also be suggested that objects of the tourist gaze can effectively be classified in terms of three key dichotomies, of which the romantic/collective is one (others are authentic/inauthentic and historical/modern). In chapter 4 particular attention was directed to the social or sociological character of the delivery of services, that customers increasingly expect and demand a particular social experience. This issue will be developed in a number of ways, particularly through considering the concept of the 'theme'.

The next section begins this complex argument by briefly analysing some salient features of postmodernism.

Postmodernism

In some ways it is difficult to address the topic of postmodernism at all. It seems as though the signifier 'postmodern' is free-floating, having few connections with anything real, no minimal shared meaning of any sort. In this section, however, I shall endeavour to outline a particular set of cultural developments, what one might call a new 'cultural paradigm', and to elaborate some of the sociological conditions that have given rise to it. I shall suggest that the term 'postmodernism' is appropriately applied to this paradigm.

Thinking of postmodernism in this way makes it clear that it is not a term which refers either to the whole of society (different therefore in scope from say 'post-industrial society'); or to one particular sphere of activity (such as architecture). It refers to a system of signs or symbols, which is specific in both time and space. Such a system is characterisable in terms of a specific regime of signification in which particular cultural objects are produced, circulated and received. Such objects involve a particular set of relations between the signifier, the signified and the referent (my account here is drawn from Lash, 1990: ch. 1, to which I am indebted).

Although I have maintained that postmodernism refers to the cultural sphere, its relationship to that sphere is somewhat idiosyncratic. As Lash expresses it, postmodernism 'is a regime of signification whose fundamental structuring trait is "de-differentiation"' (1990: 11). This argument can be elucidated in terms similar to those used in much conventional sociology. Modernism involves 'structural differentiation', the separate development of a number of institutional and normative spheres, of the economy, the family, the state, science, morality, and an aesthetic realm. Each of these becomes subject to what Weber called *Eigengesetzlichkeit*, or self-legislation (see Lash, 1990: 8–9). Each sphere develops its own conventions and mode of valuation. Value within the cultural spheres is dependent upon how well a cultural object measures up to the norms appropriate to that sphere. I shall term this horizontal differentiation.

But a further aspect needs to be considered, what I will term vertical differentiation. What is involved is that as each sphere becomes separated off horizontally, so immensely important vertical differentiations develop. Within the cultural sphere this consists of a number of distinctions: between culture and life, between high and low culture, between scholarly or auratic art and popular pleasures, and between elite and mass forms of consumption. Within building design there is the distinction between 'architecture' (which obviously takes many different styles) and various vernacular forms of building. There is also the important distinction between high-level science and the typical layperson's understanding of physical processes (as in the area of medical knowledge).

Modernism, then, is to be understood as a process of differentiation, especially as we have seen here, of the differentiation between the various cultural spheres both horizontally and vertically. Postmodernism, by contrast, involves de-differentiation (again see Lash, 1990: ch. 1 on the following). There are a number of developments.

There is a breakdown in the distinctiveness of each of these spheres of social activities, especially the cultural. Each implodes into the other, and most involve visual spectacle and play. This is seen most clearly in so-called multi-media events but much cultural production, especially via the central role of TV, is difficult to categorise and place within any particular sphere.

Such cultural spheres are no longer auratic, in Benjamin's terms (see Benjamin, 1973; Lash and Urry, 1987: ch. 9). To say that a cultural phenomenon had aura was to say that it was radically separated from the social, it proclaimed its own originality, uniqueness and singularity, and that it was based in a discourse of formal organic unity and artistic creativity. Postmodernist culture is anti-auratic. Such forms do not proclaim their uniqueness but are mechanically and electronically reproduced. There is a denial of the separation of the aesthetic from the social and of the contention that art is of a different order from life. The value placed on the unity of the artistic work is challenged through an emphasis on pastiche, collage, allegory and so on. Postmodern cultural forms are not consumed in a state of contemplation (as in the classical concert) but of distraction. Postmodern culture affects the audience via its immediate impact, through what it does for one, through regimes of pleasure, and not through the formal properties of the aesthetic material. And this serves to undermine any strong distinction between a high culture, enjoyed by an elite knowledgeable about the aesthetics of a given sphere (painting, music, literature), and the popular or low culture of the masses. Postmodernism is anti-hierarchical, opposed to such vertical differentiations.

There is a de-differentiation of the 'cultural economy'. One aspect of this is the breakdown of some at least of the differences between the cultural object and the audience so that there is an active encouragement of audience participation. Examples include the 'living theatre' and the development of game shows on TV where 'anyone can be a star for five minutes'. Another aspect is the dissolving of the boundaries between what is artistic production and what is commercial. Developments here include the growth of 'free' artistic pop videos to sell records, of pop songs appearing first within advertisements, of major artistic talents employed within the production of adverts, and the use of 'art' to sell products via sponsorship. Commerce and culture are indissolubly intertwined in the postmodern.

Postmodernism problematises the distinction between representations and reality. This results from a number of processes. Signification is increasingly figural or visual and so there is a closer, more intimate, relationship between the representation and the reality than where the signification takes place through words or music (without the advantage of a film, TV, video, pop video and so on). Further, an increasing proportion of the referents of signification, the 'reality', are themselves representations. Or as Baudrillard famously argues, what we increasingly consume are signs or representations. Social identities are constructed through the exchange of sign-values. But these are accepted in a spirit of spectacle. People know that the media, for example, are a simulation, and they in turn simulate the media. This world of sign and spectacle is one in which there is no real originality, only what Eco terms 'travels in hyper-reality' (1986). Everything is a copy, or a text upon a text, where what is fake seems more real than the real. This is a depthless world or, as Lash puts it, there is a 'new flimsiness of reality' (Lash, 1990: 15). He summarises this argument: '*modernism conceives of representations as being problematic whereas postmodernism problematises reality*' (1990: 13).

Many writers have recently demonstrated that these processes of de-differentiation have begun to characterise many aspects of contemporary culture, although by no means all (see, amongst various sources, Hebdige, 1986–7, 1988; Foster, 1985b; Lash, 1990; Kroker and Cook, 1986; I will

discuss architecture in chapter 6). Lash argues that postmodernism should
be thought of as a cultural paradigm or ideal type. To do so is to
recognise that there are *other* important cultural elements which will be
present in a given society (premodern, realist, modernist, etc.); that many
cultural phenomena embody elements of different ideal types; and that
different societies are more *or* less postmodern (US more so than Sweden)
and indeed that some regions or cities are more postmodern than other
areas within the same society (Los Angeles more so than New England).

Much of the rest of this book consists of an examination of the relationship between such postmodern developments and a wide variety of
contemporary tourist practices. Before this it should be noted that many
tourist practices, even in the past, prefigure some of the postmodern
characteristics just described (see MacCannell, 1989, on tourism and
postmodernism). Tourism has always involved spectacle. Resorts in
England have, for example, competed with each other to provide visitors
with the grandest ballroom, the longest pier, the highest tower, the most
modern amusement park, the most stylish holiday camp, the most spectacular illuminations, the most beautiful gardens, the most elegant
promenade, and so on. Because of the importance of the visual, of the
gaze, tourism has always been concerned with spectacle and with cultural
practices which partly implode into each other. Much tourist activity has
been thoroughly anti-auratic. It has been based on mechanical and electronic reproduction (beginning with 'What the butler saw' machines,
through spectacular illuminations, to *son et lumière* and laser shows); it
has been thoroughly based on popular pleasures, on an anti-elitism with
little separation of art from social life; it has typically involved not
contemplation but high levels of audience participation; and there has
been much emphasis on pastiche, or what others might call kitsch (as in
the famous Hawaiian ballroom at Maplin's holiday camp on the British
TV programme '*Hi-de-Hi*!').

What I have just been describing are some of the characteristics of what
I termed the collective tourist gaze in chapter 3. But in that chapter I also
discussed the romantic gaze, which is much more obviously auratic, concerned with the elitist – and solitary – appreciation of magnificent scenery,
an appreciation which requires considerable cultural capital especially if
particular physical objects signify specific literary texts (as with the
Lakeland poets, for example). However, even within the romantic gaze
there have been elements which we now can classify as postmodern. Much
of what is appreciated is not directly experienced reality itself but representations, particularly through the medium of photography. What people
'gaze upon' are ideal representations of the view in question that they
internalise from postcards and guidebooks (and increasingly from TV
programmes). And even when they cannot in fact 'see' the natural wonder
in question they can still sense it, see it in their mind. And even when the
object fails to live up to its representation it is the latter which will stay
in people's minds, as what they have really 'seen'.

I have suggested that there is a relatively new cultural paradigm, the postmodern; that this is particularly to be understood in terms of the processes of de-differentiation; but that a number of tourist practices have historically prefigured this paradigm. Tourism is prefiguratively postmodern because of its particular combination of the visual, the aesthetic, and the popular.

Yet there is an important sense in which much tourism has also been minimally modernist. This sense is revealed through the term *mass* tourism which is how much tourist activity has been structured since the late nineteenth century. We noted in chapter 2 certain aspects of this attempt to treat people in the same manner and not to set up invidious differentiations between people who were consumers of the same holiday camp or hotel or restaurant. Central to modernism is the view of the public as an homogeneous mass, that there is a realm of correct values which will serve to unify people. I shall consider this in more detail later, in the context of some aspects of architectural change. But within tourism modernism has been reflected in the attempt to treat people *within a socially differentiated site* as similar to each other with shared tastes and characteristics, albeit determined by the providers of the service in question. In the next section I consider how one of the key characteristics of postmodernism is people's refusal to accept treatment as part of an undifferentiated mass. Hutcheon summarises postmodernism as: 'a model that is profoundly implicated in, yet still capable of criticizing, that which it seeks to describe' (1986–7: 180). Part of postmodernism's hostility to authority is the opposition felt by many people to being seen as part of a mass. Rather, people appear to want to be treated in a much more differentiated manner and this has given rise to so-called life-style research on the part of the advertising industry (see Thurot and Thurot, 1983).

I have so far talked of different cultural paradigms without regard to the social forces that underlie them. But the development of postmodernism should be related to an analysis of the changing powers of different social classes. The weakened collective powers of the working class and the heightened powers of the service and other middle classes have generated a widespread audience for postmodern cultural forms and particularly for what some have termed 'post-tourism' (see Urry, 1988a, for a preliminary account of this argument).

My argument here is in a loose sense derived from Bourdieu's *Distinction* (1984). A number of features of this major work are relevant to the following, and especially to the analysis of the impact of the cultural practices of one class upon another. Bourdieu brings out that the powers of different social classes (and by implication other social agents) are as much symbolic as economic or political. Such symbolic goods are subject to a distinct economy, a 'cultural economy', characterised by competition, monopolisation, inflation, and different forms of capital, including especially cultural capital. Different social classes are engaged in a series of struggles with each other, to increase the volume of capital they possess vis-à-vis other classes, and to increase the valuation placed on the particular forms of capital they happen to possess. Each social class possesses a habitus, the system of classification which operates below the level of individual consciousness and which is inscribed within people's orienting practices, bodily dispositions and tastes and distastes. Classes in competition with each other attempt to impose their own system of classification on other classes and to become dominant. In such struggles a central role is played by the institutions of culture, of education and of intellectuals more generally. The cultural realm has its own logic, currency and rate of convertibility into economic capital. Cultural capital is not just a matter of abstract theoretical knowledge but the symbolic competence necessary to appreciate works of 'art' or even 'anti-art'. Differential access to the means of arts consumption is thus crucial to the reproduction of class and hence to the processes of class and broader social conflict. This differential cultural consumption both results from the class system and is a mechanism by which such classes, and other social forces, seek to establish dominance within a society (see Bourdieu, 1984, on France, as well as Lash and Urry, 1987: ch. 9; Featherstone, 1987; Lash, 1990).

I shall now try to relate this thesis to the understanding of the development of post-modernism through the following argument. First, I shall show that there have been changes in the structuring of contemporary societies which have produced a substantial increase in the size of the service class and more generally in what Bourdieu terms the 'new petty bourgeoisie'. Second, I shall note that such classes are stronger on cultural than on economic capital and they provide much of the mass audience for ever-new cultural phenomena, counterposed to the taste of more traditional bourgeois and intellectual classes. Third, I shall show that such classes possess a habitus which is relatively decentred, that is, with a weak classificatory structure and fairly unclear boundaries between it and other social classes (weak on both grid and group). And finally, it will be shown that these classes employ their relatively high levels of cultural capital to proclaim the tastelessness of much of both bourgeois and working-class culture. The former is criticised for 'elitism' (that is, not sufficiently de-differentiated); the latter for coarseness or lack of subtlety (that is, it is too close to nature, with insufficient distance or parody). Bourdieu summarises the attitude to the latter:

> The denial of lower, coarse, vulgar, venal, servile – in a word, natural – enjoyment, which constitutes the sacred sphere of culture, implies an affirmation of the superiority of those who can be satisfied with the sublimated, refined, disinterested, gratuitous, distinguished pleasures forever closed to the profane. That is why art and cultural consumption are predisposed, consciously and deliberately or not, to fulfil a social function of legitimating social differences. (1984: 7)

It is clear that in western societies there is both a major service class and, more generally, a substantial white-collar or middle class. In Britain in 1981, for example, 20.3 per cent of men and 7.5 per cent of women in employment were in professional and managerial posts ('socioeconomic groups' 1–4, 13). A further 16.8 per cent of men and a staggering 51.3 per cent of women held lower-level white-collar/clerical posts ('socio-economic groups' 5, 6; Abercrombie et al., 1988: 116).

The service class consists of that set of places within the social division of labour whose occupants (1) do not own capital or land to any substantial degree; (2) are located within a set of interlocking social institutions which collectively 'service' capital; (3) enjoy superior work and market situations generally resulting from the existence of well-defined careers, either within or between organisations; and (4) have their entry regulated by the differential possession of educational credentials. These serve to demarcate the service class from more general white-collar workers and generate distinctions of cultural capital and taste (see Goldthorpe, 1982; Abercrombie and Urry, 1983; Lash and Urry, 1987: ch. 6; Thrift, 1989; Savage et al., 1989).

It is also interesting to consider the age distribution of such a class. In the US, for example, Pfeil shows that in 1980 59 per cent of all 25–35-year-olds were employed in professional and managerial specialty occupations (not including sales clerks). Hence 'postmodernism is pre-eminently the "expressive form" of the social and material life-experience of my own generation and class, respectively designated as the "baby boom" and the "professional-managerial class" or PMC' (Pfeil, 1985: 264; cf. Ehrenreich, 1989).

What I have termed the service class is discussed by Bourdieu but in somewhat different terms. In talking of 'intellectuals' he contrasts their preference for 'aesthetic-asceticism' with a bourgeois preference for sumptuous interiors. In Britain this would be reflected in the liking for Habitat or Ikea-style interiors amongst 'intellectuals'. Of their leisure patterns Bourdieu writes: 'the most ascetic form of the aesthetic disposition and the culturally most legitimate and economically cheapest practices, e.g., museum-going, or, in sport, mountain-climbing or walking, are likely to occur particularly frequently among the fractions (relatively) poorest in economic capital' (1984: 267). Interestingly, Bourdieu talks of the symbolic subversion by intellectuals of the rituals of the bourgeois order through demonstrating 'ostentatious poverty'. This is reflected in the tendency to dress casually even when at work, to favour bare wood interiors, and activities like mountaineering, hiking and walking, which represent the intellectual's taste for 'natural, wild nature' (1984: 220). It is the intellectuals, according to Bourdieu, who most exemplify the 'romantic gaze'. The bourgeois by contrast is said to prefer 'organized, signposted cultivated nature' (Bourdieu 1984: 220).

What I have referred to as the service class and other white-collar workers would also include two newly emerging groups discussed by Bourdieu who are major consumers of the postmodern: the 'new bourgeoisie', who possess considerable amounts of both cultural and economic

capital; and the 'new petit bourgeois' of occupations involving presentation and representation. Much of the work of both categories is symbolic
– in the media, advertising, design – acting as cultural intermediaries.
Such groups have a very strong commitment to fashion, that is, to the
rapid and playful transformations of style (see Featherstone, 1987: 27).
Moreover, such groups are often downwardly mobile in terms of social
origins and are not necessarily accepted by the intellectuals and the
cultural-capital establishment. So there is here a challenge to established
culture, to high culture, while at the same time the emergence of celebrity
intellectuals has demystified (delegitimated?) traditional sources of
cultural capital. Featherstone well describes how these groups involved in
symbolic work construct the conditions for the emergence of the postmodern: 'This interchange, the alertness of intellectuals to new popular
styles and the marketability of "the new", creates conditions in which
styles travel faster, both from the avant-garde to the popular, the popular
to the avant-garde, and the popular to the jet-set' (1987: 27).

As a result there comes to be generated a kind of stylistic melting-pot,
of the old and the new, of the nostalgic and the futuristic, of the 'natural'
and the 'artificial', of the youthful and the mature, of high culture and of
low, and of modernism and the postmodern. Martin neatly summarises
how the growth of these middle-class groups has upset pre-existing cultural
patterns: 'The contemporary culture market muddles together the elite and
the vulgar, yesterday's shock and today's joke in one gloriously trivial
bricolage. Style is everything and anything can become style' (1982: 236–7).

Furthermore, Bourdieu argues, these groups also have a quite different
approach to pleasure. The old petit bourgeoisie bases its life on a morality
of duty, with 'a fear of pleasure,. . .a relation to the body made up of
"reserve", "modesty" and "restraint", and associates every satisfaction
of the forbidden impulses with guilt' (Bourdieu, 1984: 367). By contrast
the new middle-class group:

> urges a morality of pleasure as a duty. This doctrine makes it a failure, a threat
> to self-esteem, not to 'have fun' . . . . Pleasure is not only permitted but
> demanded, on ethical as much as on scientific grounds. The fear of not getting
> enough pleasure . . . is combined with the search for self-expression and 'bodily
> expression' and for communication with others. (1984: 367)

This last argument needs some clarification. Capitalist societies have
always been characterised by a strong emphasis on consumption based on
a romantic ethic. Campbell argues that romanticism has provided that
philosophy of 'recreation' necessary for a dynamic consumerism in which
the search for pleasure is viewed as desirable in and of itself (1987: 201).
Romanticism has produced the widespread taste for novelty which has
ensured the ethical support for restless and continuously changing
patterns of consumption. But Campbell's argument too is rather un-
specific and fails to suggest that important changes may be taking place
in the romantic ethic and modern consumerism, or that these could be
linked to the changing power and character of different social forces.

In particular here I want to suggest that a number of middle-class groupings are indeed in a transformed situation and are having significant effects upon the wider society. These groups have a number of important features: the central significance of symbolic work; the enormous increase in the importance of the media and of their contemporary role in structuring fashion and taste; the greater freedom and incentive of such groups to devise ever-new cultural patterns; the heightened prestige that accrues for the middle classes not from respectability but from fashionability; the greater significance of cultural capital to such groups and the continuous need to augment it; and a reduced functional need to maintain their economic capital intact (see Warde, 1988, on many of these points). An interesting exploration of how the architectural design of gentrified areas reflects the cultural capital of such a class is presented in an analysis of the 'postmodern landscape of gentrification' in Vancouver (Mills, 1988).

I shall now analyse the habitus of the service class in particular and see how and in what ways a weak grid and group have provided the basis for postmodernism. The implications of this discussion for contemporary tourism will be considered in the next section.

The media, and especially TV, have a significant impact (see Meyrowitz, 1985; Lash and Urry, 1987: ch. 9). The collective identities of different social classes (and other social forces) are structured through 'grid', the basic system of classification, and 'group', the boundaries that distinguish what is internal from what is external. Such collective indentities depend upon particular systems of information specific to a given social group. However, the growth of the media has minimised the importance of such separate and distinct systems of information. This is because individuals from all social groupings are exposed to more generally available systems of information, and because each grouping can now see some representations of the private spaces of other social groupings. The media have provided an enormously increased circulation of the representations of other people's lives, including those of elite groups and in Britain even (especially?) the royal family. This kind of institutionalised voyeurism in turn enables people to adopt the styles of other groups, to transgress boundaries between different social groupings as supposedly embodying particular values such as high culture, low culture, artistic, tasteful, tasteless. The media have also undermined what is to be thought of as properly backstage, as what should be kept private and what can be made public.

Turning specifically to the middle classes, Bourdieu argues that the new petit bourgeoisie is low on both grid and group. Such people live for the moment 'untrammelled by constraints and brakes imposed by collective memories and expectations' (Bourdieu, 1984: 317). Such people are weak on group in that many feel guilt about being middle class:

> they see themselves as unclassifiable, 'excluded' . . . anything rather than categorized, assigned to a class, a determinate place in social space. . . freed from the temporal structures imposed by domestic units, with their own life-

cycle, their long-term planning, sometimes over several generations, and their collective defences against the impact of the market. (Bourdieu, 1984: 370–1)

Martin provides a similar analysis, talking of an effectively destructured habitus amongst middle-class youth, especially from the 1960s onwards (1982). This she attributes to an immensely extended liminal zone derived from the decline in parental authority and the extension of the period when one is neither child or adult. She argues that a particularly extended period of liminality develops in the new middle class in that they have a destructured habitus not only in youth but in many occupations as well, for example the media.

A number of major cultural critics have also developed this argument. Jameson analyses the growth of pastiche rather than parody (1985). While the latter stands in a relationship to real historical time, the former does not. There is the disappearance of the original real historical referent and of an appreciation of how the past has led to the present. Jameson talks of how we seek the past instead through 'our own pop images and stereotypes about the past which remain forever out of reach' (1985: 118). Pastiche, for Jameson, fragments time into a series of 'perpetual presents' (1985: 118). People's lives in what Edgar (1987) terms 'the new era of pastiche and nostalgia' are experienced as a succession of discontinuous events. Although the individual blocks may be calculated and rational, the overall pattern is likely to be irrational. Spreading out from parts of the middle class is a 'calculating hedonism' (see Featherstone, 1987).

Cultural conservatives such as Lasch and Bell have developed a similar argument about time (Lasch, 1980; Bell, 1976). They maintain that our sense of history has been lost. As Frampton argues: 'We live in a paradoxical moment when, while we are perhaps more obsessed with history than ever before, we have, simultaneously, the feeling that a certain historical trajectory, or even for some, history itself, is coming to an end' (1988: 51).

This loss of historical sense has also been associated with a characteristic of the media: that we increasingly live in a three-minute (or five-minute!) culture. It is suggested that TV viewers keep switching from channel to channel unable to concentrate on any topic or theme for longer than a few minutes. Cultural conservatives argue that people no longer live their lives through identities imbued with the consciousness that they are the children of their parents who were in turn children of their parents, and so on. Even within generations the fascination with immediate consumption (purchased through immediate credit rather than saving) means that lifelong projects like marriage become instead a succession of marriages, 'serial monogamy' or affairs. Lawson and Samson (1988), for example, show that there has been a quite marked increase in Britain in the preparedness of younger women in particular to undertake sexual relationships outside marriage. The mean duration of marriage before an outside relationship was undertaken was 14.6 years for women married before 1960, 8.2 years for women married in the 1960s, and 4.2

years for women married since 1970 (Lawson and Samson, 1988: 432). There has been a similar but not quite so steep a decline in the mean period in the case of men.

Lawson and Samson suggest that two factors have contributed to this change: the return of many married women into paid, albeit intermittent, employment outside the home; and the widespread influence of the myth of self-actualisation, or the 'myth of me'. Some support for the significance of the second factor, from the USA, can be found in Ehrenreich's analysis of the flight from commitment of American males to marriage and responsibility (1983). She details a series of transformations which have generated a 'moral climate that endorsed irresponsibility, self-indulgence and an isolationist detachment from the claims of others – and endorsed these as middle class virtues and even as signs of health' (1983: 169). The middle-class components of this revolt against marital commitment which began in the USA in the 1950s were the establishment of *Playboy*, the Beat generation, the medical 'discovery' of stress, the new psychology of growth and self-actualisation, the counter-cultural critique of traditional masculinity, and the growth of a men's movement.

In the next section I shall return to tourism (after this rather long 'break') and show how these various cultural changes and the development of the service and middle classes have had profound effects on existing centres of tourism, especially the English seaside resort. I shall also demonstrate how postmodernism is ushering in some major new conceptions of what it is to be a contemporary tourist.

Postmodernism and post-tourism

For a number of reasons the British seaside resort had declined in popularity; in particular we saw that such resorts were no longer 'extraordinary'; their once distinctive features had become commonplace. Some, such as sand and sea, could be found in very many places, especially abroad; some, such as accommodation, had become available in many towns and cities within Britain; and some, such as leisure facilities, had developed almost everywhere. Very many places have generated different kinds of specialist service provision which compete with existing resorts. Almost everywhere has become a centre of 'spectacle and display', and as a result resorts now have relatively little to distinguish themselves from elsewhere. Indeed to the extent to which their own provision is now often somewhat derelict, the resorts have suffered further difficulties. In chapter 6 I discuss aspects of the current fascination with 'history and heritage' and show how this also serves to favour certain kinds of towns and cities – but infrequently resorts.

Here I shall link some of the arguments of the previous discussion with current developments in tourism. Indeed the way in which all sorts of places have become centres of spectacle and display and the nostalgic attraction of 'heritage' can both be seen as elements of the postmodern. It is only through the analysis of such wider cultural changes that specific tourist developments can be properly understood. I shall begin with some comments on the tastes of the service class and the impact of these on seaside resorts.

Such tastes involve the prioritisation of 'culture' over a particular construction of 'nature' or 'natural desires'. Bourdieu expresses this well: 'The nature against which culture is here constructed is nothing other than what is "popular", "low", "vulgar", "common". . . . a "social promotion" experienced as an ontological promotion, a process of "civilization". . . . a leap from nature to culture, from the animal to the human' (1984: 251).

The typical resort would thus seem the embodiment of a particular construction of nature – as uncivilised, tasteless, animalistic, to be counterposed to the civilisation of culture. Such an attitude can, interestingly, be seen even amongst socialist representatives of the service class. George Orwell imagined a modern design for Coleridge's 'Kubla Khan' as consisting of a holiday camp where air-conditioned caverns were transformed into a series of tea-grottoes in Moorish, Caucasian and Hawaiian styles. The sacred river would be turned into an artificially warmed bathing pool and muzak would be playing in the background 'to prevent the onset of that dreaded thing – thought' (quoted in Hebdige, 1988: 51). Likewise, Richard Hoggart set one of his parodies of cheap romantic fiction in what he called the Kosy Holiday Camp where there was a 'shiny barbarism', a 'spiritual dry-rot' and a 'Candy Floss World' (again see Hebdige, 1988: 52). Having good taste would involve looking down on such places and only passing through, to view them as a voyeur would (as an Orwell or a Hoggart), never to stay. The only permitted exception might be to appropriate elements from such resorts, such as McGill's postcards, in a postmodern cultural pastiche. The uncivilised resorts are not to be taken seriously, but can perhaps be played at (or with?).

Such resorts have become increasingly aware that they do not appeal to those elements in Britain who have become influenced by these tastes of the service and middle class. In Morecambe, for example, there has been a prolonged debate on whether it should continue to host the Miss Great Britain contest. A particular representation of women as 'cultureless' sex objects (women as 'nature') has increasingly come to be viewed as in bad taste and inappropriate to a civilised resort seeking to appeal to more than the traditional clientele. The competition has now ended in the town.

At the same time an alternative construction of nature is also part of the service class habitus. There is a pronounced cultural emphasis on certain aspects of the natural. When discussing Bourdieu it was argued that intellectuals subvert the bourgeois order through minimal luxury, functionalism and an ascetic aesthetics (1984: 287). This pattern is reflected in an extraordinary range of contemporary cultural symbols and practices: health foods, real ale, real bread, vegetarianism, nouvelle cuisine, traditional, non-western science and medicine, natural childbirth, wool, lace and cotton rather 'man-made' fibres, antiques rather than 'man-made' reproductions, restored houses/warehouses, jogging, swimming, cycling, mountaineering, and fell-walking rather than organised, contrived leisure. The middle-class ambivalence to the 'natural' is well captured in Ross' account of a commitment both to natural childbirth and to going to classes to learn how to give birth naturally (1989: 13; and see Campbell, 1989, on how fishing has been affected by the naturalistic myth of the 'sportsman').

A recent reflection of this attraction of the real or natural in the tourism field has been the 'Campaign for Real Holidays' conducted in one of the key newspapers of the British service class, the *Independent*. This campaign has now resulted in the novel travel guide, *The Independent Guide to Real Holidays Abroad. The Complete Directory for the Independent Traveller* (Barrett, 1989a). The author states that it is increasingly difficult to have a 'real holiday'. This is because the 'rise and rise of the package holiday has imposed on travel the same problems that mass production has inflicted on beer, bread, ice cream and many other things' (1989a: 1). It is of interest that the *Guide* argues that coach holidays, surely the paradigm case of the collective tourist gaze, 'could hardly be described as "real holidays"' (Barrett, 1989a: 2). A real holiday has to have two main characteristics. First, it involves visiting somewhere well away from where the mass of the population will be visiting; examples include the Maldives, Syria, or Bolivia. Real holidays thus involve the romantic tourist gaze, which has the effect of incorporating almost everywhere in the world as part of the 'pleasure periphery'. Second, the real holiday-maker will use small specialist agents/operators to get to their destination. The *Guide* bemoans the fact three-quarters of all foreign holidays taken by Britons are sold by five major companies. The *Guide* favours instead the development of smaller companies who have come to specialise in particular segments of the tourism market, or perhaps one should say the 'traveller market'. The *Guide* talks of the development of the 'delicatessen' travel agent – these are specialist agencies that promote particular operators to 'a discriminating, independent-minded clientele' (Barrett, 1989a: 4).

The existing major companies have not been slow in recognising the importance of this trend to real holidays, involving travel rather than tourism, the romantic rather than collective gaze, and involving small-niche suppliers rather than mass production/consumption operators. For example, British Airways is establishing 'Four Corners' travel agencies which are planned to look like Next or Laura Ashley shops and which will advertise the specialist brochures that do not normally appear in high-street agencies (see Barrett, 1989a: 5). Likewise Thomas Cook has recently been advertising a large and attractive brochure of 'Escorted Journeys' worldwide. The copy tells us that this:

is not a trip for the tourist but a voyage of discovery for the traveller . . . there is no packaging . . . Thomas Cook treats you not just as an individual but as a VIP . . . Thomas Cook provides a service that is both personal and global . . . This is truly travel à la carte. (*Thomas Cook Escorted Journeys*, Jan. 1989–Dec. 1989)

Accompanying the description of each holiday (travel experience?) is a reading list of useful books on the particular country. A number of emphases should be noted here: on travel rather than tourism, on individual choice, on avoiding the package holiday-maker, on the need to be an educated traveller, and on a global operation that permits individual care and attention – undoubtedly one kind of postmodern experience.

The service class preference for the 'real' or the 'natural' can also be seen in the increasing attraction of both visiting the countryside and protecting it. This is of course not new; Thomas, for example, points out that:

Whether or not the preoccupation with nature and rural life is in reality peculiarly English, it is certainly something which the English townsman [*sic*] has for a long time liked to think of as such; and much of the country's literature has displayed a profoundly anti-urban bias. (1973: 14; see Williams, 1973, as well as Wiener, 1981, on the nineteenth-century antipathy to the urban)

It should of course be noted that this image of the English countryside, 'a bucolic vision of an ordered, comforting, peaceful and, above all, deferential past' is a fundamentally constructed one, comprised of elements that never existed together historically (Thrift, 1989: 26). The countryside today is even less like 'ye Olde English village', even less like Gray's description of Grasmere in the Lake District: 'This little unsuspected paradise, where all is peace, rusticity and happy poverty'.

But at the moment when rural life is being fundamentally transformed, particularly because of changes taking place in modern agriculture, the image of the countryside is becoming an ever more attractive object of the tourist gaze (see Newby, 1982; Shoard, 1987). One reflection of this increased attractiveness is the enormous rise in membership of many of the organisations concerned with protecting the countryside and facilitating access. For example, between 1971 and 1987 membership of the National Trust increased by 505 per cent, the Royal Society for the Protection of Birds by 539 per cent, the Royal Society for Nature Conservation by 281 per cent, Friends of the Earth by 2,850 per cent, and so on (see Thrift, 1989: 27). Connected with this has been the proliferation of new magazines which help to construct ever more redolent signs of the fast-disappearing countryside. At least a dozen 'new traditionalist' magazines appeared in the 1980s, including *Country Homes and Interiors*, *Country Living*, *Country Homes* (Thrift, 1989: 28).

Thrift argues that it is the service class which 'seems to be the social group that has taken the countryside and heritage traditions most to heart' (1989: 31). This class has been leading the push to move into the countryside. Thrift talks of the 'service-class character of places replete with manicured countryside' (1989: 34). This is having a particular effect upon the market for country houses which has been booming for the past ten years or so, particularly in the counties surrounding London. It has also led to the building of new estates in vernacular or rustic style; such estates are usually described as 'villages'. More than half of the new houses started at the beginning of 1988 were in rural or semi-rural areas (see McGhie, 1988). With the prediction that there will be 5–6 million acres of spare agricultural land in Britain by the end of the century, it is certain that this trend will continue as many other people, following the example of the service class, seek to realise the 'village in their mind' (Pahl, 1965). One might also add that there has been a parallel movement in many towns and cities towards urban conservation, in effect to 'green the city' (see Nicholson-Lord, 1987: ch. 7, 'The Country Comes to Town').

The service class is more likely to visit the countryside. In 1986, for example, one-third of socioeconomic groups A and B (roughly the service class plus capitalists and middle-level management) made at least five visits to the countryside. This was a 50 per cent higher proportion than for skilled manual workers and twice the proportion of semi- and unskilled workers. One-third of the service class made no visits at all – but this figure was far lower than all the other groups, that for semi- and unskilled workers being over 60 per cent (see Thrift, 1989: 35).

On the face of it this attraction of the countryside seems to have little to do with postmodernism; indeed it looks like its very antithesis (for further discussion see Bagguley et al., 1990: ch. 5; and for a review of research on rural recreation, Owens, 1984). But I shall suggest here that there is indeed a relationship, albeit complex, between postmodernism and the current obsession with the countryside.

The attractions of the countryside derive in part from the disillusionment with elements of the modern, particularly with the attempt to effect wholesale reconstruction of towns and cities in the postwar period. The countryside is *thought* to embody some or all of the following features: a lack of planning and regimentation, a vernacular quaint architecture, winding lanes and a generally labyrinthine road system, and the virtues of tradition and the lack of social intervention. It hardly needs to be said that rural areas, as in Britain, have in fact been subject to a wide range of modernising processes – including large-scale agriculture (arguably Britain's *most* rationalised industry), considerable attempts at land-use planning and, especially in the 1980s, extensive private sector rural development (see Cloke, 1989).

But only certain sorts of countryside are attractive to the prospective visitor, particularly those consistent with the idea of 'landscape'. Cosgrove summarises this conception in England:

> the landscape idea was active within a process of undermining collective appropriation of nature for use. It was locked into an individualist way of seeing. . . . It is a way of seeing which separates subject and object, giving

lordship to the eye of a single observer. In this the landscape idea either denies collective experience . . . or mystifies it in an appeal to transcendental qualities of a particular area. (1984: 262)

A particular feature of this construction of the rural landscape has been to erase from it farm machinery, labourers, tractors, telegraph wires, concrete farm buildings, motorways, derelict land, polluted water, and more recently nuclear power stations. What people see is therefore highly selective, and it is the gaze which is central to people's appropriation. The countryside is there to be gazed upon, and ideally one should not be gazing upon other people, whether workers or other tourists. Raymond Williams says that: 'a working country is hardly ever a landscape. The very idea of landscape implies separation and observation' (1973: 120; see Heiman, 1989, for an analysis of the Hudson valley to illustrate this in the American context).

The service class is leading the way in sustaining the romantic gaze of the countryside. But it is a gaze which has become more complex and playful, as rural images have become central to mainstream popular culture, particularly advertising:

From such a post-modern perspective landscape seems less like a palimpsest whose 'real' or 'authentic' meanings can somehow be recovered with the correct techniques, theories or ideologies, than a flickering text . . . whose meaning can be created, extended, altered, elaborated and finally obliterated by the touch of a button. (Daniels and Cosgrove, 1988: 8)

There is an alternative approach to the countryside to that of the gaze *per se*, one in which the very term 'landscape' is inappropriate (see Cosgrove, 1984: 267–8). The inter-war period saw attempts, especially by the northern urban working class, to gain access to wild upland countryside for walking, rambling and cycling. Central to these campaigns was an element of class struggle, against the landowners who had historically restricted access. The most famous access campaign took place at Kinder Scout in the Peak District in 1932. According to Cosgrove the intentions of organisers such as Tom Stephenson 'were not to *see* landscape, so much as to experience it physically – to walk it, climb it or cycle through it' (1984: 268). There are of course similar current campaigns to ensure access, something which these days is often rejected on grounds of environmental protection. Shoard demonstrates the weakness of such arguments for sustaining such 'private pleasures' of landlords (1987: 306–7).

To the extent to which contemporary appropriations of the countryside involve treating it as a spectacle, even a 'theme', this can be seen as a postmodern attitude to the countryside, to be contrasted with an approach which emphasises its 'use'. In response to the former attitude many people living in rural areas have come to produce packaged environments whereby a relatively sanitised representation of rural life is constructed and presented to visitors:

> We seem to find it far easier to schedule areas for preservation as outstanding landscape for those who would passively view their scenery than to delegate authority for their shaping to those who live, work and actively recreate in them. . . Such preserved landscapes have in fact become a national commodity, advertised and sold abroad by the travel industry. (Cosgrove, 1984: 269)

The category of tourist is a relatively privileged one in rural areas. To be able to claim such a status it is normally necessary to be white, and to be wealthy enough to own a car and to be able to organise and purchase certain kinds of accommodation (hotel bed, caravan or recognised camp site). It is also necessary, if people are visiting as a group, to use certain kinds of transport, such as coach or train, and not others, such as a convoy of cars or motorbikes, or a hippie convoy of travellers (see Rojek, 1988, on the 'convoy of pollution'). It is also necessary to engage in certain kinds of behaviour which are deemed appropriate and not others (in Britain this is known as the 'country code': see Countryside Commission, 1988).

A number of different strands in postmodern architecture will be outlined in the next chapter. One is the partially authentic reconstruction of vernacular buildings from the past as a reaction to elements of both the modern and playful postmodern movements in architecture. There is a similar strand in recent appropriations of the countryside, which one can loosely label 'green tourism' (see Jones, A., 1987). What some people appear increasingly to want is an appropriation of the countryside that will benefit rather than harm the area visited. Research conducted in Wales suggests that what many people like is to be able to visit the 'ordinary' relatively well-preserved countryside rather than specific rural attractions apart from nature reserves (Jones, A., 1987: 355). A vital function of green tourism is to ensure the conservation of areas and their associated wildlife for future generations. The development of such a novel tourism stems from a repudiation of aspects of modern life, especially modern forms of transport, energy and industrial and agricultural production. Particular hostility has been shown to the 'modernised' planting of extensive forests of conifers, particularly by the Forestry Commission but also by private landlords. Such forests are thought to have deleterious environmental and social consequences: the loss of a distinctive wildlife including indigenous birds of prey; reduced levels of employment compared with those that would be supported by tourism; and the elimination of the wild, open and 'romantic' moors that are of such appeal. Indeed a greater influence exercised by tourists would probably preserve the open moorlands against modernised planting of more and more rows of conifers (see Shoard, 1987: 223–5 for more detail).

Thus some important features of rural tourism stem from the broader development of an environmental politics in the past two to three decades and the resistance to widespread attempts to 'modernise' particular areas or localities. The next chapter will show just how significant is this anti-modern resistance to development in both urban and rural contexts (see Lowe and Goyder, 1983, on the importance of environmental politics in Britain).

One element of the postmodern briefly mentioned above is playfulness. An interesting version of this argument in relation to tourism has been advanced by Feifer (1985). She discusses the concept of the 'post-tourist', or what one might term the 'post-(mass) tourist', and highlights three particular features. The first is that the post-tourist does not have to leave his or her house in order to *see* many of the typical objects of the tourist gaze, with TV and video all sorts of places can be gazed upon, compared, contextualised and gazed upon again. It is possible to imagine oneself 'really' there, really seeing the sunset, the mountain range or the turquoise-coloured sea. The typical tourist experience is anyway to see *named* scenes through a *frame*, such as the hotel window, the car windscreen or the window of the coach. But this can now be experienced in one's own living room, at the flick of a switch; and it can be repeated time and time again. There is much less of the sense of the authentic, the once-in-a-lifetime gaze, and much more of the endless availability of gazes through a frame at the flick of a switch. The distinctiveness of the 'tourist gaze' is lost as such gazes are irreducibly part of a postmodern popular culture.

Second, the post-tourist is aware of change and delights in the multitude of choice. According to Feifer: 'Now he [*sic*] wants to behold something sacred; now something informative, to broaden him, now something beautiful, to lift him and make him finer; and now something just different, because he's bored' (1985: 269).

The post-tourist is freed from the constraints of 'high culture' on the one hand, and the untrammelled pursuit of the 'pleasure principle' on the other. He or she can move easily from one to the other and indeed can gain pleasure from the contrasts between the two. The world is a stage and the post-tourist can delight in the multitude of games that can be played. When the miniature replica of the Eiffel Tower is purchased, it can be simultaneously enjoyed as a piece of kitsch, an exercise in geometric formalism and as a socially revealing artefact (see Feifer, 1985: 270). There is no need to make a fetish out of the correct interpretation since the post-tourist can enjoy playing at it being all three.

Third, and most important, the post-tourist knows that they are a tourist and that tourism is a game, or rather a whole series of games with multiple texts and no single, authentic tourist experience. The post-tourist thus knows that they will have to queue time and time again, that there will be hassles over foreign exchange, that the glossy brochure is a piece of pop culture, that the apparently authentic local entertainment is as socially contrived as the ethnic bar, and that the supposedly quaint and traditional fishing village could not survive without the income from tourism. According to Feifer the post-tourist knows that he [*sic*] is: 'not a time-traveller when he goes somewhere historic; not an instant noble savage when he stays on a tropical beach; not an invisible observer when he visits a native compound. Resolutely 'realistic', he cannot evade his condition of outsider (1985: 271; see Crick, 1985, for an interesting critique of the thesis that anthropologists do manage to get backstage and overcome the position of outsider).

One interesting game is that of the tourist 'as child'. This is especially clear in guided coach tours. One is told where to go, how long to go for, when one can eat, how long one has to visit the toilet, and so on. The group (or class) are also asked inane questions and much of the discourse consists of setting up imaginary hostilities between people visiting from different places. And yet such tours seem much appreciated even by those who understand that they are 'playing at being a tourist', and one of the games that has to be embraced is that of 'being a child'.

If post-tourism is of contemporary importance it will clearly have important effects on existing tourist practices. The pleasures of tourism stem from complex processes of both production and consumption. I have emphasised the socially constructed character of the tourist gaze, that both production and consumption are socially organised, and that the gaze must be directed to certain objects or features which are extraordinary, which distinguish that site/sight of the gaze from others. Normally there is something about its physical properties which makes it distinct, although these are often both manufactured and have to be learnt. But sometimes it is merely a place's historical or literary associations which make it extraordinary (such as the building in Dallas from which President Kennedy was supposedly shot, or the vicarage in Haworth, Yorkshire, where the Brontës lived).

The development of post-tourism transforms these processes by which the tourist gaze is produced and consumed. Mercer, for instance, notes that popular pleasures: 'require a wholehearted and unselfconscious involvement in a cultural event, form or text' (1983: 84). Particularly important in tourist pleasures are those that involve the energetic breaking of the mild taboos that operate on various forms of consumption, such as eating or drinking to excess, spending money recklessly, wearing outrageous clothes, keeping wildly different time patterns, and so on. As Thompson says: 'People are encouraged to spend by this *disorganisation* of the normal, "acceptable" routines of consumption' (1983: 129). But the post-tourist emphasis on playfulness, variety and self-consciousness makes it harder to find simple pleasures in such mild and socially tolerated rule-breaking. The post-tourist is above all self-conscious, 'cool' and role-distanced. Pleasure hence comes to be anticipated and experienced in different ways from before. A number of changes are occurring here.

The universal availability of the predominantly visual media in advanced western societies has resulted in a massive upward shift in the level of what is 'ordinary' and hence what people view as 'extraordinary'. Moreover, to the extent to which it is true that the media have ushered in a 'three-minute' culture, so this is also likely to encourage people to switch forms and sites of pleasures. It is almost certain that people will gain relatively less satisfaction from continuing to do what they, or more particularly their family, have always done. Thus, holidays have become less to do with the reinforcing of collective memories and experiences and more to do with immediate pleasure. As a result people keep demanding new out-of-the-ordinary experiences. Some examples include 'Eastender' holiday breaks run by Islington council in London, football weekend breaks organised in Liverpool, the Leprosy Museum in Bergen, the Japanese Death Railway in Burma, the Gestapo headquarters in Berlin, and 'boring tours' in Sydney. It is an interesting question whether it is in fact possible to construct a postmodern tourist site around absolutely any object. Mercer, though, argues that to experience pleasure in this more distanced, playful way makes all pleasures less satisfying. And in particular it makes it much harder to enjoy 'simple' pleasures such as those once found in seaside resorts.

Conclusion

Another way of expressing the effects of the postmodern is to consider the dissolving of group and grid and the impact this has on seaside resorts, which were based on strong group and grid. On the former the resort was based on a family-regulated holiday for people of roughly the same class and from similar areas. But with the postmodern dissolving of social identity, many of these forms of group identification within space and over time have vanished, and this has reduced the attractiveness of those resorts which were designed to structure the formation of pleasure in particular class-related patterns. There has been a marked growth in the variety of tourist units, many of which are not family households.

Grid too has changed. Such resorts were based on a specific division of pleasure and pain. Pleasure was associated with being away from the place in which one worked and from the boring and monotonous pain of work, especially of industrial production. Now, however, such a division is much less clear-cut. Pleasures can be enjoyed in very many places, not at all concentrated at the seaside. There has been a proliferation of objects on which to gaze, including the media. What now is tourism and what is more generally culture is relatively unclear. Pleasures and pain are everywhere, not spatially concentrated in particular sites.

Resorts will have to change quite dramatically if they are going to survive. Recent advertising by the Isle of Man on British TV indicates one possible way of responding (see Urry, 1988b). The advert states that 'You'll look forward to going back', to experiencing a seaside holiday as remembered from one's childhood. Time has supposedly stood still in the Isle of Man and the advert plays on our nostalgia for childhood, when pleasures were experienced more directly and were less contaminated by an apparent playful sophistication. Elsewhere I have argued that 'Resorts should not try to resist the trend to "nostalgia". . . . Rather than trying to be modern and failing, they would do better to embrace it self-consciously. . . . Soon there may be nothing in the Isle of Man to look forward to going back to' (Urry, 1988b; and see Cooper and Jackson, 1989, on the declining attractiveness of the Isle of Man).

The next chapter considers this issue of nostalgia and history in more detail.

6

GAZING ON HISTORY

The heritage industry

Tourist sites can be classified in terms of three dichotomies: whether they are an object of the romantic or collective tourist gaze; whether they are historical or modern; and whether they are authentic or inauthentic. Characterising sites in such terms is obviously not straightforward and the third dichotomy, authentic/inauthentic, raises many difficulties. Nevertheless it is useful to summarise the differences between such sites by employing these dichotomies.

For example, the Lake District in the north-west of England can be characterised as predominantly the object of the romantic gaze, it is historical and it is apparently authentic. By contrast, Alton Towers leisure park, again in the north-west, is the object of the collective gaze, it is mainly modern and it is predominantly inauthentic. These are fairly straightforward characterisations. But more complex are places like the refurbished Albert Dock in Liverpool, the Wigan Pier Heritage Centre in Lancashire (see Photograph 6.1) and the restored mills in Lowell, Massachusetts, the first industrial town in the USA. These are all examples of the heritage industry, a development which has generated a great deal of debate. Although they are the object of the collective gaze, it is more controversial whether such sites are really 'historical' and 'authentic', as is claimed. There is also much debate as to the causes of this contemporary fascination with gazing upon the historical or what is now known as heritage (generally here see Lowenthal, 1985, especially ch. 1 on 'nostalgia' as a physical affliction dating from the late seventeenth century).

There are indicators of this phenomenon in Britain, where it seems that a new museum opens every week or so. Of the 1,750 museums responding to a 1987 questionnaire, half had been started since 1971. There are now at least 41 heritage centres, including Ironbridge Gorge near Telford, the Wigan Pier Heritage Centre, Black Country World near Dudley, the Beamish Open Air Museum near Newcastle, and the Jorvik Viking Centre in York. In Britain there are now 464 museums possessing industrial material and 817 with collections relating to rural history. The director of the Science Museum has said of this growth in heritage that: 'You can't project that sort of rate of growth much further before the whole country becomes one big open air museum, and you just join it as you get off at Heathrow' (quoted in Hewison, 1987: 24).

Photograph 6.1   *The Wigan Pier Heritage Centre, Lancashire*

Some of the most unlikely of places have become centres of a heritage-based tourist development. Bradford, which once sent most of its holiday-makers to Morecambe, has now become a major tourist attraction in its own right. In the Rhondda valley in South Wales it is planned to locate a museum in the Lewis Merthyr coalmine and to establish a Rhondda Heritage Park (see Halsall, 1986). Almost everywhere and everything from the past may be conserved. In Lancashire environmentalists have sought to preserve the largest slag heap in Britain, which British Coal had wanted to remove. There are now 500,000 listed buildings in Britain, as well as over 5,500 conservation areas. The broadcaster Michael Wood writes: 'Now that the present seems so full of woe . . . the profusion and frankness of our nostalgia . . . suggest not merely a sense of loss . . . but a general abdication, an actual desertion from the present' (1974: 346). The seventeenth-century disease of nostalgia seems to have become an epidemic.

Some museums and heritage centres are, moreover, major developments. For example, in the period January–June 1988 £127.2 million was invested in heritage and museums in Britain. This investment was in a wide variety of sites and activities: such as a chemicals museum in Widnes, the restoration of the West Pier in Brighton, a 'Living Dockyard' attraction in Chatham, a Museum of Nursing in Lambeth, the reconstruction of Coronation Street in the Granada studios in Manchester, a new themed attraction of 'waterfront Poole' in Devon, and a 'Norfolk bygone village' in East Anglia. Until about 1970 or so most museums were publicly owned, normally by local councils. At the same time central government expenditure is considerable. It spends over £100 million a year on conserving the built environment, much of it through increasingly entrepreneurial agencies like English Heritage. One striking feature of these recent developments has been the increased privatisation of the heritage/museum industry, with 56 per cent of recently opened museums being in the private sector (on these various points see Hewison, 1987: 1, ch. 4; White, 1987; Urry, 1988a; Thrift, 1989). And these private initiatives have inspired particularly new ways of representing history, as commodifying the past.

Enormous numbers of people visit such places. In 1983–4 more people visited museums and galleries in Britain than visited the cinema, while many more visited heritage buildings than the live theatre (Myerscough, 1986: 292). The proportion of the service class visiting museum and heritage centres in any year is about three times that of manual workers. About two-thirds of the visitors to such places have white-collar occupations (Myerscough, 1986: 303–4). Seventy-five per cent of overseas visitors to Britain visited a museum/gallery during their stay in Britain. By contrast, only 40 per cent went to a theatre/concert and fewer than 20 per cent saw a film at the cinema (Myerscough, 1986: 311).

There is little doubt that similar developments are taking place in many industrial countries (see Lumley, 1988). Lowenthal says of the USA that 'the trappings of history now festoon the whole country' (1985: xv). The number of properties listed in the US National Register of Historic Places rose from 1,200 in 1968 to 37,000 in 1985 (Frieden and Sagalyn, 1989: 201). However, various critics of heritage, such as Hewison or Wright, argue that these developments are more extensive in Britain than elsewhere, although the empirical testing of such a hypothesis is clearly fraught with methodological difficulties (Hewison, 1987; Wright, 1985). What is fair to claim is the following argument.

Since the late nineteenth century in Britain there has certainly been a tradition of visiting/conserving the countryside, as was discussed in the previous chapter. This is reflected in the appreciation both of certain kinds of landscape (including villagescapes) and of the grand country houses set in attractive rural settings. On the first of these Raban talks of a recent willingness of people to present a particular impression of village England: 'nowhere outside Africa . . . were the tribespeople so willing to dress up in "traditional" costumes and cater for the entertainment of their visitors. . . . The thing had become a national industry. Year by year, England was being made more picturesquely merrie' (1986: 194–5).

Some of these events are now organised as 'costume dramas' by English Heritage, the main body concerned with the protection of heritage sites. The tendency to visit grand country houses also remains immensely popular, with 4.2 million people visiting National Trust houses in 1986 (Thrift, 1989: 29).

There has been a further interest in visiting the countryside, stemming from a widespread interest in the equipment and machinery that was used in farming, and in the patterns of life that developed in agriculture. We noted earlier that there are over 800 museums containing rural exhibits. These have been described as 'pretend farms', with wheelwrights, blacksmiths, horse breeders, farriers and so on (see Vidal, 1988). There are also many restaurants and cafés in rural areas which are in effect small agricultural museums, such as the Tithe Barn in Garstang, Lancashire.

There has been an even more remarkable increase in interest in the real lives of industrial/mining workers. MacCannell points out the irony of these changes: 'Modern Man [sic] is losing his attachments to the work bench, the neighbourhood, the town, the family, which he once called "his own" but, at the same time, he is developing an interest in the "real lives" of others' (1976: 91). This interest is particularly marked in the north of England, where much heavy industry had been located. It seems that it is such industries which are of most interest to visitors, particularly because of the apparently heroic quality of much of the work, as in a coalmine or steel works. However, this should not be overemphasised, since people also appear to find interesting the backbreaking but unheroic household tasks undertaken by women. This fascination with other people's work is bound up with the postmodern breaking down of boundaries, particularly between the front and the backstage of people's lives. Such a development is also part of what I will discuss later, namely, a postmodern museum culture in which almost anything can become an object of curiosity for visitors.

The remarkably rapid de-industrialisation of Britain in the late 1970s and early 1980s had two important effects. On the one hand, it created a profound sense of loss, both of certain kinds of technology (steam engines, blast furnaces, pit workings) and of the social life that had developed around those technologies. The rapidity of such change was greater in Britain than elsewhere and was probably more geographically concentrated in the north of England, South Wales and central Scotland. On the other hand, much of this industry had historically been based in inner-city Victorian premises, large numbers of which became available for alternative uses. Such buildings were either immensely attractive in their own right (such as Central Station that is now the G-Mex Centre in Manchester), or could be refurbished in a suitable heritage style for housing, offices, museums or restaurants. Such a style is normally picturesque, with sandblasted walls, replaced windows and attractive street furniture.

This process of de-industrialisation occurred in Britain at a time when many local authorities were developing more of a strategic role with regard to economic development and saw in tourism a way of generating jobs directly and through more general publicity about their area. A good example is Wigan; this is well represented in a publicity booklet called *I've never been to Wigan but I know what it's like* (Economic Development, Wigan, undated). The first five pictures in black and white are of back-to-back terraced housing, mines and elderly residents walking along narrow alleyways. But we are then asked if we are sure this is really what Wigan is now like. The following twelve photos, all in colour, demonstrate the contemporary Wigan, which is revealed as possessing countless tourist sites, Wigan Pier, a colourful market and elegant shops, excellent sports facilities, attractive pubs and restaurants, and delightful canalside walkways. Selling Wigan to tourists is part of the process of selling Wigan to potential investors, who are going to be particularly concerned about the availability of various kinds of services for their employees.

Yet this was also a period in which the proportion of smaller enterprises was beginning to grow for the first time for many years (see Lash and Urry, 1987: ch. 7). Much emphasis was also placed on small firms in central government policy and in the encouragement provided by local authority economic development programmes. Developing new enterprises in the tourist field, many of which are relatively small, became commonplace in Britain in the 1980s.

With the tendencies to globalisation I discussed in chapter 3, different countries have come to specialise in different sectors of the holiday market for overseas visitors: Spain for cheaper packaged holidays, Thailand for 'exotic' holidays, Switzerland for skiing and mountaineering holidays, and so on. Britain has come to specialise in holidays that emphasise the historical and the quaint (north Americans often refer to Britain as that 'quaint country' or that 'old country'). This emphasis can be seen in the way that overseas visitors tend to remain inland in Britain, rarely visiting either the coast or much of the countryside. Such visitors cannot know about more than a handful of sights worth visiting and, apart from London, these will normally include Oxford, Cambridge, Stratford, York, Edinburgh, and increasingly some of the sites of industrial tourism mentioned above (see Urry, 1988a). This location within the global division of tourism has further reinforced the particular strength of the heritage phenomenon in Britain.

The preservation of heritage has been particularly marked in Britain because of the mostly unattractive character of the modern architecture produced in the UK. The characteristic modern buildings of the postwar period have been undistinguished office blocks and public housing towers, many with concrete as the most visible building material. Such buildings have proved to be remarkably disliked by most of the population, which has seen modern architecture as 'American'. Yet the contrast with the often striking and elegant north American skyscrapers located in the downstream areas is particularly noticeable. In addition Britain had a very

large stock of pre-1914 houses and public buildings suitable for conservation, once the fashion for the modern had begun to dissolve in the early
1970s. An interesting example of this can be seen in the changing attitude
towards conservation, particularly of the Regency façades in Cheltenham,
which is now one of the prime townscapes being strenuously preserved
even though much of it had been scheduled for 'redevelopment' (Cowen,
1990).

So for a number of reasons heritage is playing a particularly important
role in British tourism, and it is somehow more central to the gaze in
Britain than in many other countries. But what is meant by heritage,
particularly in relationship to notions of history and authenticity (see
Uzzell, 1989, on the recent professional literature on heritage)? A lively
public debate has been raging in Britain concerned with evaluating the
causes and consequences of heritage.

This debate was stimulated by Hewison's book on the heritage industry,
which was subtitled *Britain in a Climate of Decline* (1987). He begins with
the provocative comment that increasingly, instead of manufacturing
goods, Britain is manufacturing heritage. This has come about because of
the perception that Britain is in some kind of terminal decline. And the
development of heritage not only involves the reassertion of values which
are anti-democratic, but the heightening of decline through a stifling of
the culture of the present. A critical culture based on the understanding
of history is what is needed, not a set of heritage fantasies.

Hewison is concerned with analysing the conditions in which nostalgia
is generated. He argues that it is felt most strongly at a time of discontent,
anxiety or disappointment. And yet the times for which we feel most
nostalgia were themselves periods of considerable disturbance. Furthermore, nostalgic memory is quite different from total recall; it is a socially
organised construction. The question is not whether we should or should
not preserve the past, but what kind of past we have chosen to preserve.
Roy Strong wrote perceptively in 1978 that:

> We are all aware of problems and troubles, of changes within the structure of
> society, of the dissolution of old values and standards. . . . The heritage
> represents some kind of security, a point of reference, a refuge perhaps,
> something visible and tangible which . . . seems stable and unchanged. Our
> environmental heritage . . . is a deeply stabilising and unifying element within
> our society. (quoted in Hewison, 1987: 46–7)

(Incidentally both Marx and Nietzsche might be said to have a similarly
critical attitude to 'nostalgia': see Lowenthal, 1985: 65.) Hewison notes
something distinctive about some contemporary developments. Much
contemporary nostalgia is for the industrial past. The first major battle
in Britain was fought – and lost – in 1962 over the elegant neoclassical
arch at the entrance to Euston station. But this gave rise to a survey of
industrial monuments by the Council for British Archaeology and a major
conference in 1969. Four years later the Association for Industrial
Archaeology was founded and by the 1980s industrial museums were

developing almost everywhere in the northern half of Britain. Hewison makes much of the contrasts between the development of the industrial museum at Beamish and the devastation brought about by the closure of the steel works at Consett, just ten miles away. The protection of the past conceals the destruction of the present. There is an absolute distinction between authentic history (continuing and therefore dangerous) and heritage (past, dead and safe). The latter, in short, conceals social and spatial inequalities, masks a shallow commercialism and consumerism, and may in part at least destroy elements of the buildings or artefacts supposedly being conserved. Hewison argues that: 'If we really are interested in our history, then we may have to preserve it from the conservationists' (1987: 98). Heritage is bogus history.

Obviously there is much value in many of Hewison's comments. It seems that one commentator has even suggested that Britain will 'soon be appointing a Curator instead of a Prime Minister' (quoted in Lowenthal, 1985: 4). Similarly Tom Wolfe has recently proposed that the entire British population service a national Disneyland for foreign tourists. Most of the buildings would be fibreglass replicas designed by Quinlan Terry and made in Taiwan (see Stamp, 1987). There are, however, some serious difficulties raised by Hewison's argument.

These criticisms of heritage bear a remarkable similarity to the critique of the so-called mass society thesis. Indeed social scientists may well be prone to a kind of nostalgia themselves, that is, for a Golden Age when the mass of the population were supposedly not taken in by the new distorting cultural forms (see Stauth and Turner, 1988; and more generally here Bagguley et al., 1990: ch. 5). There has, of course, never been such a period.

Hewison ignores the enormously important popular bases of the conservation movement. For example, like Patrick Wright he sees the National Trust as a gigantic system of outdoor relief for the old upper classes to maintain their stately homes. But this is to ignore the widespread support for such conservation. Indeed Samuel points out that the National Trust with nearly 1.5 million members is the largest mass organisation in Britain (1987a). Moreover, much of the early conservation movement was plebeian in character – for example railway preservation, industrial archaeology, steam traction rallies and the like in the 1960s, well before more obvious indicators of economic decline materialised in Britain. Even Covent Garden, which might be thought of as the ultimate 'yuppified heritage playground', was only transformed into a tourist site because of a major conservation campaign by local residents (see Januszczak, 1987, who also misses this point). Likewise the preservation of some derelict coalmines in Wales has resulted from pressure by local groups of miners and their families who have sought to hold on to aspects of 'their' history; indeed visitors to Big Pit in South Wales, for example, are said to be pleased that it has not been made pretty for visitors. Oral history also has played a role in preservation, not just of artefacts, but of memories. Generally Hewison and his fellow critics fail to link the pressure for conservation with the much broader development of environmental politics in the 1980s. In Britain Marcus Binney is a key figure here, as reflected in his book *Our Vanishing Heritage* (1984; see Stamp, 1987). One might also ask whether Hewison is actually suggesting that most of the unused industrial buildings should in fact have been demolished over the last decade or two.

Hewison links nostalgia for our industrial past with the growth of postmodernism. But although they are undoubtedly connected one needs to make some distinctions. This can be seen in Chester, where the expansion of a Roman centre ('Diva') will involve the demolition of a listed Georgian house. Local conservationists wish to save the house and to prevent the development of what will be a Roman theme park (with Roman coins, Roman food etc.; see Stamp, 1987). Hewison conflates the two sides. Mainly, however, he concentrates his critique on scholarly museums and heritage centres, which often employ academic historians to research the background to the site (see Rose, 1978, for an official history of the Gregs who developed the Quarry Bank Mill, now an industrial museum in Cheshire). Hewison's case could have been made much more easily against the Camelot theme park, the proposed Roman theme park in Chester, or the possible construction of Clegg Hall heritage park near Rochdale which will involve the compulsory purchase of some of the existing terraced houses. In the USA there is a similar distinction between the scholarly representation of Lowell as part of a National Park and the construction of Main St in Disneyland. Another distinction that might be made is between 'crafts' and 'trades'. The former is clearly part of the constructed heritage industry, even to the extent that the craftspeople become part of the exhibit. But this kind of construction can be distinguished from various 'trades' and the historical reconstruction of the authentic methods and techniques used, by, say, harness-makers or wheelwrights (see discussion in Vidal, 1988). Hewison's critique is more apposite to the former than the latter. An interesting example here is the Jewellery Quarter in Birmingham and the attempt to transform a 'trade' area into a 'crafts' area.

Hewison presumes a rather simple model by which certain meanings, such as nostalgia for times past, are unambiguously transferred to the visitor. There is no sense of the complexity by which different visitors can gaze upon the same set of objects and read them in a quite different way. There is ultimately something condescending about Hewison's view that such a presentation of heritage cannot be interpreted in different ways, or that the fact that the experience may be enjoyable means that it cannot also be educational. It is also not very clear that the examples Hewison discusses are unambiguous in their meaning anyway. The Wigan Pier Centre is, after all, scholarly and educational; it presents a history of intense popular struggle; it identifies the bosses as partly to blame for mining disasters; it celebrates a non-elite popular culture; and it is organised by a council with the objective of glorifying 'heroic labour'.

Compared with most people's understanding of history it surely conveys something of the social processes involved, even if it is hard to see how to build on that history in the future. Indeed, it is not at all clear just what understanding of history most people have. In the absence of the heritage industry just how is the past normally appropriated? It certainly is not through the academic study of 'history' as such (see Lowenthal, 1985: 411). For many people it will be acquired at best through reading biographies and historical novels. It is not obvious that the heritage industry's account is any more misleading.

What does need to be emphasised is that heritage history is distorted because of the predominant emphasis on visualisation, on presenting visitors with an array of artefacts, including buildings (either 'real' or 'manufactured'), and then trying to visualise the patterns of life that would have emerged around them. This is an essentially 'artefactual' history, in which a whole variety of social experiences are necessarily ignored or trivialised, such as war, exploitation, hunger, disease, the law, and so on (see Jordanova, 1989).

Overall Lowenthal's judgement on history seems right: 'We must concede the ancients their place. . . . But their place is not simply back there, in a separate and foreign country; it is assimilated in ourselves, and resurrected into an ever-changing present' (1985: 412).

The following three sections explore certain aspects of heritage in more detail: in relation to its use as part of a local strategy for economic regeneration; in its interconnections with recent trends in design and postmodern architecture; and its role is the development of what I shall term the postmodern museum.

Tourism and the local state

In the previous discussion of the heritage industry it was noted that there is often considerable local support for conservation. I shall consider more fully here the relationship between local areas and tourism development. In that relationship there are three key elements. First, there are local people who are often concerned to conserve features of the environment which seem in some ways to stand for or signify the locality in which they live. Second, there are a variety of private sector owners and potential owners of tourist-related services. And third, there is the local state, which is comprised of local authorities as well as the local/regional representatives of various national-level bodies, including tourist boards.

An interesting example which illustrates this complexity of elements is the Winter Gardens theatre in Morecambe, which has recently been debated in the national press (see Binney, 1988). This theatre closed in the late 1970s and will cost £2–5 million to repair (there is galloping dry rot). It is widely agreed that the theatre, built in 1897, is architecturally superb. English Heritage describes it as 'outstanding', while John Earl of the

Theatres Trust has characterised it as the Albert Hall of the north. It may be conserved, although this is by no means certain. If it is, there is little doubt that amongst other uses will be the staging of old-time music hall (as well as pop/classical concerts), hence conveying nostalgic memories of a somewhat imprecise golden age of pre-TV entertainment.

Clearly such a refurbishment would be subject to criticism as yet another example of the heritage industry. However, it should be noted that without a great deal of local support for conservation the theatre might already have been demolished. There is an extremely energetic action group convinced that this currently semi-derelict building symbolises Morecambe – that if it is allowed to be demolished, that would be the end of the town itself. It is certain that there is widespread popular support for increasing the attractiveness of Morecambe, to make it more congested and more subject to the tourist gaze. Indeed potential tourists to any site cannot contribute to environmental concern: that has to be expressed by local residents. Although the building is currently privately owned, it is quite clear that it will only be refurbished with much support from public bodies, including English Heritage, the European Community, Lancashire County Council and Lancaster City Council. The last of these will almost certainly be involved in putting together an appropriate funding package. The role of the local state may well be crucial.

This example demonstrates two important points about contemporary tourist development: the impact of local conservation groups whose heritage-preserving actions will often increase tourism in an area, sometimes as an unintended consequence; and the central organising role of the local state.

On the first of these, it is important to note that the strength of conservation groups varies very considerably between different places. For example, in 1980 while there were 5.1 members of 'amenity societies' per 1,000 population in the UK as a whole, the ratio was over 20 per 1,000 in Hampshire and over 10 per 1,000 in most of the counties around London, in Devon, in North Yorkshire and in Cumbria (see Lowe and Goyder, 1983: 28–30 for more detail). Clearly part of the rationale of such groups is to prevent new developments taking place that will harm the supposed 'character' of the locality (in the south-east especially through low-cost housing schemes). The role of the service and middle classes in such groups is crucial – and is a major means by which those possessing positional goods, such as a nice house in a nice village, seek to preserve their advantages. However, conservation movements can often have fairly broad objectives: not merely to prevent development, but to bring about the refurbishment of existing public buildings and more generally to 'museumify' the villagescape or townscape. Moreover, even if the objectives of the movement have nothing to do with tourism, the effect will almost certainly be to increase the attractiveness of the locality to tourists.

An interesting negative example of this can be seen in New Zealand.

Close to the largest city in the South Island, Christchurch, is the port of Lyttleton. As this is located within an extinct volcano, there is a superb natural harbour and scenic backdrop to the port. The town consists of mainly unexceptional low-level buildings but with very attractive façades. To the European it looks a typical town of the inter-war period. What is striking about Lyttleton is how undeveloped it is, although potentially it is an excellent tourist site. At present it does not look quaint, merely old. In Hewison's terms it has not been conserved, only preserved. For it to become an object of the tourist gaze, it needs a conservation movement to ensure that these façades are not demolished; an infusion of new capital to transform some of the premises into 'tourist-friendly' shops and cafés; and a strategic plan by the local authority to co-ordinate activities. At present there is nothing but a single, badly signposted small museum.

A factor which has helped to strengthen conservation movements is the apparently lower rate of geographical mobility of at least the male members of the service class (see Savage, 1988). As a result such people are likely to develop more of an attachment to place than previously. One can talk therefore of the 'localisation of the service class' and this will have its impact, through the forming of amenity groups, on the level of conservation (see Bagguley et al., 1989: 151–2). To the extent that such groups are successful, this will make the place more attractive to tourists. Thus the preservation of the quaint villagescape or townscape in particular, through middle-class collective action, is almost certain to increase the number of tourists and the resulting degree of congestion experienced by residents. One place where this has been particularly marked is Cheltenham. Because of concerted conservation pressure in the late 1960s the formal development policy was dropped in 1974. Since then a conservation policy has been adopted and there has been wholesale rehabilitation of the Regency housing stock for both housing and prestige office accommodation (see Cowen, 1990).

Before considering the various ways in which local states have responded to such pressures, and more generally how they have in recent years attempted to reconstruct the objects of the tourist gaze, I will note some reasons why local states have recently become centrally involved in both developing and promoting tourism.

As many local authorities moved into local economic intervention during a period of rapid de-industrialisation, so it seemed that tourism presented one of the only opportunities available for generating employment. Indeed it has been estimated that the cost of one new job in tourism is £4,000, compared with £32,000 in manufacturing industry and £300,000 in mechanical engineering (see Lumley, 1988: 22). The chairman of the South-East Tourist Board, for example, concludes that:

> I am heartily encouraged that County Councils are now giving tourism the recognition it deserves. It features strongly in most county structure plans. This is, of course, only right, given that it is one of the few growth elements in our economy. (English Tourist Board, no date: 4)

It was also noted that many such authorities have found themselves with a particular legacy, of derelict buildings, such as the Albert Dock in Liverpool, and/or derelict land, such as that which now comprises the Salford Quays development in Manchester. Converting such derelict property into sites which would have a tourist aspect directly or indirectly has been almost the only alternative available.

Earlier we saw just how much more competitive the tourist market has become in recent years, particularly as all sorts of places are competing to attract the increasingly selective and choosy post-tourist. As with many other commodities, the market has become more differentiated and particular places have been forced to develop coherent strategies. These have included taking an audit of local facilities, developing a plan of action and targeting appropriate marketing for the identified market niche. In some cases this has involved the local state starting a tourist industry almost from scratch – as in the case of Bradford, as will be seen later. In some parts of the south-east it has led to the development of a self-conscious 'post-tourist' strategy (see Landry et al., 1989).

Local authorities also play an important role because of the structure of ownership in tourist towns. This is often fragmented and it is difficult to get local capital to agree on appropriate actions from the viewpoint of the locality as a whole. The council is often the only agent with the capacity to invest in new infrastructure (such as sea defences, conference centres, harbours), or to provide the sort of facilities which must be found in any such centre (entertainments, museums, swimming pools). This has led in some of the older resorts, such as those on the Isle of Thanet, to the development of 'municipal Conservatism', a combination of small-scale entrepreneurialism and council intervention (see Buck et al., 1989: 188–9). In the last few years in Britain many Labour councils have enthusiastically embraced local tourist initiatives, having once dismissed tourism as providing only 'candy-floss jobs' (again see Landry et al., 1989, for an example of this argument; Glasgow would be a good illustration).

Finally, local councils have been willing to engage in promoting tourism because in a period of central government constraint this has been one area where there are sources of funding to initiate projects which may also benefit local residents. This certainly applies to some activities, such as swimming pools, leisure centres or the major refurbishment of derelict properties, although less so to others, such as running concerts at a loss, as Thanet Council has apparently done (see Buck et al., 1989). Furthermore, such facilities are important since they may attract prospective employees and employers and then keep them satisfied. This seems to have happened in Wigan following the establishment of the Wigan Pier Centre. The chairman of the North-West Tourist Board argues that:

> The growth of the tourism industry has a great deal to do with the growth of every other industry or business: the opening up of the regions as fine places to visit means they're better places to live in – and thus better places to work . . . a higher quality of life benefits employees. (quoted in Reynolds, 1988)

It is problematic to assess the economic impact of any particular tourism initiative. This results from the difficulty of assessing the so-called multiplier. If we consider the question of income generation, the impact of the expansion of tourism cannot be assessed simply in terms of how much income is spent by 'tourists' in hotels, camp sites, restaurants, pubs, and so on. It also depends upon what and where the recipients of that income, such as suppliers to the hotel or bar staff in the pubs, spend it, and in turn where those recipients spend it, and so on. There are some further problems in assessing such multipliers for a local economy: the linkages between firms are particularly complex and opaque partly because of the multitude of small enterprises involved; leakages from the economy are often very difficult to assess; there is no clear and agreed-upon definition of just what is a 'tourist' and hence what is tourist expenditure; the definition of the 'local economy' is in any case contentious so that the larger the geographical unit the higher the *apparent* multiplier. For all these difficulties it does seem that tourist expenditure has a fairly high local multiplier compared with other kinds of expenditure that might occur locally. Most studies show that something like half of tourism expenditure will remain in the locality, from its direct and indirect effects (see Williams and Shaw, 1988c: 88). However, such income remains highly unequally distributed since tourism areas are notable for their low wages level, even amongst those not even employed in the tourism industry as such (see Taylor, 1988, on the effects in tourism-rich Blackpool).

Local states in the UK have undertaken initiatives concerned to reconstruct and re-present whole places as objects of the tourist gaze. A useful summary of the actual agencies involved, and the complex conflicts and contradictions between them is to be found in Houston (1986); on the US see Frieden and Sagalyn (1989).

By no means all local authorities have been concerned to develop their localities as tourist centres. It has probably been most marked in the Midlands, the north of England, and Wales, rather less so in Scotland, Northern Ireland and the south-east. Moreover, the reorganisation of local government in the mid-1970s had the effect in some cases of merging resorts with other areas, which is believed to have reduced the support for specifically tourist initiatives, at least within the resorts themselves. Examples include the way that Broadstairs, Margate, Ramsgate and a rural hinterland were merged into the Isle of Thanet local authority (see Buck et al., 1989), or Morecambe was merged with the more prosperous Lancaster and an extensive rural area (Bagguley et al., 1990), or Rothesay became part of Argyll and Bute District Council (Houston, 1986: 19).

A number of local authorities, especially in England, have recently been successful in the tourism field. An interesting example in the north is Hebden Bridge, a small west Yorkshire town (see Waterhouse, R., 1989). Its nadir was in the mid-1960s, when half the native population had left in the previous ten years following the closure of thirty-three clothing works. A strategy came to be formulated to break with the industrial past, to promote Hebden as a place to visit and to convert some of the visitors into new residents. There had been plans for a major development scheme but this was thrown out in 1967. A heritage-led growth strategy was devised instead, a strategy influenced by an early environmental movement in the town. The place is now booming, with a considerable shortage of housing. There are now twice as many newcomers as original residents.

Some other places that have pursued a similar strategy have been assisted by the English Tourist Board scheme to establish Tourism Development Action Programmes (TDAPs). These are integrated programmes, lasting between one and three years, which involve research, development and marketing (see Davies, 1987). The English Tourist Board serves as a catalyst, forming a partnership between the local authority, the private sector and often other agencies (such as the Training Commission). The emphasis is on taking action. Some of the places that have experienced such a programme are cities, such as Bradford, Tyne and Wear, Lancaster, Gosport and Portsmouth, rural areas such as Exmoor and Kielder Water, and seaside resorts such as Bridlington and Torbay.

The Lancaster TDAP consists of a partnership between the two relevant local authorities, Lancaster City Council and Lancashire County Council, together with Lancashire Enterprises Limited (a publicly funded enterprise board) and the North-West Tourist Board. The objectives are to develop and implement a marketing strategy, to improve the heritage attractions, to develop links with the countryside and coast, to enhance visitors' experience of Lancaster, and to expand and improve the provision of accommodation. It is clearly recognised that enhancing the tourist potential of Lancaster will simultaneously make the place more attractive to inward investment. In the *Position Statement* for the programme it is stated that:

> in addition to creating new tourism jobs locally, the development of tourism in Lancaster will help to up-grade the local environment and improve facilities which will assist industrial promotion generally. The City's appearance and the range of facilities it offers are critical to the attraction of new companies to Lancaster. (Special Projects Group, Lancaster City Council, 1987: para 1.20)

It is interesting that this *Position Statement* is entitled *Lancaster – Heritage City*. It would seem that three conditions are necessary if Lancaster is to set about constructing itself as a heritage city. First, there would have to be a number of attractive and reasonably well-preserved buildings from a range of historical periods. In Lancaster's case these were medieval (a castle), Georgian (the customs house and many townhouses) and Victorian (old mills).

Second, such buildings would have to be used for activities in some ways consistent with the tourist gaze. An interesting example concerns Lancaster Castle, which has a magnificent Norman gate. Most of the castle is currently closed to the public because it is used as a prison. Now although castles often operated historically as prisons (Lancaster Castle indeed has some famous dungeons), there is thought to be something inappropriate about tourists gazing upon a building which still functions as a prison. Hence the castle has not fulfilled its potential as a tourist site. the TDAP has been partly concerned with planning how to capitalise on the castle when it will stop functioning as a prison in the early 1990s. It will then be available for more 'appropriate' uses, such as a hotel, museum or shopping area.

The third condition for Lancaster to become a plausible heritage city is that the buildings should in some sense have been significant historically, that they stand for or signify important historical events, people or processes. Thus in the TDAP *Position Statement* Lancaster is described as:

> an ancient settlement steeped in history, with Roman origins, an important medieval past. . . . Through the Duchy of Lancaster it has close associations with the Monarchy. . . . The City's many attractions, based on its rich history and fine buildings, together with its royal associations, combine for the promotion and marketing of Lancaster's heritage. (Special Projects Group, Lancaster City Council, 1987: paras 4.3, 4.4)

It is worth considering the use of 'history' in the quotation: that because there has been a 'rich' history the old buildings appear not merely old but historically important; and in turn the buildings signify that the place is properly old – that it is indeed steeped in history. There must therefore be a coherent relationship between the built environment and the presumed atmosphere or character of the place concerned. In the case of the Lancaster TDAP the aim is to develop and market an appropriate representation of that heritage.

One considerable advantage of a TDAP is that it is likely to stimulate an overall strategy for the area concerned and to make it more likely that there is some consistency in the image being constructed. We will see in the next chapter how that was important in the recent successful development of Bradford's tourism. The contrasting example of Manchester illustrates what can happen without co-ordination. A huge redevelopment programme is currently taking place in Manchester, which many consider to be the most promising tourism site in Britain. But with the abolition of the Greater Manchester County Council there is no co-ordinating authority. Current and competing players involved in tourist development in Manchester include: Salford, Trafford and Manchester Councils, Central Manchester and Trafford Park Development Corporations, the English Tourist Board, the consultants Land Design and Research, and property developers Merlin Properties, Rosehaugh, and the Manchester Ship Canal Company (Pearman, 1989).

One way in which a number of cities have been more successful in constructing a relatively coherent tourist image is through so-called cultural tourism. It is calculated that about £2 billion of tourist expenditure in the UK is specifically attributable to the arts. In London, for example, 44 per cent of museum attendance is made up of tourists, compared with 21 per cent outside London. Tourists form 40 per cent of the audience at London's theatres and concerts, while an incredible 37 per cent of those at West End theatres are overseas tourists. It is calculated that overall 25 per cent of all tourist spending is arts-related (although there are immense problems of definition here; see Myerscough, 1988: ch. 5 for more detail).

In addition to Glasgow, which I will briefly discuss in chapter 7, Liverpool is another city which has successfully capitalised on its particular cultural heritage. Strongly featured in the *Discover Merseyside 1988* brochure is the daily 'Beatles Magical History Tour'. The brochure talks of 'Beatleland', which includes the 'Cavern Walks' shopping centre, the John Lennon Memorial Club, the Beatles Shop, Tommy Steele's statue of Eleanor Rigby, and so on. Details are also included of the annual Beatles Convention. Another cultural advantage of Merseyside increasingly featuring in its tourism literature is soccer, something which again illustrates how the boundaries between different activities are dissolving, the de-differentiation referred to earlier. Liverpool describes itself as '*The Football Capital of the World*' and there are well-organised 'Soccer City Weekend' packages where Goodison Park and Anfield constitute important objects of the tourist gaze.

Two other features of Liverpool's recent tourism strategy are of more general relevance: the garden festival and waterfront development. On the former, Liverpool's festival in 1984 was the first in Britain, to be followed by Stoke and Glasgow. The Liverpool site is now derelict and although popular at the time it has not had much long-term effect. Elsewhere, though, such festivals have helped to reinforce a conservative pastoral image, to declare that manufacturing industry has gone for good. Roberts suggests that the festivals represent an attempt to impose a predominantly southern conception on the north: 'The image of the South as predominantly green is imported into the North as a collective vision of a United Green and Pleasant Kingdom' (1989).

The Liverpool festival site was on the waterfront. And in recent years almost every town and city in Britain has been producing mixed development waterfront schemes in which tourist appeal is one element. In London the Docklands Development has become a major tourist attraction although there is not much there apart from housing, offices and water. The model for such waterfront development has been the USA, beginning with Baltimore's Harbourplace, which attracts 29 million visitors a year. Other examples worldwide include Boston's Fanueil Hall Marketplace and associated Harborwalk, South Street Seaport in New York, and Sydney's Darling Harbour. The last of these was developed by Sydney property developers, Merlin, who are also involved in Manchester and in the Sheriff's Court Fashion Centre in Glasgow (see Wilsher, 1988). In Britain current waterfront projects include the Albert Dock (with 3 million visitors a year), Bristol (as part of a TDAP), Birmingham Canal (including the National Indoor Arena), Gloucester Docks (in addition to the National Waterways Museum), and

Salford Quays (once described as the least promising development site in Britain).

The inspiration for development in Britain has arisen from the striking ways in which the downtown areas of American cities have been transformed, mainly by private developers but with a fair degree of public coordination. The main features found in the USA are the 'festival marketplace', particularly by the developer James Rouse as in Fanueil Hall in Boston; historical preservation, as in Lowell, Massachusetts; the development of new open spaces or plazas, such as Harborplace in Baltimore; waterfront developments, such as Battery City Park in New York; cultural centres, such as a performing arts centre in Los Angeles; renovation of old hotels, such as the Willard Inter-Continental in Washington DC; refurbished housing, as on Beacon Hill, Boston; and new public transportation systems, even in Los Angeles, the ultimate automobile city (see Fondersmith, 1988; Frieden and Sagalyn, 1989: 210–12).

In the next section I shall consider in more detail the design and architecture of these various developments. Tourism is about finding certain sorts of place pleasant and interesting to gaze upon, and that necessarily comes up against the design of the buildings and their relationship to natural phenomena. Without the right design no amount of local state involvement will attract tourists. It will be seen that much of the architecture of these developments is in different senses *post*modern.

Designing for the gaze

Given the emphasis on tourist consumption as visual, and the significance of buildings as objects upon which the gaze is directed, it is essential to consider changing patterns and forms that those buildings might take. Moreover, it is of course impossible to consider postmodernism without consideration of the built environment, surely the sphere which many would say best demonstrates such a cultural paradigm.

I shall argue, first, that there are a number of postmodern architectures; second, that the impact of these different architectures depends upon whether we are considering private or public buildings; third, that architects and architectural practices are of major importance in shaping the contemporary tourist gaze; fourth, that tourist practices have to be taken much more seriously by commentators on building design; and fifth, that tourists are socially differentiated and hence gaze selectively upon these different architectural styles.

The first point can be approached by considering what is meant by *post* in postmodern. There are three senses: *after* the modern; *return* to the premodern; and *anti* the modern. I shall now briefly summarise the architectural style associated with each of these (see Harris and Lipman, 1986, for an alternative classification).

After the modern is what one could also term 'consumerist postmodernism'. This takes its cue from Venturi's famous cry to 'learn from Las Vegas' (1972; Jencks, 1977; Frampton, 1988). Caesar's Palace at Las Vegas or Disneyland are the icons of this architecture, which proudly celebrates commercial vulgarity (see Harris and Lipman, 1986: 844–5). Art and life are fused or pastiched in the playful and shameless borrowing of ornamental style. Previous elements of high culture are mass-produced, and no longer signify anything in particular. This is an architecture of surfaces and appearances, of playfulness and pastiche. It is mannerist – as if all the historical styles and conventions of architecture are there to be endlessly drawn on, juxtaposed and drawn on yet again. However, a distinction should be made between the literal consumerism of Las Vegas and the manner in which some postmodern architects have hijacked such styles to construct something of an auratic architecture appealing to the cognoscenti (as in James Stirling's Stuttgart gallery). In Britain Ian Pollard is one of the best-known postmodernists. A particularly striking building of his is the *Observer*'s Marco Polo House in Battersea, with its massive porticoes, broken pediments and banded ceramic towers (see Jenkins, 1987). An illustrative controversy has recently occurred over one of his other designs, a do-it-yourself store in west London built for Sainsbury (see Pearman, 1988). At the entrance to this store Pollard had playfully designed a massive Corinthian arch. Sainsbury, however, even before the store was open, found the design, with its abundance of Egyptian motifs and postmodern ornamentation, far too jokey for a serious retailer. A spokesman for the company condemned it as 'this pastiche of a design' and the arch was demolished before the store was opened.

After this débâcle Sainsbury is reassessing its design practices, since the company takes the architecture of its stores seriously, more so than other retailers. In general it favours two styles: certain kinds of modernism, as found in Norman Foster's plans for a hypermarket in Eastleigh or Nick Grimshaw's cantilevered supermarket in Camden Town (see Photograph 6.2); and local vernacular styles, such as Sainsbury's Lancaster store which is built around the façade of the old public baths, or its Wolverhampton shop which is built around an old church, or its new Grimsby shop which is to be part of a fishing heritage centre. The vernacular styles are more common in the north, modernism in the south. However, the extension to the National Gallery that the Sainsburys are funding is being designed by Robert Venturi, and although is less colourful than expected it is nevertheless thoroughly postmodern, that is, *after* the modern (see Pawley, 1987).

Much of the debate about postmodernism has tended to concentrate on significant public buildings, such as Terry Farrell's TV-AM headquarters, Philip Johnson's AT-&-T building, and James Stirling's Stuttgart gallery. There is less investigation of the impact of such a style on the everyday architecture of particular towns and cities. This is an important issue, since historically most architecture has been partly eclectic, drawing on

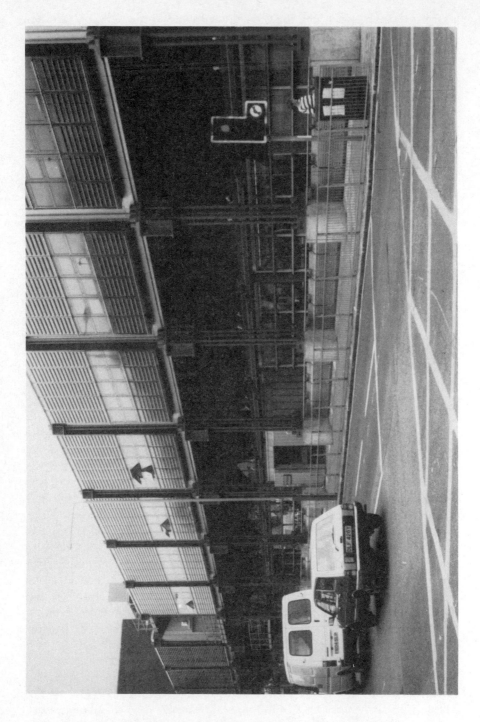

Photograph 6.2   *Sainsbury's supermarket in Camden Town, designed by Nick Grimshaw*

earlier traditions, such as the Gothic style favoured by the Victorians, or the Egyptian motifs popular with the Art Deco movement (on the latter see Bagguley, 1990: ch. 5; more generally, see Lowenthal, 1985: 309–21). The one exception was the modern movement and its perhaps unique rejection of all previous architectural mannerisms. Interestingly, even during the heyday of modernism (say 1930–70 in Britain) two other styles were common: red-brick neo-Georgian shopping parades, and neo-Tudor half-timbered suburban housing.

One useful series of studies has been conducted on the impact of different architectural styles and on the different social forces which generated them (see Freeman, 1986, on the following; for a related study see Larkham, 1986). The architectural history of two towns was investigated: Aylesbury and Wembley. Modern architecture dominated the centres of both towns in the postwar period. This changed in Aylesbury in the early 1970s and in Wembley in the 1980s. Since then most town-centre building has been postmodern. Brick has become the predominant building material during the postmodern period; concrete, glass and brick were all common during the modern period. The earlier break with modernism in Aylesbury rather than Wembley appears to have resulted from the nature of the architectural practices involved:

> In Aylesbury, local firms, perhaps endowed with a rich historical and architectural heritage, were primary adopters of this style [postmodernism] in the early years. The continuing existence of local initiators and architects may, therefore, have been a reason why the dominance of Modernism with its monolithic designs ended so much sooner in Aylesbury than in Wembley. (Freeman, 1986: 75)

But Freeman treats as postmodern a wide range of different styles: what I earlier have termed 'consumerist postmodernism' and what I will go on to discuss as 'patrician postmodernism' and 'vernacular postmodernism'.

Patrician postmodernism involves a *return* to the premodern. Here what is celebrated is the classical form, the architecture of an elite. Leon Krier summarises its attraction: 'People never protested against the tradition of classical architecture. . . . Architecture has reached its highest possible form in the classical principles and orders . . . [which] have the same inexhaustible capacities as the principles which govern nature and the universe itself' (1984: 87, 119).

This reconstructed classicism springs from individuals who believe they have distinct powers of insight, who will be able to return to the aura of the fine building. Architecture here is a self-determining practice, an autonomous discipline able to reproduce the three classical orders. This is linked to the belief that such classicism is really what people want if only their choices were not distorted by modernism. In Britain, Prince Charles in part demonstrates this position, of appearing to speak on behalf of the people who know they do not like modernism and who really want only to gaze on nothing but uninterrupted classical buildings. Roger Scruton's position is somewhat similar (and as we will see less ambiguous than the

Prince's; see Scruton, 1979). As Wright says: 'While Scruton certainly approaches everyday life, he does so in such a way as to freeze it over. What emerges is an aestheticized, and indeed severely 'classical', definition of *appropriate* everyday life' (1985: 30–1). It is no accident that it is Krier who has been commissioned by the Prince to devise the site plan for the western expansion of Dorchester, a proposal in effect to put Prince Charles' theories into practice. One interesting feature is the rejection of the idea of zoning activities. In Poundbury shops will be found in arcades under flats, and workshops will be located next to housing.

The British architect who has become best known for his implementation of the classical tradition is Quinlan Terry, particularly in a series of elegant private houses, which are usually located in pleasant countryside. More recently he has been responsible for the extensive and controversial Richmond development, which consists of fifteen separate buildings built in a variety of classical styles. Terry's properties are expensive since they embody large amounts of craft labour on the exteriors, although the interiors are standardly modern. They are to do with 'an elitist and austere *return* to style and a cult of the unique' and yet compared with a modernist towerblock 'Terry's classy and expensive classical buildings may indeed, in a limited . . . sense, form a "popular" style of architecture' (Wright, 1985: 31). Certainly, to the extent to which such contemporary classical buildings mirror in particular the Georgian style, they will be immensely popular objects of the tourist gaze. If there is a single style of house which tourists in Britain want to gaze upon it is the classical country house (see Hewison, 1987: ch. 3). There is even now a handbook instructing people how to furnish and entertain in such Georgian houses, *The Official New Georgians Handbook* (Artley and Robinson, 1985).

A considerable amount of such building is preserved in many towns and cities in Britain. The most striking Georgian townscape is Bath, where the housing stock is a positional good. One could describe many of the residents as living in a museum and simultaneously surrounded by museums. The city is almost definitive of good taste and a setting in which part of the cultural capital possessed by its residents is the knowledge of such housing and of the skills necessary to improve it while at the same time appearing to conserve it. The contemporary renaissance of Bath is just as important an icon of the postmodern (in the return to the premodern sense) as is the latest jokey theme park or shopping mall.

There is a third variant of postmodern architecture. This is not simply after the modern, or involving a return to the premodern – it is *against* the modern. It has much in common with Frampton's concept of 'critical regionalism' (1988) and Foster's notion of a 'critical postmodernism' (1985b). The latter defines the critique of modernism as a Eurocentric and phallocentric set of discourses (see Hebdige, 1986–7: 8–9). It is argued that modernism (like of course premodern classicism) privileges the metropolitan centre over provincial towns and cities, the developed world over developing countries, the north Atlantic rim over the Pacific rim, western art forms over those from the 'east' and the 'south', men's art over women's art, the professional over the people, and so on. There is one variant of the postmodern which involves challenging these dominant discourses: in architecture it can be characterised as vernacular postmodernism. Hebdige well characterises the spatial correlates of this shift. He says that there is: 'not so much a lowering of expectations as a shift towards a total transformation in historical time . . . to the piecemeal habitation of finite space – the space in which we live' (1986–7: 12).

Space in vernacular postmodernism is localised, specific, context-dependent, and particularistic – by contrast with modernist space which is absolute, generalised, and independent of context (see Harvey, 1989, more generally here). Leon Krier talks of the need to create 'localities of human dignity' (1984: 87). In Britain one of the clearest examples of this has been the 'community architecture' movement which Prince Charles has also done much to foster. This movement began with the restoration of Black Road in Macclesfield designed by Rod Hackney. The main principle of such a movement is 'that the environment works better if the people who live, work and play in it are actively involved in its creation and maintenance' (Wates and Krevitt, 1987: 18). This involves much emphasis on the process of design rather than on the end product, on reducing the power of the architecture vis-à-vis clients, on channelling resources to local residents and communities, and on restoration, or where new building is involved, ensuring it is appropriate to local historical context (see Hutchinson, 1989, for a critique of this movement).

The locality is central to such an architecture. And there are important resistances in contemporary societies which have made local vernacular architecture particularly popular, at least outside the metropolitan centres. There is the apparent desire of people living in particular places to conserve or to develop buildings, at least in their public spaces, which express the particular locality in which they live. Such old buildings appear to have a number of characteristics: solidity, since they have survived wars, erosions, developers, town planning etc.; continuity, since they provide links between past generations and the present; authority, since they signify that age and tradition are worthy or preservation; and craft, since they were mostly built using otherwise underrated premodern techniques and materials (see Lowenthal, 1985: 52–63).

And because of the universalisation of the tourist gaze, all sorts of places (indeed almost everywhere) have come to construct themselves as objects of the tourist gaze; in other words, not as centres of production or symbols of power but as sites of pleasure. Once people visit places outside capital cities and other major centres, what they find pleasurable are buildings which seem appropriate to place and which mark that place off from others. One of the very strong objections to modernism was that it generated uniformity, or placelessness, and was therefore unlikely to generate large numbers of buildings attractive to potential tourists who want to gaze upon the distinct. The only exceptions are to be found in major cities, such as Richard Rogers' Lloyds building in London, or his high-tech Pompidou Centre in Paris, which now attracts more visitors than the Louvre. Outside the major cities the universalisation of the tourist gaze has made most other places enhance difference through the rediscovery of local vernacular styles. These styles moreover convey particular histories. As Lynch asks 'what time is this place?' (1973). In other words, places indicate particular times or histories and in that process vernacular postmodernism is centrally important. Wright talks of the 'abstract and artificial aestheticisation of the ordinary and the old', although it can be noted that different places signify very different 'old' times (1985: 230).

It should not be forgotten that each such place will be viewed from a variety of perspectives. There will be differences between what visitors and locals 'see' in a place, and between the viewpoints of old and new residents: 'People live in different worlds even though they share the same locality: *there is no single community or quarter*. What is pleasantly old for one person is decayed and broken for another' (Wright, 1985: 237).

So far I have talked about various kinds of architecture and how these do or do not coincide with the likely gazes of both local residents and visitors; earlier I made some comments about the likely role of the state. What I have not yet considered are the respective influences of architects and developers in the construction of different tourist sites, although in the comparative study of Aylesbury and Wembley the role of locally based architects was noted in the case of the former. There is also evidence in the USA that there has been expanding employment of architects in small and medium-sized towns where an expanding middle class has given rise to localities with high incomes, environmental sensitivity and a consciousness of design (see Knox, 1987; Blau, 1988). The same appears to be true of many of the smaller cities in Britain, such as Bath, Chester, Lancaster or York, cities which are or are becoming important tourist sites (see Bagguley et al., 1990: ch. 5).

I will conclude by making some points about architects, developers and the changing objects of the tourist gaze. Partly influenced by some of these locally based architects, a more participatory and activist-influenced planning developed, 'aimed not only at halting renewal schemes but also at preserving and enhancing the neighborhood lifeworld' (Knox, 1988: 5). The effectiveness has of course varied enormously and quite often schemes for the desired conservation of an area turn out to have quite different consequences. The renewal of Covent Garden as a result of a planning decision influenced by activists concerned to conserve the buildings has had the consequence of generating an immensely successful tourist site (with resulting congestion, inflated prices and piles of uncollected rubbish).

According to Raphael Samuel a similar fate might befall Spitalfields in east London. Samuel argues that what is being planned in Spitalfields is an alliance of conservationists and developers working together. One effect of the proposed scheme would be to turn much of Spitalfields into a tourist site, which it is not at present. Samuel writes dismissively:

> Conservation here is typically pastiche in which, as in a costume drama, items are treasured for their period effect. . . . 'Georgianised' Spitalfields, with its immaculate brickwork, restored lintels and tasteful interiors. . . . What meaning does conservation have . . . when a building is frozen in historical limbo? (1987b)

A sustained attack was mounted in Britain in the 1980s on the systems of planning control that had been established since the war. A crucial Circular 22/80 from the Department of the Environment asserted the superiority of developer 'patronage' over the democratic system of planning control. Design was to be left to developers, except in certain areas, such as National Parks, Areas of Outstanding Natural Beauty, Conservation Areas and so on (see Punter, 1986–7). What came to be established was a two-tier system. Punter summarises the way this met the apparently conflicting objectives of Conservative policy:

> to retain those escapist elements of aesthetic control which protect the interests and property values [and we may add the tourist sites] of their supporters – the gentrified Georgian, Victorian and Edwardian suburbs, the picture postcard villages and 'unspoilt' countryside so sought after by long distance commuters. . . . In crude terms the remainder of the country is to be left to the mercies of the developers. (1986–7: 10)

This policy tries to overcome contradictions in Conservative attitudes to development. One way of effecting this will be to compensate farmers in rural areas for not damaging areas or features of acknowledged environmental significance (see Cloke, 1989: 44). But the most significant test of this policy is in the London Docklands. So far it seems that there is an extraordinary clutter of diverse and conflicting architectural styles, what has been referred to as an architectural zoo (see Wolmar, 1989). There has also been a lack of consultation with the local boroughs and communities and a failure to implement various social objectives. Sir Andrew Derbyshire, former chairman of the London Docklands Planning Committee, has been particularly critical of the architectural consequences: 'We have learnt from Docklands that the free play of market forces is not going to produce the best results in terms of quality. The good architects have lost out' (quoted in Wolmar, 1989: 5). It should be noted that the Docklands has nevertheless already become a major tourist site.

In the 1980s a number of new flamboyant developers have emerged in most western countries. Some have international interests, such as Donald Trump from New York with his postmodern Trump Tower. In Britain a number of more regionally oriented developers have recently emerged and are taking advantage of the increased discretion available to developers. The best known is John Hall, from the north-east, who was responsible for building the enormous Metrocentre in a deregulated enterprise zone in Gateshead in north-east England (see Hattersley, 1989). Hall sees himself as a representative of the region and has drawn on the local culture to underpin his activities. His vision is based on the centrality of family life and on the need to provide families with a centre that integrates leisure and shops; in such a place people will spend prolifically. More recently he has been developing Winyard Hall, a mixed leisure/residential development, with two golf courses, a nature reserve, hotel, expensive housing, and so on. Another north-country developer is John Broome, who has been responsible for Alton Towers, the closest thing in Britain to Disneyland. For the last couple of years he had been developing the Battersea, a multi-purpose postmodern leisure complex which was to have been based within the old Battersea Power Station (see Grove, 1988).

But it should not be assumed that all these developments will be financially successful. Two mentioned here, the London Docklands and the Battersea, were in serious financial difficulties in 1989. In the USA there has been overinvestment in shopping malls in Texas and hotels in Atlanta, while Virginia's waterfront development is a financial failure. Harvey provocatively asks: 'How many museums, cultural centres, convention and exhibition halls, hotels, marinas, shopping malls, waterfront developments can we stand? (1988).

Here I have thus shown how the universalisation of the tourist gaze is reaping its postmodern harvest in almost every village, town and city in Britain and in many other western countries as well. I will now turn to one particular kind of building – the museum.

Postmodern museums

We have seen a spectacular growth in the number of museums in western countries. This is clearly part of the process by which the past has come to be much more highly valued by comparison with both the present and the future. Also, the past has become particularly valued in the UK because of the way in which international tourism in this country has come to specialise in the construction of historical quaintness. And the attraction of museums increases as people get older – thus the 'greying' of the population in the west is also adding to the number and range of museums.

I have strongly argued for the significance of the gaze to tourist activities. This is not to say that all the other senses are insignificant in the tourist experience. But I have tried to establish that there has to be something distinctive to gaze upon, otherwise a particular experience will not function as a tourist experience. There has to be something extra-ordinary about the gaze.

On the face of it this seems a relatively straightforward thesis. But it is not – because of the complex nature of visual perception. We do not literally 'see' things. Particularly as tourists we see objects which are constituted as signs. They stand for something else. When we gaze as tourists what we see are various signs or tourist clichés. Some such signs function metaphorically. A pretty English village can be read as representing the continuities and traditions of England from the Middle Ages to the present day. By contrast the use of the term 'fun' in the advertising for a Club-Med holiday is a metaphor for sex. Other signs, such as lovers in Paris, function metonymically. Here what happens is the substitution of some feature or effect or cause of the phenomenon for the phenomenon itself. The ex-miner, now employed at the former coalmine to show tourists around, is a metonym for the structural change in the economy from one based on heavy industry to one based on services. The development of the industrial museum in an old mill is a metonymic sign of the development of a post-industrial society.

There have of course been museums open to the public since the early nineteenth century, beginning with the Louvre in Paris, the Prado in Madrid and the Altes Museum in Berlin. And since the *Michelin Guides* first appeared museums have been central to the tourist experience. Horne describes the contemporary tourist as a modern pilgrim, carrying guidebooks as devotional texts (1984). What matters, he says, is what people are told they are seeing. The fame of the object becomes its meaning. There is thus a ceremonial agenda, in which it is established what we should see and sometimes even the order in which they should be seen.

Such museums were based on a very special sense of aura. Horne summarises the typical tourist experience, in which the museum has functioned as a metaphor for the power of the state, the learning of the scholar and the genius of the artist:

> tourists with little or no knowledge of painting are expected to pay their respects solely to the fame, costliness and authenticity of these sacred objects, remote in their frames. As 'works of art' from which tourists must keep their distance, the value of paintings can depend not on their nature, but on their authenticated scarcity. The gap between 'art' and the tourist's own environment is thereby maintained. (1984: 16)

Museums have thus been premised upon the aura of the authentic historical artefact, and particularly upon those which are immensely scarce because of the supposed genius of their creator. Horne argues that what can be especially problematic about museums is their attribution of reverence to objects simply because of their aura of authenticity (1984: 249). How we gaze within museums has changed in three central ways. The sense of aura that Horne describes has been undermined through the development of the postmodern museum. This involves quite different modes of representation and signification. What we 'see' in the museum has been transformed.

First, there has been a marked broadening of the objects deemed worthy of being preserved. This stems from a changed conception of history. There has been a decline in the strength of a given national history, which the national museums then exemplify. Instead a proliferation of alternative or vernacular histories has developed – social, economic, populist, feminist, ethnic, industrial and so on. There is a pluralisation and indeed a contemporarisation of history. This has produced in Britain a 150 per cent increase in the number of museums over the past twenty years (see White, 1987). The British Tourist Authority has calculated that there could be up to 12,000 museum-type venues in Britain (see Baxter, 1989). Museums are concerned with 'representations' of history, and what has happened is a remarkable increase in the range of histories worthy of being represented. I have already noted some of these, especially the development of rural and industrial museums. It is now almost as though the worse the previous historical experience, the more authentic and appealing the resulting tourist attraction (see Urry, 1988a: 50). No longer are people only interested in seeing either great works of art or artefacts from very distant historical periods. People increasingly seem attracted by representations of the 'ordinary', of modest houses and of mundane forms of work. Glass-blowing, engine driving, shop working, candle-making, cotton spinning, salt-making, cobbling, chemical manufacture, holiday-making, lace-making, domestic chores, coalmining and so on, are all deemed worthy of being represented in contemporary museums, as are the often mundane artefacts associated with each of these activities (see West, 1988, on Ironbridge Gorge; Bennett, 1988, on Beamish; and Hewison, 1987, on Wigan Pier). There has been a quite stunning fascination with the popular and a tendency to treat all kinds of object, whether it is the *Mona Lisa* or the old cake tin of a Lancashire cotton worker, as almost equally interesting. One could summarise this shift as being 'from aura to nostalgia', and it reflects the anti-elitism of postmodernism (see Edgar, 1987). It should also be noted that all sorts of other phenomena are now preserved in museums, including moving images, radio, television, photographs, cinema, the environment and even the sets of TV soap operas (Lumley, 1988; and see Goodwin, 1989, on the Granada museum of the *Coronation Street* set).

There has also been a marked change in the nature of museums themselves. No longer are visitors expected to stand in awe of the exhibits. More emphasis is being placed on a degree of participation by visitors in the exhibits themselves. 'Living' museums replace 'dead' museums, open-air museums replace those under cover, sound replaces hushed silence, and visitors are not separated from the exhibits by glass. The publicity for the Tyne and Wear museum well expresses this new trend towards participation:

> In our museum, the emphasis is on action, participation and fun. Out are the endless old-fashioned glass cases you pored over in hushed silence. In are professionally designed displays, working models to play with, complete period room settings to browse through and sound effects to complete the picture. (quoted in White, 1987: 10)

Hooper-Greenhill notes a number of further attitudinal changes taking place in Britain's museums which are making them much more aware of the public and of how to improve the experience of visiting the particular museum (1988). In Leicester, for example, some acknowledgement is now made that visitors will come from different ethnic groups and that the museum staff must concern themselves with the various ways in which such visitors may interact with the displays and with the different accounts of histories they present (Hooper-Greenhill, 1988: 228–30).

There are further ways in which the museum display is now far less auratic. It is now quite common for it to be revealed how a particular exhibit was prepared for exhibition, and in some cases even how it was made to appear 'authentic', there are also now a number of museums where actors play various historical roles and interact with the visitors, even to the extent of participating in various historical sketches. At Beamish, for example, there are people acting out various roles in the different shops, while at Wigan Pier visitors are encouraged to experience a simulated school lesson. Elsewhere ex-miners describe mining work to visitors, and people run machinery which does not actually produce anything but simply demonstrates the machinery – 'the working non-working industry' (White, 1987: 11). Lumley summarises these changes overall by arguing that they involve replacing the notion that the museum is a collection for scholarly use with the idea that it is a means of communication (1988: 15).

In addition there is a changed relationship between what is considered a museum and various other social institutions. Those other institutions have now become more like museums. Some shops, for example, now look like museums with elaborate displays of high-quality goods where people will be attracted into the shop in order to wander and to gaze. In places like the Albert Dock in Liverpool, which contains the Tate Gallery of the North, a maritime museum and many stylish shops, it is difficult to see quite what is distinctive about the shops as such since people seem to regard their contents as 'exhibits'. Stephen Bayley, from the new Museum of Design in the London Docklands, has remarked:

> the old nineteenth century museum was somewhat like a shop . . . a place where you go and look at values and ideas, and I think shopping really is becoming one of the great cultural experiences of the late twentieth century. . . . The two things are merging. So you have museums becoming more commercial, shops becoming more intelligent and more cultural. (quoted in Hewison 1987: 139)

It has also been suggested recently that 'factory tourism' should be developed in Britain, that factories should in effect be viewed as museum-like. Ministers believe that there would be considerable interest in visiting plants producing cars, planes, processed food, submarines and so on (Jones, G., 1987). Certainly when factories do organise 'open days' they are very successful. Recently the Sellafield nuclear reprocessing plant in Cumbria has become a major tourist attraction. The English Tourist Board calculates that up to 6 million people visit a factory each year and

that this figure will soon rise to 10 million. What is happening is that the
factory is becoming more like a museum. Likewise, in the 1980s there has
been an extensive 'museumification' of English pubs, many of which have
become 'mock Imperial Victorian' and undergone 'ye olde-ing' (see
Norman, 1988). Small collections of apparently authentic exhibits are now
to be found in many pubs and restaurants.

At the same time, museums have become more like commercial
businesses:

> the enterprise and flair of the High St is diffusing in the world of
> museums. . . . Packaging means establishing a corporate identity. . . . Shop-
> ping is not just making a purchase, it is about the whole experience, including
> the ambience of the shop, the style of the staff. (Pemberton, quoted in Lumley,
> 1988: 20)

This poses particular difficulties for museum staff, who should be trying
to fashion an identity for museums different from that of commercial
enterprises. The problem has arisen because of the growth of tourist and
leisure industries (see Morton, 1988). Theme parks, shopping malls and
heritage centres have all forced museums to compete, to become much
more market-oriented, certainly to run a prominent museum 'shop' and
café, but also to mount spectacular displays as in the exceptional
historical reconstructions in the new Canadian Museum of Civilization.
The new-style heritage centres, such as the Jorvik Viking Centre in York
or the Pilgrim's Way in Canterbury, are competitors with existing
museums and challenge given notions of authenticity. In such centres
there is a curious mixing of the museum and the theatre. Everything is
meant to be authentic, even down to the smells, but nothing actually is
authentic. These centres are the product of a York-based company
Heritage Projects, whose work is perhaps the most challenging to existing
museums who will be forced to adapt even further (see Davenport, 1987).

The sovereignty of the consumer and trends in popular taste are
colluding to transform the museum's social role. It is much less the
embodiment of a single unambiguous high culture from which the over-
whelming mass of the population is excluded. Museums have become
more accessible, especially to the service and middle classes (see
Merriman, 1989, for a recent UK survey, and Heinich, 1988, on the
Pompidou Centre). In the leisure of such classes, Merriman (1989)
suggests, museum visiting, with its previously high cultural associations,
enables the acquisition of a certain cultural capital, an acquisition made
possible by the increased degree to which people are now able to 'read'
museums. This has helped museums to become important in defining
good taste, particularly as we saw earlier, the 'heritage' look. A rural
version of this is the 'country decor' look, the parameters of which are
partly defined in terms of rural museums and the 'charming' manner in
which the various quaint rooms are set out.

It is worth asking whether it is now possible to construct a museum or
heritage centre preserving just any set of objects. It certainly seems

Photograph 6.3   *Museum of the former Gestapo cells in Berlin*

possible. Some apparently unlikely museums which nevertheless succeed
are a pencil museum in Keswick, a museum of the chemical industry in
Widnes, a former Gestapo prison cells museum in Berlin (see Photograph
6.3), a Japanese prisoner-of-war museum in Singapore, a dental museum
in London, and a shoe museum in Street. However, such museums appear
to work because some connections between the past and the present are
usually provided by place. It may sometimes be provided by occupation,
industry, famous person or event. However, some museums/heritage
centres do not work, such as a wild West heritage park which was located
in the Rhondda Valley in South Wales; it seems that potential visitors did
not view this as an appropriate location.

So it is clear that museums cannot be created about anything anywhere.
But a museum on almost any topic can be created somewhere. A lot more
museums will emerge in the next few years although whether we should
still refer to them as 'museums' is increasingly doubtful. The very term
'museum' stems from a period of high art and auratic culture well before
'heritage' had been invented.

7

TOURISM, CULTURE AND SOCIAL INEQUALITY

Introduction

I have shown some of the connections between tourist practices and many other social phenomena. These are complex, partly because of the diverse nature of tourism and partly because other social phenomena increasingly involve elements of the tourist gaze. There is a universalisation of the tourist gaze in postmodern cultures – a universalisation which in Britain mainly takes the form of a vernacular and heritage reshaping of much of the urban and rural landscape.

None of the theories outlined in chapter 1 are in themselves adequate to grasp the 'essence' of tourism, which is multi-faceted and particularly bound up with many other social and cultural elements in contemporary societies. It is inappropriate to think that it is possible to devise 'the theory of tourist behaviour'. Instead what is required is a range of concepts and arguments which capture both what is specific to tourism and what is common to tourist and certain non-tourist social practices. The concept of the tourist gaze attempts to do this. I categorised objects of the gaze in terms of romantic/collective, historical/modern, and authentic/inauthentic. Central to such objects is some notion of departure, particularly that there are distinct contrasts between what people routinely see and experience and what is extraordinary, the extraordinary sometimes taking the form of a liminal zone. The following are relevant to understanding the changing sociology of the tourist gaze: the social tone of different places; the globalisation and the universalisation of the tourist gaze; the processes of consuming tourist services; tourist meanings and signs; modernism and postmodernism; history, heritage and the vernacular; and post-tourism and play. Different gazes and hence different tourist practices are authorised in terms of a variety of discourses. These include education, as in the Grand Tour; enlightenment, as in much individual 'travel' and cultural tourism; health, as in tourism designed to 'restore' the individual to healthy functioning; group solidarity, as in many Japanese tourist practices; and play, as in the case of the post-tourist.

I shall now consider what is meant by the visual aspects of the gaze, by the idea of seeing and in turn being seen, and will bring together the various arguments on social divisions and tourism, especially with regard to gender and ethnicity. I will reconsider the simulated character of the contemporary cultural experience, so-called 'hyper-reality' and the construction of themes and the notions of cultural and educational tourism – developments which bring us back to the certain elements of the Grand Tour and which imply that further transformations are occurring in the complex relationships between work, leisure and holidays.

Seeing and being seen

Mass tourism is a characteristic of modern societies. It could only develop when a variety of economic, urban, infrastructural and attitudinal changes had transformed the social experiences of large sections of the population of European societies during the course of the nineteenth century. The way these changes worked themselves out in Britain were illustrated by analysing the causes and consequences of the growth of a new urban form, the seaside resort.

But there was one aspect of nineteenth-century developments which I did not describe in any detail. This concerns the emergence of relatively novel modes of visual perception which became part of the modern experience of living and visiting new urban centres, particularly the grand capital cities. Here I shall show the nature of this new mode of visual perception, the connections between it and the growth of the tourist gaze, and the centrality of photography to these processes. The immensely expanding popularity of photography in the later nineteenth century indicates the importance of these new forms of visual perception, and their role in structuring the tourist gaze that was emerging in this period. This new mode of visual experience has been eloquently characterised by Berman, who sees in the rebuilding of Paris during the Second Empire in the mid-nineteenth century the construction of the conditions for the quintessentially modern experience (see Berman, 1983: section 3). It is also one of the most celebrated of tourist gazes.

For Berman what is of central importance to Paris in this period is the reconstruction of urban space which permits new ways of seeing and being seen. This was engendered by the massive rebuilding of Paris by Haussmann, who blasted a vast network of new boulevards through the heart of the old medieval city. The rebuilding of Paris displaced 350,000 people; by 1870 one-fifth of the streets of central Paris were Haussmann's creation; and at the height of the reconstruction one in five of all workers in the capital was employed in construction (see Clark, 1984: 37).

The boulevards were central to this planned reconstruction – they were like arteries in a massive circulatory system, and were partly at least to be functional for rapid troop movements. However, they also restructured what could be seen or gazed upon. Haussmann's plan entailed the building of markets, bridges, parks, the Opera and other cultural palaces, with many located at the end of the various boulevards. Such boulevards came to structure the gaze, both of Parisians and later of visitors. For the first time in a major city people could see well into the distance and indeed see where they were going and where they had come from. Great sweeping vistas were designed so that each walk led to a dramatic climax. As Berman says: 'All these qualities helped to make Paris a uniquely enticing spectacle, a visual and sensual feast . . . after centuries of life as a cluster of isolated cells, Paris was becoming a unified physical and human space' (1983: 151). Certain of these spectacular views have come to be signifiers of the entity 'Paris' (as opposed to the individual districts).

These boulevards brought enormous numbers of people together in ways that were relatively novel. The street level was lined with many small businesses, shops and especially cafés. The last of these have come to be known all over the world as signs of *la vie Parisienne*, particularly as generations of painters, writers and photographers have represented the patterns of life in and around them, beginning with the Impressionists in the 1860s (see Berman, 1983: 151; Clark, 1984).

In particular Berman talks of the way in which the boulevards and cafés created a new kind of space, especially one where lovers could be 'private in public', intimately together without being physically alone (1983: 152). Lovers caught up in the extraordinary movement of modern Paris in the 1860s and 1870s could experience their emotional commitment particularly intensely. It was the traffic of people and horses that transformed social experience in this modern urban area. Urban life was both exceptionally rich and full of possibilities; and at the same time it was dangerous and frightening. As Baudelaire wrote: 'I was crossing the boulevard, in a great hurry, in the midst of a moving chaos, with death galloping at me from every side' (Berman, 1983: 159). To be private in the midst of such danger and chaos created the perfect romantic setting of modern times; and millions of visitors have attempted to re-experience that particular quality among the boulevards and cafés of Paris.

This romantic experience could be felt especially intensely in front of the endless parades of strangers moving up and down the boulevards – it was those strangers they gazed upon and who in turn gazed at them. Part then of the gaze in the new modern city of Paris was of the multitude of passers-by, who both enhanced the lovers' vision of themselves and in turn provided an endlessly fascinating source of curiosity.

> They could weave veils of fantasy around the multitude of passers-by: who were these people, where did they come from and where were they going, what did they want, whom did they love? The more they saw of others and showed themselves to others – the more they participated in the extended 'family of eyes' – the richer became their vision of themselves. (Berman, 1983: 152)

Haussmann's reconstruction of Paris was not of course without its intense critics (see Clark, 1984: 41–50). It was very forcibly pointed out that demolishing the old *quartiers* meant that much of the working class was forced out of the centre of Paris, particularly because of the exceptionally high rents charged in the lavish apartment blocks that lined the new boulevards. Reconstruction therefore led to rapid residential segregation and to the worst signs of deprivation and squalor being removed from the gaze of richer Parisians and, later in the century, of visitors. Second, Paris was said to be increasingly a city of vice, vulgarity and display – ostentation not luxury, frippery not fashion, consumption not trade (see Clark, 1984: 46–7). It was a city of uncertainty in which there were too many surfaces, too few boundaries. It was the city of the *flâneur* or stroller. The anonymity of the crowd provided an asylum for those on the margins of society who were able to move about unnoticed, observing and being observed, but never really interacting with those encountered. The *flâneur* was the modern hero, able to travel, to arrive, to gaze, to move on, to be anonymous, to be in a liminal zone (see Benjamin, 1973; Wolff, 1985).

The *flâneur* was invariably male and this rendered invisible the different ways in which women were both more restricted to the private sphere and at the same time were coming to colonise other emerging public spheres in the late nineteenth century, especially the department store (see Wolff, 1985). The strolling *flâneur* was a forerunner of the twentieth-century tourist and in particular of *the* activity which has in a way become emblematic of the tourist: the democratised taking of photographs – of being seen and recorded and seeing others and recording them.

Sontag explicitly makes this link between the *flâneur* and photography. The latter:

> first comes into its own as an extension of the eye of the middle-class *flâneur*. . . . The photographer is an armed version of the solitary walker reconnoitering, stalking, cruising the urban inferno, the voyeuristic stroller who discovers the city as a landscape of voluptuous extremes. Adept of the joys of watching, connoisseur of empathy, the *flâneur* finds the world 'picturesque'. (1979: 55)

While the middle-class *flâneur* was attracted to the city's dark seamy corners, the twentieth-century photographer is attracted everywhere, to every possible object, event and person. And at the same time the photographer is also observed and photographed. One is both see-er and seen. To be a photographer in the twentieth century, and that is so much part of travel and tourism, is also to be seen and photographed.

There has been an enormous proliferation of photographic images since the invention of photography in 1839. Over that century and a half there has been an utter insatiability of the photographing eye, an insatiability that teaches new ways of looking at the world and new forms of authority for doing so. But it is crucial to understand that photography is a socially constructed way of seeing and recording. As such it has a number of central characteristics (on the following see Sontag, 1979; Berger, 1972; Barthes, 1981; Albers and James, 1988).

1 To photograph is in some way to appropriate the object being photographed. It is a power/knowledge relationship. To have visual

knowledge of an object is in part to have power, even if only momentarily, over it. Photography tames the object of the gaze, the most striking examples being of exotic cultures. In the USA the railway companies did much to create 'Indian' attractions to be photographed, carefully selecting those tribes with a particularly 'picturesque and ancient' appearance (see Albers and James, 1988: 151).

2   Photography *seems* to be a means of transcribing reality. The images produced appear to be not statements about the world but pieces of it, or even miniature slices of reality. A photograph thus seems to furnish evidence that something did indeed happen – that someone really was there or that the mountain actually was that large. It is thought that the camera does not lie.

3   Yet in fact photographs are the outcome of an active signifying practice in which those taking the photo select, structure and shape what is going to be taken. In particular there is the attempt to construct idealised images which beautify the object being photographed. Sontag summarises: 'the aestheticizing tendency of photography is such that the medium which conveys distress ends by neutralizing it' (1979: 109).

4   The power of the photograph thus stems from its ability to pass itself off as a miniaturisation of the real, without revealing either its constructed nature or its ideological content.

5   As everyone becomes a photographer so everyone also becomes an amateur semiotician. One learns that a thatched cottage with roses round the door represents 'ye olde England'; or that waves crashing on to rocks signifies 'wild, untamed nature'; or, especially, that a person with a camera draped around his/her neck is clearly a 'tourist'.

6   Photography involves the democratisation of all forms of human experience, both by turning everything into photographic images and by enabling anyone to photograph them. Photography is then part of the process of postmodernisation. Each thing or person photographed becomes equivalent to the other, equally interesting or uninteresting. Barthes notes that photography began with photographs of the notable and has ended up making notable whatever is photographed (1981: 34, and see Sontag, 1979: 111). Photography is a promiscuous way of seeing which cannot be limited to an elite, as art. Sontag talks of photography's 'zeal for debunking the high culture of the past . . . its conscientious courting of vulgarity . . . its skill in reconciling avant-garde ambitions with the rewards of commercialism . . . its transformation of art into cultural document' (1979: 131).

7   Photography gives shape to travel. It is the reason for stopping, to take (snap) a photograph, and then to move on. Photography involves obligations. People feel that they must not miss seeing particular scenes since otherwise the photo-opportunities will be missed. Tourist agencies spend much time indicating where photographs should be taken (so-called viewing points). Indeed much tourism becomes in effect a search for the photogenic; travel is a strategy for the accumulation of photographs. This

seems particularly to appeal to those cultures with a very strong work ethic. Japanese, Americans and Germans all seem to 'have' to take photographs – it is a kind of leisure equivalent of the distorting obligations of a strong workplace culture (see Sontag, 1979).

8   Involved in much tourism is a kind of hermeneutic circle. What is sought for in a holiday is a set of photographic images, as seen in tour company brochures or on TV programmes. While the tourist is away, this then moves on to a tracking down and capturing of those images for oneself. And it ends up with travellers demonstrating that they really have been there by showing their version of the images that they had seen originally before they set off.

Photography is thus intimately bound up with the tourist gaze. Photographic images organise our anticipation or daydreaming about the places we might gaze upon. When we are away we record images of what we have gazed upon. And we partly choose where to go in order to capture places on film. The obtaining of photographic images in part organises our experience as tourists. And our memories of places are largely structured through photographic images and the mainly verbal text we weave around images when they are on show to others. The tourist gaze thus irreducibly involves the rapid circulation of photographic images.

Social divisions and the tourist gaze

In much of the earlier discussion I emphasised the importance of social class divisions in structuring how tourist developments occurred in different ways in different places. For example, the respective social tone of different resorts and the patterns of landholding; the importance of the aristocratic connection in constructing the fashionability of certain places; the growth of the middle-class family holiday and the development of the bungalow as a specialised building form by the seaside; the importance of the 'romantic gaze' and its role in constructing nature as an absolutely central positional good; the character of the 'collective' gaze and the role of others like oneself in constituting the attraction of certain places; and the enhanced cultural capital of the service class and its impact in heightening the appeal of rural and industrial heritage, and of postmodernism.

I shall now broaden this discussion to consider some of the ways that generation, gender and ethnicity interconnect with class. These interconnections are important in forming the preferences that different social groupings develop about where to visit and in structuring the effects of such visits upon host populations. There are two key issues here: the social composition of fellow tourists and the social composition of those living in the places visited. These are important because of the way that most tourist practices involve movement into and through various sorts of public space – such as beaches, shops, restaurants, hotels, pump rooms, promenades, airports, swimming pools and squares. In such spaces people both gaze at and are gazed upon by others (and photograph and are photographed). Complex preferences have come to develop for the range of appropriate others that different social groups expect to look at in different places; and in turn different expectations are held by different social groups about who are appropriate others to gaze at oneself. Part of what is involved in tourism is the purchase of a particular social experience, and this depends upon a specifiable composition of the others with whom that experience is being shared in one way or another.

However, these preferences cannot be reduced solely to issues of social class. One different kind of argument was developed in chapter 3 with regard to the development of sex-tourism in certain South-East Asian societies. Here the combination of relations of gender and ethnic subordination had colluded to help construct very young Asian women as objects of a tourist/sexual gaze for male visitors from other societies which are in a sense ethnically dominant. The resulting tourist patterns cannot be analysed separately from relations of gender and racial subordination.

The importance of gender inequalities can be seen in another way. It is clear that in most societies men have enjoyed a higher standard of living than women. In Britain this has resulted from a privileged treatment in the household's distribution of food, heat and other material resources; and from the ability to escape the home to spend large amounts of leisure time in the 'masculine republic' of the pub, where at least 15 per cent of the household income was spent (see Hart, 1989, for an insightful analysis of the implications of this for politics). To the extent to which contemporary leisure patterns are more 'privatised' and shared, this may involve a reduced inequality of both household income and leisure time.

This relates in an important way to the development of holidays. Until the nineteenth century access to travel was largely the preserve of men. But this changed with the development of 'Victorian lady travellers', some of whom visited countries that were at the time considered 'uncivilised' and 'uncharted' (see Enloe, 1989: ch. 2). Other women took advantage of Cook's tours. As one woman wrote: 'We would venture anywhere with such a guide and guardian as Mr Cook' (quoted in Enloe, 1989: 29). From then onwards access to holidays has not been so unequally distributed as has access to some other forms of leisure, especially leisure time spent in the pub or bar. Working-class holidays to English seaside resorts were normally undertaken by couples. Moreover, the fact that such holidays developed first in industrial Lancashire was partly the result of high levels of female employment in the cotton textile industry, especially in weaving. This meant that household earnings were higher than in other areas and women had more say over its distribution. So there is a sense that the development of the couple-based holiday has been a major mechansim for reducing some of the obvious inequalities of leisure access between the sexes and is something that has partly resulted from women's own economic activities.

The early forms of mass tourism were based around the heterosexual couple; during the course of the nineteenth century the holiday unit had increasingly come to be made up of such a couple plus their children. And by the inter-war period the family holiday had become very much child-centred. This was given a significant boost by the development of the holiday camp in the 1930s in which child-based activities were central. Their development was of benefit to women since it meant that a considerable amount of child care was undertaken by paid workers. The more recent growth of self-catering has moved in the opposite direction. Only a minority of holidays in Britain are now taken in serviced accommodation.

It is important to note how holiday-making could be described as overwhelmingly heterosexual, involving actual couples, with or without children, or potential couples. In the material produced by tour operators there are three predominant advertising images. These are the 'family holiday', that is a couple with two or three healthy school-age children; the 'romantic holiday', that is a heterosexual couple on their own gazing at the sunset (indeed the sunset is a signifier for romance); and the 'fun holiday', that is same-sex groups each looking for other-sex partners for 'fun'. There is also, as we have noted, the 'sex holiday' for men. It is well known that social groups that do not fall into any of these particular categories are poorly served by the tourist industry. Many criticisms have been made of how difficult holiday-making is for single people, sole-parent families, homosexual couples or groups, and those who are disabled.

Another social category is partly excluded from conventional holiday-making, namely black Britons. The advertising material produced by holiday companies shows that tourist are white; there are simply no black faces amongst the holiday-makers. Indeed if there are any non-white faces in the photographs it is presumed that they are the 'exotic natives' being gazed upon. The same process would seem to occur in those areas in Britain which attract large numbers of foreign tourists. If black or Asian people are seen there it would be presumed that they were visitors from overseas, or perhaps service workers, but not British residents themselves on holiday. The countryside particularly is constructed as 'white'.

An interesting question is the degree to which members of ethnic minorities do undertake western-type holidays. Clearly, relatively low incomes will make the rate of non-holiday-making higher than the UK average of 30 per cent (in any year). But it is also the case that aspects of the western holiday, in which one travels elsewhere simply because of the sun, hotel or scenery, form a cultural practice which must seem rather idiosyncratic at least to recent immigrants to Britain. The obsession of white people to darken their skins and thereby increase the possibilities of acquiring skin cancer must leave black and Asian people both excluded and perplexed. Many recent immigrants at least would consider that travel should have a more serious purpose than this: to look for work, to join the rest of one's family, or to visit relatives.

Many of the recent tourist developments discussed in this book are also likely to exclude many ethnic groups. On the one hand are the temples of consumerism, the new shopping centres, which I will discuss later. These clearly require considerable income for full participation; they also require a strong commitment to the values of a credit-based consumerism. This is certainly likely to make many citizens from Asia feel remarkably estranged. On the other hand, there is the heritage industry discussed in the previous chapter. It was noted that such a heritage is overwhelmingly populated by white faces. For example, in the new award-winning Maritime Museum in the Albert Dock in Liverpool there is a substantial section on the trade union history of the docks, but nothing on the complex patterns of ethnic subordination which has produced in Liverpool one of the most racist cities in Britain. Moreover, the first heritage attraction in Britain portraying black culture is now planned for Birkenhead, near Liverpool. Astonishingly, it will reconstruct life on board a ship built locally for the slavery-supporting Confederates in the American Civil War. One might also wonder whether part of the attraction of heritage for many white visitors is precisely the fact that it is seen as predominantly white – while many larger cities are disapprovingly viewed as having become 'multicultural'.

Ethnic groups are not unimportant in the British tourist industry, and in some respects play a key role. They are likely to be employed in those enterprises concerned with servicing visitors, especially in the major cities, apart incidentally from Liverpool. Almost 10 per cent of workers from Pakistan and Bangladesh, and 20 per cent of workers from the Mediterranean, the Middle East and Latin American countries are employed in the hotel and catering industry (Bagguley, 1987). In some parts of Britain there is a remarkable concentration. In central London hotels, for example, 45 per cent of those employed are from 'black' ethnic groups. This is partly for the general reason that the majority of these jobs are badly paid, with poor conditions of employment and low levels of unionisation. White workers will tend to avoid such jobs; they are concentrated in other sectors of the economy where structural racial disadvantage discriminates against 'blacks'. The concentration of employment is also because a number of employers in hotel and catering in the past specifically recruited abroad, such as Grand Metropolitan. Such firms provided both transport and work permits for migrant workers. Although this does not now happen so clearly, there are still about 115,000 foreign nationals employed in the hotel and catering industry (Bagguley, 1987: 35).

In recent years certain ethnic groups have come to be constructed as part of the 'attraction' of some places. This is most common in the case of Asian rather than Afro-Caribbean groups. In Manchester this has occurred around its collection of outstanding restaurants in a small localised area, and resulted from the internationalisation of British culinary taste in the postwar period (although this is less pronounced than in the USA; see Frieden and Sagalyn, 1989: 199–201), as well as from a cultural reinterpretation of racial difference. By the 1980s city planners were committed to a new vision of 'Chinatown', reconstructed and conserved as a now desirable object of the tourist gaze (see Anderson, 1988, on the similar process in Vancouver).

Bradford is a more distinctive example, since it had no tourist industry until 1980. It was a prime example of an industrial city of dark satanic mills. The setting up of a tourism initiative was self-consciously undertaken when it was realised that Bradford had a number of ingredients likely to appeal to the short-break holiday-maker. These were, apart from plenty of hotel beds, proximity to internationally renowned attractions such as Haworth and the Dales and Moors; a substantially intact industrial heritage of buildings, railways and canals derived from Bradford's status as 'Worstedopolis'; its location within the high-profile county of Yorkshire; and the existence of a large and vigorous Asian community which had generated a plethora of small enterprises.

The city council, moreover, realised that turning Bradford into a tourist mecca was itself a newsworthy item. They received considerable free publicity in the early 1980s as they launched their tourism initiative (such publicity being worth at least £250,000). One element in later campaigns has been to market the Asian community as a major visitor attraction. A separate booklet was produced entitled 'Flavours of Asia'. This details fifty 'Asian' restaurants, the largest Asian store in Europe, various curry tours, a dozen sari centres as well as a brief history of various Asian religions and of the patterns of immigration to Bradford. Consideration is now being given to developing a museum and a festival to complete the visitor's Asian experience in Bradford (see Davies, 1987).

Further analysis of this would need to explore the social effects for those of Asian origin of becoming constructed as an exotic object and whether this distorts patterns of economic and political development; and the effects on the white population of coming to view those of Asian origin as not so much threatening or even inferior but as exotic, as curiously different and possessing a rich and in part attractive culture. Such debates are developing in the context of a number of cultures taken to be exotically different. These issues arise not only in the case of those exceptionally inauthentic ethnic constructions but also where the representations are reasonably scholarly.

Themes and malls

If an ethnic group living in an area is sometimes constructed and presented as a visitor attraction, another way of expressing this is to say that ethnic difference, the 'exotic', may sometimes function as a 'theme'. In this section I shall discuss the themed character of urban and rural life directly, considering some aspects of recent theme parks before turning to the themed character of contemporary retailing, noting especially the features of the ubiquitous shopping mall.

There is an increasingly pervasive tendency to divide up Britain spatially. A series of new place names has been invented for the tourist. In the north of England there is 'Last of the Summer Wine Country', 'Emmerdale Farm Country', 'James Herriot Country', 'Robin Hood Country', 'Catherine Cookson Country', 'Brontë Country' and so on. Space is divided up in terms of signs which signify particular themes – but not themes that necessarily relate to actual historical or geographical processes. A similar process can be seen in Canada where the theme of 'Maritimicity' has been clearly developed since the 1920s as a result of the provincial state and private capital seeking to develop modern tourism in Nova Scotia. McKay describes it as 'a peculiar petit-bourgeois rhetoric of lobster pots, grizzled fishermen, wharves and schooners . . . a Golden Age mythology in a region that has become economically dependent on tourism' (1988: 30). In particular Peggy's Cove has over the years become a purer and purer simulacrum, a copy of a prosperous and tranquil fishing village which never existed.

Even stranger is the case of the recently opened Granada Studios in Manchester. Part of the display consists of a mock-up of certain sets from the soap opera *Coronation Street*, including the famous Rover's Return public house (see Photograph 7.1). This is very popular with visitors, who are keen to photograph it. But as one commentator noted: 'when we develop our photos of that Rover's Return scenario we will consume a representation of a representation of a representation' (Goodwin, 1989). This set is part of the 'Coronation Street Experience' in which the Rover's Return is given a fictional history, starting in 1902.

Other recently developed themed attractions in Britain include the Jorvik Centre in York, the Chessington World of Adventures, the Camelot theme park in Lancashire, the American Adventure in the Peak District, Frontierland in Morecambe, the Oxford Story, the Crusades experience in Winchester ('history brought to life'), a planned Tudor theme park in Avebury, and the Pilgrim's Way in Canterbury. The last is described in the advertising material as 'a pilgrimage to the past'. However, the sense of history is exceptionally distorted. Faulks summarises one bizarre aspect: 'a man on children's television is the model for a dummy who is the adjunct to a non-existent scene in a mediaeval religious poem, none of whose words you hear' (Faulks, 1988).

Another distinctive example is to be found in Llandrindod Wells in Wales. Once a year most of the population dress up in Edwardian costume, but it has recently been suggested that the population could be dressed that way *for the entire year*. Thus the whole town and its population would be turned into a permanent Edwardian themed town. Already Visby in Sweden, an island in the Baltic, experiences a 'medieval week' when everyone dresses up in medieval costume.

Photograph 7.1   *Coronation Street*

This is, in Debord's terms, a 'society of the spectacle' (1983) or what Eco describes as 'travels in hyper-reality' (1986). In such themed areas the objects observed must seem real and absolutely authentic. Those responsible for Jorvik or the Oxford Story have attempted to make the experience authentic, through the use of smells as well as visual and aural simulation. The scenes are in a sense more real than the original, hyper-real in other words. Or at least the surfaces, as grasped through the immediate senses, are more real. Lowenthal notes that 'habituation to replicas tends to persuade us that antiquities should look complete and "new"' (1985: 293). The representations thus approximate more closely to our expectations of reality, of the signs that we carry around waiting to be instantiated: 'Disneyland tells us that faked nature corresponds much more to our daydream demands . . . Disneyland tells us that technology can give us more reality than nature can' (Eco, 1986: 44).

This is currently being taken to the extreme in New Zealand. A popular nineteenth-century tourist attraction was a set of pink and white terraces rising up above Lake Rotomahana. These were destroyed by volcanic eruptions in 1886 although photographs of them have remained popular ever since. They are a well-known attraction even if they have not existed for a century. Now, however, there is a plan to recreate the physical attraction by running geothermal water over artificially built terraces in an entirely different location, but one close to existing tourist facilities. This set of what might be called themed terraces will look more authentic than the original which is only known about because of the hundred-year-old photographic images.

This technological ability to create new themes which appear more real than the original has now spread from tourist attractions *per se*, beginning with Disneyland, to shopping centres or malls. Some north American malls are now extraordinary tourist attractions in their own right and represent an exceptional degree of cultural de-differentiation, as discussed in chapter 5. See Photograph 7.2 and consider the following publicity material for the West Edmonton Mall:

> Imagine visiting Disneyland, Malibu Beach, Bourbon Street, the San Diego Zoo, Rodeo Drive in Beverly Hills and Australia's Great Barrier Reef. . .in one weekend – and under one roof. . . . Billed as the world's largest shopping complex of its kind, the Mall covers 110 acres and features 828 stores, 110 restaurants, 19 theatres. . .a five-acre water park with a glass dome that is over 19 storeys high. . . . Contemplate the Mall's indoor lake complete with four submarines from which you can view sharks, octopi, tropical marine life, and a replica of the Great Barrier Reef. . . . Fantasyland Hotel has given its rooms a variety of themes: one floor holds Classical Roman rooms, another '1001 Nights' Arabian rooms, another, Polynesian rooms. . . . (Travel Alberta, undated)

The mall has been stunningly successful. In 1987 it attracted over 9 million tourists, making it the third most popular tourist attraction in north America after Walt Disney World and Disneyland. It represents a symbolic rejection of the normally understood world geography in which there are distant centres with Edmonton on the periphery. What is being asserted is a new collective sense of place based on transcending the geographical barrier of distance and of place. The real-space relations of the globe are thus replaced by imaginary-space relations (Shields, 1989: 153).

This has only been possible because of the pervasiveness of tourist signs, of the rapid circulation of photographic images in particular. It is this exchange of signs which makes possible the construction of a pastiche of themes, each of which seems more real than the original, particularly because of the way that shopping malls in general emphasise newness and cleanliness: 'It is a world where Spanish galleons sail up Main Street past Marks and Spencer to put in at 'New Orleans', where everything is tame and happy shoppers mingle with smiling dolphins' (Shields, 1989: 154).

The closest to this phenomenon in Europe is the Metrocentre in Gateshead, interestingly again located in a place that has normally been considered peripheral to British and European life. It was constructed on derelict land which is part of an Enterprise Zone. The Centre was established by John Hall, a regional entrepreneur and is now owned,

Photograph 7.2 *West Edmonton shopping mall*

somewhat improbably, by the Church Commissioners. It contains 3 miles of shopping malls with 300 shops, 40 restaurants, a 10-screen cinema, a bowling alley, an enormous fantasy kingdom of fairground rides and entertainments, a crèche, and three themed areas. These themes are 'Antique Village', with a phoney waterwheel and plastic ducks on the village pond; a 'Roman Forum', with areas on which to recline Roman-style; and a 'Mediterranean Village', with Italian, Greek and Lebanese restaurants lining a windingly quaint Mediterranean street (see Photograph 7.3). Shopping is clearly here only part of the appeal of the mall, which is as much concerned with leisure and with tourism. Within a few minutes' walk one can consume a range of tourist themes, can stroll gazing and being gazed upon as though 'on holiday', and can experience an enormous range of entertainment services (on malls in general, see Shields, 1989).

Malls represent membership of a community of consumers. To be in attendance at the 'court of commodities' is to assert one's existence and to be recognised as a citizen in contemporary society, that is, as a consumer. However, the recent marketing philosophy for the 1980s has been to develop spectacles of 'diversity and market segmentation', although this is less clear in the case of mass middle-class malls such as the Metrocentre. The development of such differentiation in particular centres is 'because the display of difference will today increase a centre's "tourist" appeal to everyone else from elsewhere' (Morris, 1988: 205). The 'everyone else' means everyone within the same market segment. Trump Tower in New York is the ultimate upper-middle-class white shopping mall (see Photograph 7.5)

Developments of this sort also represent the changing nature of public space in contemporary societies. An increasingly central role is being played by privately owned and controlled consumption spaces. These involve high levels of surveillance where certain types of behaviour, clothing and comportment are expected, such as not sitting on the floor. The entrance and pathways of malls are 'policed' and undesirable categories of the population, such as the homeless or ethnic minorities, can be excluded. The Metrocentre boasts that it is safest place in Britain to shop. There are some analogies between Bentham's panopticon prison and the visual and electronic surveillance found in these malls. They are also conspicuous for cleanliness and newness, with no space for untidy litter, the old, the shabby or the worn. Malls have to exude up-to-dateness and fashionability which is why they have to be regularly refurbished (see Fiske, 1989: 39–42).

It is suggested that malls attract their share of 'post-shoppers', people who play at being consumers in complex, self-conscious mockery. Users should not be seen simply as victims of consumerism, as 'credit card junkies', but also as being able to assert their independence from the mall developers. This is achieved by *flânerie*, by continuing to stroll, to gaze, and to be gazed upon: 'Their wandering footsteps, the modes of their

Photograph 7.3   *The Mediterranean Village in the Metrocentre,*
Gateshead

Photograph 7.4   South Street Seaport, New York (basically a new
shopping centre designed to look 'historic')

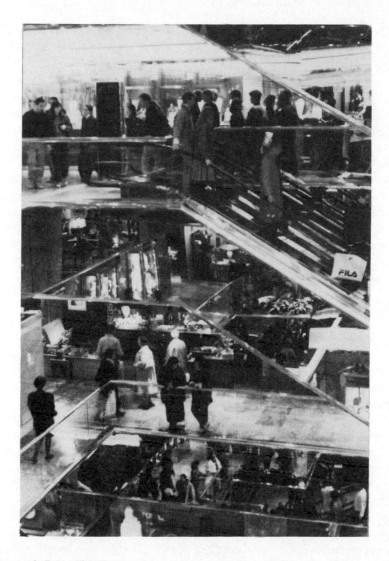

Photograph 7.5   *The Trump Tower, New York*

crowd practice constitute that certain urban ambiance: a continuous
reassertion of the rights and freedoms of the marketplace, the
communitas of the carnival' (Shields, 1989: 161).

In an Australian study Pressdee showed that in spite of the control
mechanisms in such malls 80 per cent of unemployed young people visited
them at least once a week, and that more or less 100 per cent of young
unemployed women were regular visitors (1986). Late-night shopping on
Thursday was a particular occasion when the mall was invaded by young

people with little intention to buy. The youths consumed images and space instead of commodities. Fiske talks of:

> a kind of sensuous consumption that did not create profits. The positive pleasure of parading up and down, of offending 'real' consumers and the gents of law and order, of asserting their difference within, and different use of, the cathedral of consumerism became an oppositional cultural practice. (1989: 17)

Fiske also points out the central importance of shops as public, or at least semi-public, spaces which are particularly attractive to women (1989; and see Morris, 1988). I noted earlier the importance of the nineteenth-century development of the department store in this respect, that it was both respectable and safe for unattached women. Zola described the department store as: 'a temple to women, making a legion of shop assistants burn incense before her' (quoted in Pevsner, 1970: 269). The mall is somewhat similar, and indeed shopping is a sphere of social activity in which women are empowered. It links together the public and the domestic and involves activity in which women are permitted to demonstrate competence.

Finally, one should note a further setting for themed environments which have become particularly popular in the last decade or two: world fairs, which have developed into enormous international tourist attractions. For example, over 22 million people attended the 1986 Expo in Vancouver (see Ley and Olds, 1988, for further analysis). The development and popularity of these fairs represent the growing intrusion of leisure, tourism and the aesthetic into the urban landscape. They provide further examples of the de-differentiation of leisure, tourism, shopping, culture, education, eating, and so on.

Most of the 1988 Expo in Brisbane was organised around different national displays. There were well over fifty themed environments based on different national stereotypes, such as the British pub, American achievement in sport, the German beer garden and South Sea Islands exotic dancing. Such themes were designed to demonstrate national pride in the cultural activities presumed specific to that country. Generally this pride was demonstrated either in repackaging aspects of that country's traditions and heritage or in demonstrating the high level of modern technology achieved. The display generally thought the most interesting (measured by the length of the queues to enter) was that of the Japanese, which combined both aspects, with, for example, high-technology representations of traditionally venerated dancing animals.

As with the Vancouver Expo, no single hegemonic set of messages was conveyed by the fair. Indeed they are such obviously postmodern phenomena that this would be difficult to achieve. Such fairs are, if anything, a kind of micro-version of international tourism. Rather than tourists having to travel worldwide to experience and gaze upon these different signs, they are conveniently brought together in one location, simply on a larger scale than the West Edmonton mall. Harvey says more generally:

'it is now possible to experience the world's geography vicariously, as a simulacrum' (1989: 300). This can be seen from the entertainment provided at such world fairs. At Vancouver there were 43,000 free on-site performances given by an incredible 80,000 performers (Ley and Olds, 1988: 203). Although there was high culture, including a presentation from La Scala to an audience of 40,000, most entertainment consisted of folk or popular forms, all in all a postmodern cultural pastiche, rather like the availability of cuisines from around the world in most major American cities (see Harvey, 1989: 300). Most performances were recognisably from a specific country and consisted of the sort of ethnic entertainment that is provided for tourists in each country that they visit. The difference here was that the visitors only had to walk from one tent or display to the next in order to gaze upon another cultural event signifying a further nation.

What people thus do in such a fair is to stroll, to be a *flâneur*, and what they stroll between are signs of different cultures. Therefore whether they are locals or visitors from outside the city hosting the fair, they are acting as tourists, gazing upon the signs of different cultures. People can do in an afternoon what otherwise takes a lifetime: gaze upon and collect signs of dozens of different cultures – the built environment, cultural artefacts, meals, and live, ethnic entertainment.

Many of the displays purport to be educational, and indeed groups of school-age children constitute a major category of visitors. And this is a further feature of the de-differentiation of the cultural spheres noted earlier. Education and entertainment are becoming merged, a process very much assisted by the increasingly central role of the visual media in both. Indeed some of the latest theme parks are involved in the provision of 'edu-tainment'. It is this topic, the relationships of tourism and education and culture that I shall now consider.

Education and entertainment

In chapter 1 it was noted that the development of mass tourism was an aspect of the separation of work and leisure that characterised social development in the nineteenth century, as both work and leisure became characterised by increasing rationalisation. The emergence of mass tourism at the end of the century was a further aspect of this separation. Tourism came to be systematised and organised. It was the antithesis of work and of education and learning.

The main exception to these patterns had been in the Grand Tour, undertaken mainly by the sons of the wealthy. Such 'tourism' was not a leisure activity undertaken while away from work since those involved were not in work; and it did not involve an absence of learning and education – these were important elements of the tour.

I shall bring the argument full circle by suggesting that contemporary

tourism is in part taking on some of these characteristics of the Grand
Tour. This can be seen in the way that a substantial proportion of the
population enjoys increased periods of time away from paid work. Often
this is described as increased 'leisure' time. But this is a misleading term,
since, especially for women, 'leisure' involves 'work'. However, there is
for many people more time away from paid work, because of increased
paid holidays for those in paid work, a rising proportion of the population who are in retirement, a high number of people unemployed or
underemployed, and an increasing proportion of people in part-time
work, particularly women. Work and non-work are more variable and
flexible in comparison with the past, especially in the case of men.
Holidays therefore do not have to offer such dramatic contrasts with paid
work as previously. They need not only involve two weeks of 'seaside
fun'.

Holidays are not so straightforwardly contrasted with education and
learning as in the past. In a wide variety of ways much tourism is coming
to be more closely interwoven with learning. I have already noted the
increasing popularity of museums, the fascination with the lives of
industrial workers in particular, and the popularity of hyper-real historical
re-creations. Some developments are the increased desire to learn a new
sport on holiday (such as skiing, watersports, hang-gliding); the development of arts and cultural tourism; the heightened attraction of unusual
industrial sites, such as Sellafield nuclear reprocessing plant which now
attracts 150,000 visitors a year; and the substantial increase in educational
holidays (in schools, universities and hotels). Trusthouse Forte now offers
a wide range of educational breaks at various hotels. Amongst the
subjects that can be studied are arts and antiques, bridge, watercolour
painting, archery, clay pigeon shooting, fly fishing, golf and pony-
trekking.

One interesting tourist site symptomatic of these new developments is
the Quarry Bank Mill at Styal in Cheshire. This water-powered cotton-
spinning mill was built by Samuel Greg in 1784. Surrounding the mill
were the buildings of an entire factory community, two chapels, a school,
shop, houses for mill workers, and an apprentice house, all of which have
remained physically well preserved. The museum was founded in 1976. It
is described as 'a museum of the factory system', aiming to bring to life
the role of the workforce, the Greg family and the circumstances which
began the industrial revolution in the textile industry. The museum houses
a number of displays on textile finishing and water power. Demon-
strators, some dressed in appropriate clothing, show visitors how to spin
cotton on a spinning jenny, how to hand-weave, how a carding machine
operated, the workings of a weaving mule, and the domestic routines
involved in cooking, cleaning and washing for the child workforce.

A great deal of research by professional historians has been undertaken
to produce both the displays and the large number of supporting
documents, given to or sold to visitors. Engineers have also been centrally

involved in the development of the museum, in order to get the often derelict machinery reworking.

Half of the visitors to the site are parties of schoolchildren and so the staff of the museum are directly involved in education. The mill has produced a range of supporting material for such visitors, including a 'Resource and Document Pack'. Up to 100 guides are employed in explaining aspects of the mill's workings to such visitors. There are also a number of other educational activities undertaken by the museum. Courses run by the mill include weaving, spinning, patchwork and quilting, embroidery and lace, experimental textiles, fashion and clothing, design for textiles, dyeing and printing, and knitting.

At the same time the mill is making energetic efforts to attract the 'non-museum visiting public' by specifically increasing the entertainment elements of display. This is partly achieved by the use of people to demonstrate many of the processes and to interact in a role-playing way with the visitors. It is also assisted by organising a variety of special events: Mothering Sunday lunches, a tent-making project, St George's Day celebration, Spooky tours, Apprentices' Christmas and so on. However, there is an obvious danger of both being seen as over-commercial and of actually being over-commercial. The commercialisation of the mill is a reflection of the tendencies towards the postmodern museum discussed in chapter 6.

The mill has had to grapple with the issue of authenticity. Although the building is genuine and has not been particularly cleaned up, the machinery does not of course stem from the eighteenth century. Some items had been in the mill since the nineteenth or early twentieth centuries, while quite a lot of it, including the immense waterwheel, has been imported from other, often derelict, industrial sites. The work on the machinery has involved using 'traditional' techniques which have had to be specially learnt. The mill does try to make explicit what is authentic, although this is not a straightforward exercise since what is thought to be authentic depends upon which particular period is being considered. Also, of course, existing 'authentic' factories contain machines from a variety of periods. What Quarry Bank Mill ultimately shows is that there is no simple 'authentic' reconstruction of history but that all involve various kinds of accommodation and reinterpretation.

Finally, the mill does not present an overly romanticised view of working-class life. There is plenty of evidence on the ill-health and squalor of much industrial work. However, the mill literature also draws considerable attention to the views of contemporaries which suggested that conditions in rural factory communities, such as Styal, were considerably better than those in the huge industrial cities, such as neighbouring Manchester and Salford. Thus there seem to have been lower levels of industrial unrest, although this could also be related to forms of surveillance and control available locally. It was also suggested by the curator that visitors would not necessarily return for further visits if an overly depressing account of factory life was represented. However, unlike some other industrial museums, Quarry Bank Mill is not a shrine to technology – if anything the textile machinery is likely to be regarded by visitors as noisy, dangerous and dirty.

The most surprising way in which the development of tourism is transforming the urban environment is in those places where a newly established cultural tourism has taken root. The best example of this in Britain is the transformation of Glasgow and its emergence as one of the centres of cultural tourism. It has been designated as the 'European City of Culture for 1990': 'Glasgow's regeneration has been largely arts-led, with the Mayfest and the opening of the Burrell collection all helping to change the city's image from a decaying industrial backwater to a dynamic growth area [attractive to tourists]' (quoted in McKellar, 1988: 14).

Two-thirds of visitors now consider that there is a wide variety of interesting museums and art galleries to visit in the city. And at least one-third think that there are so many cultural activities available that they wish they were able to stay longer. Fewer than one-fifth consider that Glasgow is the rough and depressing place to visit that once would have been the case (Myerscough, 1988: 88–9). Mysteriously but dramatically, Glasgow has become the kind of place that people now want to visit, to see and to be seen in. It has become a preferred object of the gaze of many tourists.

This transformation of Glasgow as an object of the gaze is the result of economic restructuring, social change, policy intervention and cultural re-evaluation. And part of that transformation has entailed tourism coming to be of central economic and social significance in western societies as the twenty-first century approaches. If Glasgow can be remade as a tourist attraction, one might wonder whether there are in fact any limits to the tourist, or post-tourist, gaze. And if there are few such limits what are the effects on societies whose built environment, conceptions of history, cultural symbols, social patterns and political processes, can all be in part remade as objects of the gaze?

It is already clear that the trajectories of some countries are significantly determined by tourism, such as Spain, Austria, Greece, the West Indies and Bali. But what now is happening, as tourism develops into the largest industry worldwide, is that many, or even most, other countries will become engulfed by a tourist tidal wave. This is a wave that is not confined to particular places but where almost all spaces, histories and social activities can be materially and symbolically remade for the endlessly devouring gaze, a gaze that in 1989 is partly responsible for bringing down some of the boundaries between East and West, as those in Eastern Europe have demanded the right to travel and to gaze upon those in the west. To return to Foucault, contemporary societies are developing less on the basis of surveillance and the normalisation of individuals, and more on the basis of the democratisation of the tourist gaze and the spectacle-isation of place.

BIBLIOGRAPHY

Abercrombie, N. and Urry, J. (1983) *Capital, Labour and the Middle Classes*. London: Allen & Unwin.

Abercrombie, N., Warde, A., Soothill, K., Urry J., and Walby, S. (1988) *Contemporary British Society*. Cambridge: Polity.

Adler, J. (1989) 'Origins of sightseeing', *Annals of Tourism Research*, 16: 7–29.

Aglietta, M. (1987) *A Theory of Capitalist Regulation: the US Experience*. London: Verso.

Albers, P. and James, W. (1988) 'Travel photography: a methodological approach', *Annals of Tourism Research*, 15: 134–58.

Anderson, K. (1988) 'Cultural hegemony and the race-definition process in Chinatown, Vancouver: 1880–1980', *Environment and Planning D: Society and Space*, 6: 127–49.

Artley, A. and Robinson, J. (1985) *The Official New Georgians Handbook*. London: Ebury Press.

Ashworth, P. (1986) 'Nottingham-by-Sea', *The Guardian*, 21 June.

Atkinson, J. (1984) 'Manpower strategies for flexible organisations', *Personnel Management*, August: 28–31.

Bagguley, P. (1987) *Flexibility, Restructuring and Gender. Changing Employment In Britain's Hotels*. Lancaster Regionalism Group Working Paper no. 24

Bagguley, P. (1990) 'Gender and labour flexibility in hotel and catering', *Services Industries Journal*, 10: forthcoming.

Bagguley, P., Mark-Lawson, J., Shapiro, D., Urry, J., Walby, S., Warde, A. (1989) 'Restructuring Lancaster', in Cooke P. (ed.) *Localities*. London: Unwin Hyman. pp. 129–65.

Bagguley, P., Mark-Lawson, J., Shapiro, D., Urry, J., Walby, S., Warde, A. (1990) *Restructuring. Place, Class and Gender*. London: Sage.

Ball, R. (1988) 'Seasonality: a problem for workers in the tourism labour market', *Service Industries Journal*, 8: 501–13.

Barrett, F. (1989a) *The Independent Guide to Real Holidays Abroad*. London: *The Independent*.

Barrett, F. (1989b) 'Why the tour operators may face their last supper', *The Independent*, 7 November.

Barthes, R. (1972) *Mythologies*. London: Jonathan Cape.

Barthes, R. (1979) 'The Eiffel Tower', in *The Eiffel Tower and Other Mythologies*. New York: Hill & Wang. pp. 3–17.

Barthes, R. (1981) *Camera Lucida*. New York: Hill & Wang.

Baudrillard, J. (1985) 'The ecstacy of communication', in H. Foster (ed.) *Postmodern Culture*. London: Pluto. pp. 126–34.

Baudrillard, J. (1988) *America*. London: Verso.

Baxter, L. (1989) 'Nostalgia's booming future', *The Daily Telegraph*, 21 July.

Beckerman, W. (1974) *In Defence of Economic Growth*. London: Jonathan Cape.

Bell, D. (1976) *The Cultural Contradictions of Capitalism*. London: Heinemann.

Benjamin, W. (1973) 'The work of art in the age of mechanical reproduction', in *Illuminations*. London: Fontana. pp. 219–54.

Bennett, T. (1983) 'A thousand and one troubles: Blackpool Pleasure Beach', in *Formations of Pleasure*. London: Routledge. pp. 138–55.

Bennett, T. (1986) 'Hegemony, ideology, pleasure: Blackpool', in T. Bennett, C. Mercer and J. Woollacott (eds) *Popular Culture and Social Relations*. Milton Keynes: Open University Press. pp. 135–55.

Bennett, T. (1988) 'Museums and "the people"', in R. Lumley (ed.) *The Museum Time-Machine*. London: Routledge. pp. 63–86.

Berger, J. (1972) *Ways of Escape*. Harmondsworth: Penguin.

Berman, M. (1983) *All that is Solid Melts into Air*. London: Verso.

Binney, M. (1984) *Our Vanishing Heritage*. London: Arlington Books.

Binney, M. (1988) 'Will Morecambe be wise?', *The Sunday Telegraph*, 30 October.

Blau, J. (1988) 'Where architects work: a change analysis 1970–80', in P. Knox (ed.) *The Design Professions and the Built Environment*. London: Croom Helm. pp. 127–46.

Bodgener, J. (1988) 'Bright spot on the landscape', *Financial Times*, 8 December.

Boorstin, D. (1964) *The Image: A Guide to Pseudo-Events in America*. New York: Harper.

Bourdieu, P. (1984) *Distinction*. London: Routledge & Kegan Paul.

Bruce, M. (1987) 'New technology and the future of tourism', *Tourism Management*, June: 115–20.

Brunner, E. (1945) *Holiday Making and the Holiday Trades*. Oxford: Oxford University Press.

BTA/ETB (1985) *Hotel Development in the UK*, mimeo.

BTA/ETB Research Services (1988a) *Overseas Visitor Survey*. London: BTA/ETB Research Services.

BTA/ETB (1988b) *Tourism Investment Report, Jan.–June 1988*. London: BTA/ETB.

Buck, M. (1988) 'The role of travel agent and tour operator', in B. Goodall and G. Ashworth *Marketing in the Tourism Industry*. London: Croom Helm. pp. 67–74.

Buck, N., Gordon, I., Pickvance, C. and Taylor-Gooby, P. (1989) 'The Isle of Thanet: restructuring and municipal conservatism', in P. Cooke (ed.) *Localities*. London: Unwin Hyman. pp. 166–97.

Burkart, A.J. and Medlik, S. (1974) *Tourism, Past, Present, and Future*. London: Heinemann.

Burton, R. (1989) 'Yorkshire tea and fat rascals', *The Guardian*, 25 March.

Cabinet Office (Enterprise Unit) (1983) *Pleasure, Leisure and Jobs. The Business of Tourism*. London: HMSO.

Callan, R. (1989) 'Small country hotels and hotel award schemes as a measurement of service quality', *Service Industries Journal*, 9: 223–46.

Campbell, C. (1987) *The Romantic Ethic and the Spirit of Modern Consumerism*. Oxford: Basil Blackwell.

Campbell, M. (1989) 'Fishing lore. The construction of the "Sportsman"', *Annals of Tourism Research*, 16: 76–88.

Carlzon, J. (1987) *Moments of Truth*. Cambridge, MA: Ballinger.

Chivers, T. (1973) 'The proletarianisation of a service worker', *Sociological Review*, 21: 633–56.

Clark, P. (1983) *The English Alehouse: a Social History, 1200–1830*. London: Longman.

Clark, T.J. (1984) *The Painting of Modern Life*. London: Thames & Hudson.

Clarke, J. and Critcher, C. (1985) *The Devil Makes Work*. London: Macmillan.

Cloke, P. (1989) 'Land-use planning in rural Britain', in P. Cloke (ed.) *Rural Land-Use Planning in Developed Nations*. London: Unwin Hyman. pp. 18–46.

Cohen, E. (1972) 'Towards a sociology of international tourism', *Social Research*, 39: 164–82.

Cohen, E. (1979) 'A phenomenology of tourist types', *Sociology*, 13: 179–201.

Cohen, E. (1988) 'Traditions in the qualitative sociology of tourism', *Annals of Tourism Research. Special Issue*, 15: 29–46.

Colson, F. (1926) *The Week*. Cambridge: Cambridge University Press.

Cooper, C. and Jackson, S. (1989) 'Destination life cycle. The Isle of Man study', *Annals of Tourism Research*, 16: 377–98.

Cosgrove, D. (1984) *Social Formation and Symbolic Landscape*. London: Croom Helm.

Cosgrove, I. and Jackson, R. (1972) *The Geography of Recreation and Tourism*. London: Hutchinson.

Countryside Commission (1988) *Out in the Country*. Cheltenham: Countryside Commission.

Cowen, H. (1990) 'Regency icons: Marketing Cheltenham's built environment', in M. Harloe, C. Pickvance and J. Urry (eds) *Place, Politics and Policy. Do Localities Matter?* London: Unwin Hyman. pp. 128–45.

Crick, M. (1985) '"Tracing" the anthropological self', *Social Analysis*, 17: 71–92.

Crick, M. (1988) 'Sun, sex, sights, savings and servility', *Criticism, Heresy and Interpretation*, 1: 37–76.

Culler, J. (1981) 'Semiotics of Tourism', *American Journal of Semiotics*, 1: 127–40.

Cunningham, H. (1980) *Leisure in the Industrial Revolution*. London: Croom Helm.

Daniels, S. and Cosgrove, D. (1988) 'Introduction: iconography and landscape', in D. Cosgrove and S. Daniels (eds) *The Iconography of Landscape*. Cambridge: Cambridge University Press. pp. 1–10.

Davenport, P. (1987) 'A fine future behind us', *The Times*, 3 November.

Davies, L. (1987) 'If you've got it, flaunt it', *Employment Gazette*, April: 167–71.

Deane, P. and Cole, W.A. (1962) *British Economic Growth, 1688–1959*. Cambridge: Cambridge University Press.

Debord, G. (1983) *Society of the Spectacle*. Detroit, IL: Black & Red.

Denison-Edson, P.W. (1967) 'Some aspects of a historical geography of Morecambe', BA dissertation, University of Cambridge.

Dent, K. (1975) 'Travel as education: the English landed classes in the eighteenth century', *Educational Studies*, 1: 171–80.

Dept of Employment (1971) *Manpower Studies No 10: Hotels*. London: HMSO.

Dept of Employment (1987) 'Historical supplement', *Employment Gazette*, February.

Dept of Employment (1988) *Overseas Travel and Tourism – September 1988*. Employment Dept press notice.

Dept of Transport (1988) *National Travel Survey: 1985/6 Report – Part 1. An Analysis of Personal Travel*. London: HMSO.

Dogan, H. (1989) 'Forms of adjustment. Sociocultural impacts of tourism', *Annals of Tourism Research*, 16: 216–36.

Douglas, M. (1973) *Natural Symbols; Explorations in Cosmology*. London: Barrie and Jenkins.

Eco, U. (1986): *Travels in Hyper-Reality*. London: Picador.

Economic Development (n.d.) *'I've Never Been to Wigan, but I Know What It's Like'*. Wigan: Economic Development.

Edgar, D. (1987) 'The new nostalgia', *Marxism Today*, March: 30–5.

Ehrenreich, B. (1983) *The Hearts of Men*. London: Pluto.

Ehrenreich, B. (1989) *Fear of Falling*. New York: Pantheon.

Ellis A. and Heath, A. (1983) 'Positional competition, or an offer you can't refuse', in A. Ellis and K. Kumar (1983). pp. 1–22.

Ellis, A. and Kumar, K. (eds) (1983) *Dilemmas of Liberal Democracies*. London: Tavistock.

English Tourist Board (n.d.) *Tourism Enterprise by Local Authorities*. London: English Tourist Board.

Enloe, C. (1989) *Bananas, Beaches and Bases*. London: Pandora.

ETAC (Education and Training Advisory Council) (1983) *Hotel and Catering Skills – Now and in the Future: Part II, Jobs and Skills*. Wembley: Hotel and Catering Industry Training Board.

Farrant, S. (1987) 'London by the sea: resort development on the south coast of England, 1880–1939', *Journal of Contemporary History*, 22: 137–62.

Faulks, S. (1988) 'Disney comes to Chaucerland', *The Independent*, 11 June.

Featherstone, M. (1987) 'Consumer culture, symbolic power and universalism', in G. Stauth and S. Zubaida (eds) *Mass Culture, Popular Culture, and Social Life in the Middle East*. Frankfurt: Campus. pp. 17–46.

Feifer, M. (1985) *Going Places*. London: Macmillan.

Fiske, J. (1989) *Reading the Popular*. Boston: Unwin Hyman.

Fondersmith, J. (1988) 'Downtown 2040: making cities fun', *The Futurist*, March/April: 9–17.

Foster, H. (1985a) 'Postmodernism: a preface', in H. Foster (ed.) (1985b). pp. ix–xvi.

Foster, H. (ed.) (1985b) *Postmodern Culture*. London: Pluto.

Foucault, M. (1976) *The Birth of the Clinic*. London: Tavistock.

Frampton, K. (1988) 'Place-form and cultural identity', in J. Thackara (ed.) *Design after Postmodernism*. London: Thames & Hudson. pp. 51–66.

Freeman, M. (1986) *Town-Centre Redevelopment: Architectural Styles and the Roles of Developers and Architects*. University of Birmingham Dept of Geography, Occasional Publication no. 20.

Frieden, B. and Sagalyn, L. (1989) *Downtown, Inc. How America Rebuilds Cities*. Cambridge, MA: MIT Press.

Gabriel, Y. (1988) *Working Lives in Catering*. London: Routledge.

Gershuny, J. (1987) 'The future of service employment', in O. Giarini (ed.) *The Emerging Service Economy*. Oxford: Oxford University Press. pp. 105–24.

Giddens, A. (1984) *The Constitution of Society*. Cambridge: Polity.

Glancey, J. (1988) 'Hello campers', *Landscape*, July/August: 54–5.

Goffee, R. and Scase, R. (1983) 'Class entrepreneurship and the service sector: towards a conceptual clarification', *Service Industries Journal*, 3: 146–60.

Goldthorpe, J. (1982) 'On the service class: its formation and future', in A. Giddens and G. Mackenzie (eds) *Social Class and the Division of Labour*. Cambridge: Cambridge University Press. pp. 162–85.

Goodall, B. (1988) 'Changing patterns and structures of European tourism', in B. Goodall and G. Ashworth (eds) *Marketing in the Tourism Industry*. London: Croom Helm. pp. 18–38.

Goodwin, A. (1989) 'Nothing like the real thing', *New Statesman and Society*, 12 August.

Gottlieb, A. (1982) 'Americans' vacations', *Annals of Tourism Research*, 9: 165–87.

Grass, J. (1972) 'Morecambe: The People's Pleasure. The Development of a Holiday Resort, 1880–1902', MA dissertation, University of Lancaster.

Gratton, C. and Taylor, P. (1987) *Leisure Industries. An Overview*. London: Comedia.

Graves, R. (1965) *Majorca Observed*. London: Cassell.

Greene, M. (1982) *Marketing Hotels into the 90s*. London: Heinemann.

Grove, V. (1988) 'One man's dream of a stately pleasure dome', *The Sunday Times*, 12 June.

Guerrier, Y. and Lockwood, A. (1989) 'Core and peripheral employees in hotel operations', *Personnel Review*, 18: 9–15.

Hall, S. (1988) 'Brave new world', *Marxism Today*, October: 24–9.

Halsall, M. (1986) 'Through the valley of the shadow', *The Guardian*, 27 December.

Harris, H. and Lipman, A. (1986) 'Viewpoint: A culture and despair: reflections on "postmodern" architecture', *Sociological Review*, 34: 837–54.

Harrison, B. (1971) *Drink and the Victorians*. London: Faber & Faber.

Hart, J. (1988) 'A package for Christmas', *Signature*, November/December: 18–19.

Hart, N. (1989) 'Gender and the rise and fall of class politics', *New Left Review*, 175: 19–47.

Harvey, D. (1987) 'Flexible accumulation through urbanism: reflections on "postmodernism" in the American city', *Antipode*, 19: 260–86.

Harvey, D. (1988) 'Voodoo cities', *New Statesman and Society*, 30 September: 33–5.

Harvey, D. (1989) *The Condition of Postmodernity*. Oxford: Blackwell.

Hattersley, R. (1989) 'A canny lad', *The Listener*, 19 January.

Hebdige, D. (1986–7) 'A report from the Western Front'. *Block* 12: 4–26.

Hebdige, D. (1988) *Hiding in the Light*. London: Routledge.

Heiman, M. (1989) 'Production confronts consumption: landscape perception and social conflict', *Society and Space*, 7: 165–78.

Heinich, N. (1988) 'The Pompidou Centre and its public: the limits of a utopian site', in R. Lumley (ed.) *The Museum Time-Machine*. London: Routledge. pp. 199–212.

Hennessy, S., Greenwood, J., Shaw, G. and Williams, A. (1986) *The Role of Tourism in Local Economies: a Pilot Study of Looe, Cornwall*. Tourism in Cornwall Project, Dept of Geography, University of Exeter.

Hern, A. (1967) *The Seaside Holiday*. London: Cresset Press.

Hewison, R. (1987) *The Heritage Industry*. London: Methuen.

Hirsch, F. (1978) *Social Limits to Growth*. London: Routledge & Kegan Paul.

Hirschhorn, L. (1984) *Beyond Mechanization*. Cambridge, MA: MIT Press.

Hochschild, A. (1983) *The Managed Heart, Commercialization of Human Feeling*. Berkeley: University of California Press.

Hooper-Greenhill, E. (1988) 'Counting visitors or visitors who count', in R. Lumley (ed.) *The Museum Time-Machine*. London: Routledge. pp. 213–32.

Horne, D. (1984) *The Great Museum*. London: Pluto.

Houston, L. (1986) *Strategy and Opportunities for Tourism Development*. Glasgow: Planning Exchange.

Howell, S. (1974) *The Seaside*. London: Collier Macmillan.

Hutcheon, L. (1986–7) 'The politics of postmodernism: parody and history', *Cultural Critique*, 5: 179–297.

Hutchinson, M. (1989) *The Prince of Wales: Right or Wrong?* London: Faber & Faber.

IMF (1986) *Balance of Payments Statistics*, 37, Part 2. Washington: IMF.

Jakle, J. (1985) *The Tourist*. Lincoln: University of Nebraska Press.

James, N. (1989) 'Emotional labour: skill and work in the social regulation of feelings', *Sociological Review*, 37: 15–42.

Jameson, F. (1985) 'Postmodernism and consumer culture', in H. Foster (ed.) *Postmodern Culture*. London: Pluto. pp. 111–25.

Jamieson, B. (1989) 'Bass checks into the Penthouse Suite', *The Sunday Telegraph*, 27 August.

Januszczak, W. (1987) 'Romancing the grime', *The Guardian*, 2 September.

Jeffrey, D. and Hubbard, N. (1988) 'Foreign tourism, the hotel industry and regional economic performance', *Regional Studies*, 22: 319–30.

Jencks, C. (1977) *The Language of Post-Modern Architecture*. New York: Academy.

Jenkins, S. (1987) 'Art makes a return to architecture', *The Sunday Times*, 15 November.

Johnson J. and Pooley, C. (eds) (1982) *The Structure of Nineteenth Century Cities*. London: Croom Helm.

Johnson, K. and Mignot, K. (1982) 'Marketing trade unionism to service industries: an historical analysis of the hotel industry', *Service Industries Journal*, 2: 5–23.

Jones, A. (1987) 'Green tourism', *Tourism Management*, December: 354–6.

Jones, G. (1987) 'Factories seen as attractions for tourists', *Daily Telegraph*, 28 December.

Jordonova, L. (1989) 'Objects of knowledge: a historical perspective on museums', in P. Vergo, *The New Museology*. London: Reaktion. pp. 21–40.

de Kadt, E. (1979) *Tourism: Passport to Development*. Oxford: Oxford University Press.

Key Note Report (1986) *Tourism in the UK*. London: Key Note Publications.

Key Note Report (1987) *Tourism in the UK*. London: Key Note Publications.

King, A. (1984) *The Bungalow*. London: Routledge.

Knox, P. (1987) 'The social production of the built environment', *Progress in Human Geography*, 11: 354–77.

Knox, P. (1988) 'The design professions and the built environment in a postmodern epoch', in P. Knox. (ed.) *The Design Professions and the Built Environment*. London: Croom Helm. pp. 1–11.

Krier, L. (1984) 'Berlin-Tagel' and 'Building and architecture', *Architectural Design*, 54: 87, 119.

Kroker, A. and Cook, D. (1986) *The Postmodern Scene*. New York: St Martin's.

Lancashire County Council (1987) *A Strategy for Tourism in Lancashire. Vol 4. Review and Assessment*. Preston: Lancashire County Council.

Landry, C., Montgomery, J., Worpole, K., Gratton, C. and Murray, R. (1989) *The Last Resort*. London: Comedia Consultancy/SEEDS (South East Economic Development Strategy).

Larkham, P. (1986) *The Agents of Urban Change*. University of Birmingham Dept of Geography, Occasional Publication no. 21.

Lasch, C. (1980) *The Culture of Narcissism*. London: Sphere.

Lash, S. (1990) *Sociology of Postmodernism*. London: Routledge.

Lash, S. and Urry, J. (1987) *The End of Organized Capitalism*. Cambridge: Polity.

Lawson, A. and Samson, C. (1988) 'Age, gender and adultery', *British Journal of Sociology*, 39: 409–40.

Lea, J. (1988) *Tourism and Development in the Third World*. London: Routledge.

Leadbetter, C. (1988) 'Power to the person', *Marxism Today*, October: 14–19.

Lee, J. (1988) *Press Notice*. Employment Dept, 30 November.

Leidner, R. (1987) 'Scripting service work: case studies of fast food and insurance sales', *Society for the Study of Social Problems*, Chicago, August.

Lett, J. (1983) 'Ludic and liminoid aspects of charter yacht tourism in the Caribbean', *Annals of Tourism Research*, 10: 35–56.

Levitt, T. (1981) 'Marketing intangible products and product intangibles', *The Cornell HRA Quarterly*, August: 37–44.

Lewis, B. and Outram, M. (1986) 'Customer satisfaction with package holidays', in B. Moores (ed.) *Are They Being Served?* Oxford: Philip Allan. pp. 201–13.

Ley, D. and Olds, K. (1988) 'Landscape as spectacle: world's fairs and the culture of heroic consumption', *Environment and Planning D: Society and Space*, 6: 191–212.

Lickorish, L.J. and Kershaw, A.G. (1975) 'Tourism between 1840 and 1940', in A.J. Burkart and S. Medlik (eds) *The Management of Tourism*. London: Heinemann. pp. 11–26.

Litteljohn, D. (1982) 'The role of hotel consortia in Great Britain', *Service Industries Journal*, 2: 79–91.

Lowe, P. and Goyder, J. (1983) *Environmental Groups in Politics*. London: Allen & Unwin.

Lowenthal, D. (1985) *The Past is a Foreign Country*. Cambridge: Cambridge University Press.

Lumley, R. (ed.) (1988) *The Museum Time-Machine*. London: Routledge.

Lunn, T. (1989) 'How to swing unused talent into action', *The Sunday Times*, 20 August.

Lynch, K. (1973) *What Time is this Place?* Cambridge, MA: MIT Press.

MacCannell, D. (1973) 'Staged authenticity: arrangements of social space in tourist settings', *American Sociological Review*, 79: 589–603.

MacCannell, D. (1976) *The Tourist: A New Theory of the Leisure Class*. London: Macmillan.

MacCannell, D. (1989): 'Introduction to the 1989 edition', in *The Tourist*. London: Macmillan. pp. ix–xx.

Mars, G. and Nicod, M. (1984) *The World of Waiters*. London: Allen & Unwin.

Marshall, G. (1986) 'The workplace culture of a licensed restaurant', *Theory, Culture and Society*, 3: 33–48.

Martin, B. (1982) *A Sociology of Contemporary Popular Culture*. Oxford: Blackwell.

Martin, B. and Mason, S. (1987) 'Current trends in leisure', *Leisure Studies*, 6: 93–7.

McKay, I. (1988) 'Twilight at Peggy's Cove: towards a genealogy of "maritimicity" in Nova Scotia', *Borderlines*, Summer: 29–37.

McKellar, S. (1988) 'The enterprise of culture', *Local Work*, June: 14–17.

McGhie, C. (1988) 'Lure of the village piles on pressure', *The Sunday Times*, 15 May.

McRae, H. (1989) 'The clouds gather over the sea and sun package', *The Guardian*, 12 August.

Mennell, S. (1985) *All Manners of Food*. Oxford: Blackwell.

Mercer, C. (1983) 'A poverty of desire: pleasure and popular politics', in T. Bennett (ed.) *Formations of Pleasure*. London: Routledge & Kegan Paul. pp. 84–101.

Merriman, N. (1989) 'Museum visiting as a cultural phenomenon', in P. Vergo, *The New Museology*. London: Reaktion. pp. 149–71.

Metcalf, H. (1988) 'Careers and training in tourism and leisure', *Employment Gazette*, February: 84–93.

Meyrowitz, J. (1985) *No Sense of Place. The Impact of Electronic Media on Social Behaviour*. New York: Oxford University Press.

Mills, C.A. (1988). '"Life on the upslope": the postmodern landscape of gentrification', *Environment and Planning D: Society and Space*, 6: 169–89.

Mills, S. (1989) 'Tourism and leisure – setting the scene', *Tourism Today*, 6: 18–21.

Milner, M. (1987) 'Where the squeeze is not only on holidaymakers', *The Guardian*, 20 August.

Mishan, E. (1969) *The Costs of Economic Growth*. Harmondsworth: Penguin.

Mitchinson, A. (1988) 'New Society database. Holidays', *New Society*, 22 April.

Mitford, N. (1959) 'The tourist', *Encounter*, 13 (October): 3–7.

Mitter, S. (1986) *Common Fate, Common Road*. London: Pluto.

Morris, M. (1988) 'Things to do with shopping centres', in S. Sheridan (ed.) *Grafts*. London: Verso. pp. 193–225.

Morton, A. (1988) 'Tomorrow's yesterdays: science museums and the future', in R. Lumley (ed.) *The Museum Time-Machine*. London: Routledge. pp. 128–43.

Myerscough, J. (1974): 'The recent history of the use of leisure time', in I. Appleton (ed.) *Leisure Research and Policy*. Edinburgh: Scottish Academic Press. pp. 3–16.

Myerscough, J. (1986) *Facts About The Arts. 1986 Edition*. London: Policy Studies Institute.

Myerscough, J. (1988) *The Economic Importance of the Arts in Britain*. London: Policy Studies Institute.

NEDO (National Economic Development Office) (1986) *Changing Working Patterns*. London: NEDO.

Newby, H. (1982) *Green and Pleasant Land*. Harmondsworth: Penguin.

Newby. P. (1981) 'Literature and the fashioning of tourist taste', in D. Pocock (ed.) *Humanistic Geography and Literature*. London: Croom Helm. pp. 130–41.

Nicholson-Lord, D. (1987) *The Greening of the Cities*. London: Routledge.

Norman, P. (1988) 'Faking the present'. *The Guardian*, 10–11 December.

Owens, P. (1984) 'Rural leisure and recreation research', *Progress in Human Geography*, 8: 157–88.

Pahl, R. (1965) *Urbs in Rure. The Metropolitan Fringe in Hertfordshire*. London: LSE Geography Dept.

Parry, K. (1983) *Resorts of the Lancashire Coast*. Newton Abbot: David & Charles.

Pawley, M. (1987) 'The man who learned', *Intercity*, November/December.

Pearce, P. (1982) *The Social Psychology of Tourist Behaviour*. Oxford: Pergamon.

Pearce, P. and Moscardo, G. (1986) 'The concept of authenticity in tourist experiences', *Australian and New Zealand Journal of Sociology*, 22: 121–32.

Pearman, H. (1988) 'Setting store by its designs', *The Sunday Times*, 3 August.

Pearman, H. (1989) 'Manchester gets a mix 'n' match revival', *The Sunday Times*, 16 April.

Percy, S. and Lamb, H. (1987) 'The squalor behind the bright fast food lights', *The Guardian*, 22 August.

Perkin, H. (1976) 'The "social tone" of Victorian seaside resorts in the north-west', *Northern History*, II: 180–94.

Pevsner, N. (1970) *A History of Building Types*. London: Thames & Hudson.

Pfeil, F. (1985) 'Makin' flippy-floppy: postmodernism and the baby-boom PMC', in M. Davis, F. Pfeil and M. Spinker (eds) *The Year Left. An American Socialist Yearbook 1985*. London: Verso. pp. 263–95.

Phelps-Brown, E.H. (1968) *A Century of Pay*. London: Macmillan.

Pickvance, C. (1990) 'Council economic intervention and political conflict in a declining resort: the Isle of Thanet', in M. Harloe, C. Pickvance and J. Urry (eds) *Place, Politics, Policy. Do Localities Matter?* London: Unwin Hyman. pp. 165–86.

Pile, S. (1987) 'You'll have no fun rushing to the sun', *The Observer*, 16 May.

Pimlott, J. (1947) *The Englishman's Holiday*. London: Faber & Faber.

Pine, R. (1987) *Management of Technological Change in the Catering Industry*. Aldershot: Avebury.

Piore, M. and Sabel, C. (1984) *The Second Industrial Divide*. New York: Basic Books.

Pollard, S. (1965) *The Genesis of Modern Management*. London: Edward Arnold.

Pollert, A. (1988) 'The "flexible firm": fixation or fact', *Work, Employment and Society*, 2: 281–316.

Poon, A. (1989) 'Competitive strategies for a "new tourism"', in C. Cooper (ed.) *Progress in Tourism, Recreation and Hospitality Management* vol. 1. London: Belhaven Press. pp. 91–102.

Pressdee, M. (1986) 'Agony or ecstacy: broken transitions and new social state of working-class youth in Australia', Occasional papers, South Australia College of Adult Education, Magill, S. Australia.

Punter, J. (1986–7) 'The contradictions of aesthetic control under the Conservatives', *Planning Practice and Research*, 1: 8–13.

Quick, R.C. (1962) *The History of Morecambe and Heysham*. Morecambe: Morecambe Times.

Raban, J. (1986) *Coasting*. London: Picador.

Reynolds, B. (1989) *The 100 Best Companies to Work for in the UK*. London: Fontana/Collins.

Reynolds, H. (1988) '"Leisure revolution" prime engines of regional recovery'. *The Daily Telegraph* 2 December.

Richards, J. and MacKenzie, J. (1986) *The Railway Station*. Oxford: Oxford University Press.

Richter, C. (1987) 'Tourism services', in O. Giarini (ed.) *The Emerging Service Economy*. Oxford: Pergamon. pp. 213–44.

Roberts, J. (1989) 'Green mantle', *The Guardian*, 17–18 June.

Robinson, H. (1976) *A Geography of Tourism*. Plymouth: Macdonald & Evans.

Rocca, T. (1989) 'Bardot scorns "Black tide of filth" in St Tropez', *The Guardian*, 10 August.

Rojek, C. (1988) 'The convoy of pollution', *Leisure Studies*, 7: 21–31.

Rojek, C. (1990) *Ways of Escape*. London: Macmillan.

Rose, M. (1978) *The Gregs of Styal*. Cheshire: Quarry Bank Mill Development Trust.

Ross, A. (1989) *No Respect*. London: Routledge.

Ryan, C. (1989) 'Trends past and present in the package holiday industry', *Service Industries Journal*, 9: 61–78.

Samuel, R. (1987a) 'History that's over', *The Guardian*, 9 October.

Samuel, R. (1987b) 'A plaque on all your houses', *The Guardian*, 17 October.

Sasser, W. and Arbeit, S. (1976) 'Selling jobs in the service sector', *Business Horizons*, 19: 61–5.

Savage, M. (1988) 'The missing link? The relationship between spatial mobility and social mobility', *British Journal of Sociology*, 39: 554–77.

Savage, M., Dickens, P. and Fielding, T. (1989) 'Some social and political implications of the contemporary fragmentation of the "service class"', *International Journal of Urban and Regional Research*, 3: 455–76.

Scott, A. (1988) *The Good Beach Guide*. London: Ebury Press.

Scruton, R. (1979) *The Aesthetics of Architecture*. Princeton, NJ: Princeton University Press.

Shamoon, S. (1989) 'Shares for sale in Euro Disneyland', *The Observer*, 5 March.

Shaw, G., Greenwood, J. and Williams, A. (1988) 'The United Kingdom: market responses and public policy', in A. Williams and G. Shaw (eds) *Tourism and Economic Development*. London: Belhaven Press. pp. 162–79.

Shields, R. (1989) 'Social spatialization and the built environment: the West Edmonton Mall', *Environment and Planning D: Society and Space*, 7: 147–64.

Shields, R. (1990) *Places on the Margin*. London: Routledge.

Shoard, M. (1987) *The Land is Our Land*. London: Paladin.

Slattery, P. and Roper, A. (1986) *The UK Hotel Groups Directory: 1986–7*. London: Cassell.

Slattery, P., Roper, A. and Boer, A. (1985) 'Hotel consortia: their activities, structure and growth', *Service Industries Journal*, 2: 192–9.

Smith, A. (1986) 'Miscellaneous services', in A. Smith (ed.) *Commercial Service Industries*. Aldershot: Gower. pp. 1–54.

Smith, D. (1988) 'A fine old stew in the kitchens', *The Guardian*, 12 November.

Smith, V. (1978) 'Introduction', in *Hosts and Guests*. Oxford: Blackwell. pp. 1–14.

Sontag, S. (1979) *On Photography*. Harmondsworth: Penguin.

Special Projects Group, Lancaster City Council (1987) *Lancaster – Heritage City. Position Statement*. Lancaster: Lancaster City Council.

Stallinbrass, C. (1980) 'Seaside resorts and the hotel accommodation industry', *Progress in Planning*, 13: 103–74.

Stamp, G. (1987) 'A right old Roman carry-on', *The Daily Telegraph*, 28 December.

Stauth, G. and Turner, B. (1988) 'Nostalgia, postmodernism and the critique of mass culture', *Theory, Culture and Society*, 2/3: 509–26.

SWET (Society of West End Theatres) (1982) *Britain at its Best: Overseas Tourism and the West End Theatre*. London: SWET.

Taylor, I. (1988) 'Down beside the seaside', *Marxism Today*, October: 43.

Thomas, K. (1973) *Man and the Natural World: Changing Attitudes in England, 1500–1800*. London: Allen Lane.

Thompson, E.P. (1967) 'Time, work-discipline, and industrial capitalism', *Past and Present*, 38: 56–97.

Thompson, G. (1981) 'Holidays', Unit 11 of *Popular Culture and Everyday Life* (2). Milton Keynes: Open University Press.

Thompson, G. (1983) 'Carnival and the calculable: consumption and play at Blackpool', in T. Bennett (ed.) *Formations of Pleasure*. London: Routledge. pp. 124–36.

Thrift, N. (1989) 'Images of social change', in C. Hamnett, L. McDowell and P. Sarre (eds) *The Changing Social Structure*. London: Sage. pp. 12–42.

Thurot, J. and Thurot, G. (1983) 'The ideology of class and tourism', *Annals of Tourism Research*, 10: 173–89.

Towner, J. (1985) 'The Grand Tour. a key phase in the history of tourism', *Annals of Tourism Research*, 12: 297–33.

Towner, J. (1988) 'Approaches to tourism history', *Annals of Tourism History*, 15: 47–62.

Travel Alberta (n.d.) *West Edmonton Mall*. Edmonton: Alberta Tourism.

Turner, C. and Manning, P. (1988) 'Placing authenticity – on being a tourist: a reply to Pearce and Manning', *Australian and New Zealand Journal of Sociology*, 24: 136–8.

Turner, L. and Ash, J. (1975) *The Golden Hordes*. London: Constable.

Turner, V. (1973) 'The center out there: pilgrim's goal', *History of Religions*, 12: 191–230.

Turner, V. (1974) *The Ritual Process*. Harmondsworth: Penguin.

Turner, V. and Turner, E. (1978): *Image and Pilgrimage in Christian Culture*. New York: Columbia University Press.

Urry, J. (1987) 'Some social and spatial aspects of services', *Environment and Planning D: Society and Space*, 5: 5–26.

Urry, J. (1988a) 'Cultural change and contemporary holiday-making', *Theory, Culture and Society*, 5: 35–55.

Urry, J. (1988b) 'Wish you were here', *Landscape*, July/August: 64–5.

Urry, J. (1990) 'The consumption of "tourism"', *Sociology*, 24: 23–35.

Uzzell, D. (1989) *Heritage Interpretation. Vol 2*. London: Belhaven Press.

Valenzuela, M. (1988) 'Spain: the phenomenon of mass tourism', in A. Williams and G. Shaw (eds) *Tourism and Economic Development*. London: Belhaven Press. pp. 39–57.

Venturi, R. (1972) *Learning from Las Vegas*. Cambridge, MA: MIT Press.

Vidal, J. (1988) 'No room here for Mickey Mouse', *The Guardian*, 19 March.

Vulliamy, E. (1988) 'Squalid renaissance', *The Guardian*, 16 April.

Walby, S. (1987) *Flexibility and the Changing Sexual Division of Labour*, Lancaster Regionalism Group Working Paper no. 36.

Walter, J. (1982) 'Social limits to tourism', *Leisure Studies*, 1: 295–304.

Walton, J. (1978) *The Blackpool Landlady*. Manchester: Manchester University Press.

Walton, J. (1979) 'Railways and resort development in Victorian England: the case of Silloth', *Northern History*, 15: 191–209.

Walton, J. (1981) 'The demand for working class seaside holidays in Victorian England', *Economic History Review*, 34: 249–65.

Walton, J. (1983) *The English Seaside Resort: A Social History, 1750–1914*. Leicester: Leicester University Press.

Walton, J. and Poole, R. (1982) 'The Lancashire wakes in the nineteenth century', in R. Storch (ed.) *Popular Culture and Customs in the Nineteenth Century*. London: Croom Helm. pp. 100–24.

Walvin, J. (1978) *Beside the Seaside*. London: Allen Lane.

Ward, M. and Hardy, D. (1986) *Goodnight Campers! The History of the British Holiday Camp*. London: Mansell.

Warde, A. (1988) 'Explaining gentrification and theories of consumption', mimeo, Dept of Sociology, Lancaster University.

Waterhouse, K. (1989a) 'Wish you were here', *The Listener*, 12 January.

Waterhouse, K. (1989b) *Theory and Practice of Travel*. London: Hodder & Stoughton.

Waterhouse, R. (1989) 'Town abandons trousers for sake of tourism', *Financial Times*, 8 July.

Waters, S. (1967) 'Trends in international tourism', *Development Digest*, 5: 57–61.

Wates, N. and Krevitt, C. (1987) *Community Architecture*. Harmondsworth: Penguin.

Welsh, E. (1988) 'Are locals selling out for a bowl of gruel?' *The Sunday Times*, 11 December.

Welsh, E. (1989) 'Unmasking the special agents', *The Sunday Times*, 26 February.

West, B. (1988) 'The making of the English working past: a critical view of the Ironbridge Gorge museum', in R. Lumley (ed.) *The Museum Time-Machine*. London: Routledge. pp. 36–62.

Whitaker, R. (1988) 'Welcome to the Costa del Kebab', *The Independent*, 27 February.

White, D. (1987) 'The born-again museum', *New Society*, 1 May: 10–14.

Whyte, W.F. (1948) *Human Relations in the Restaurant Industry*. New York: McGraw-Hill.

Wickers, D. (1987) 'Splashing out', *The Guardian*, 20 June.

Wickers, D. and Charlton, G. (1988) 'Oh, we do like to be by the seaside', *The Sunday Times*, 5 June.

Wiener, M. (1981) *English Culture and the Decline of the Industrial Spirit*. Cambridge: Cambridge University Press.

Williams, A. and Shaw, G. (1988a) 'Tourism and development: introduction', in A. Williams and G. Shaw (eds) *Tourism and Economic Development*. London: Belhaven Press. pp. 1–11.

Williams, A. and Shaw, G. (1988b) 'Western European tourism in perspective', in A. Williams and G. Shaw (eds) *Tourism and Economic Development*. London: Belhaven Press. pp. 12–38.

Williams, A. and Shaw, G. (1988c) 'Tourism: candyfloss industry or job creator', *Town Planning Review*, 59: 81–103.

Williams, A., Shaw, G., Greenwood, J., and Hennessy, S. (1986) *Tourism and Economic Development: a Review of Experiences in Western Europe*, Tourism in Cornwall Project, Dept of Geography, University of Exeter.

Williams, I. (1988) 'Profits take a holiday', *The Sunday Times* 30 June.

Williams, R. (1973) *The Country and the City*. London: Paladin.

Wilsher, P. (1988) 'How they put sparkle back into cities', *The Sunday Times*, 15 May.

Wilson, A. (1988) 'The view from the road: nature tourism in the postwar years', *Borderlines*, 12: 10–14.

Wolff, J. (1985) 'The invisible flâneuse: women and the literature of modernity', *Theory, Culture and Society*, 2: 37–48.

Wolmar, C. (1989) 'The new East Enders', *The Guardian*, 8–9 April.

Wood, M. (1974) 'Nostalgia or never: you can't go home again', *New Society*, 7 November: 343–6.

Wouters, C. (1989) 'The sociology of emotions and flight attendants: Hochschild's *Managed Heart*', *Theory, Culture and Society*, 6: 95–124.

Wright, P. (1985) *On Living in an Old Country*. London: Verso.

Younger, G. (1973) *Tourism: Blessing or Blight?* Harmondsworth: Penguin.

INDEX

Index compiled by Peva Keane